From the first dawn of consciousness, death has been a mystery to mankind. . . .

The more than fifty literary selections in this anthology illuminate human attitudes toward death over the past five thousand years and bring to the reader a fresh understanding of how acceptance of death can enrich your life.

Here are selections from the Bible and folktales, and from Shakespeare, Dickinson, Tolstoy, Flaubert, Kipling, Mishima, Dorothy Parker, James Weldon Johnson, Aldous Huxley, Tom Paxton, Jackson Browne, and many other great writers.

"Nowhere else have I read such a wide-ranging examination of this vital issue. I'm pleased that this book has been published, and I recommend it enthusiastically."
—Lynn Caine, author of *Widow*

D1572189

WE ARE BUT A MOMENT'S SUNLIGHT

Understanding Death

Edited by
Charles S. Adler, M.D.
Gene Stanford, Ph.D.
Sheila Morrissey Adler, Ph.D.

A KANGAROO BOOK
PUBLISHED BY POCKET BOOKS NEW YORK

WE ARE BUT A MOMENT'S SUNLIGHT

WASHINGTON SQUARE PRESS edition published December, 1976

2nd printing..........August, 1977

Published by
POCKET BOOKS, a Simon & Schuster Division of
GULF & WESTERN CORPORATION
1230 Avenue of the Americas, New York, N.Y. 10020.

WASHINGTON SQUARE PRESS editions are distributed
in the U.S. by Simon & Schuster, Inc., 1230 Avenue of the
Americas, New York, N.Y. 10020, and in Canada by Simon
& Schuster of Canada, Ltd., Markham, Ontario, Canada.

Printed in the U.S.A.

ACKNOWLEDGMENTS

The title of the book, *We Are But a Moment's Sunlight,* is a line from the song "Get Together" by Chet Powers.

Thanks are due for permission to include the following selections, listed by author.

Conrad Aiken: "Blind Date," from *Collected Poems* by Conrad Aiken. Copyright 1953, © 1970 by Conrad Aiken. Reprinted by permission of Oxford University Press, Inc.

Anonymous: "Man Chooses Death," from *African Myths and Tales* by Susan Taubes. Copyright © 1963 by Dell Publishing Co., Inc. Reprinted by permission of Dell Publishing Co., Inc.

Samuel Beckett: "Malone Dies," excerpted from *Malone Dies* by Samuel Beckett. Copyright © 1956 by Grove Press Inc. Reprinted by permission of Grove Press Inc.

Ingmar Bergman: Excerpt from *The Seventh Seal* by Ingmar Bergman. Copyright © 1960 by Ingmar Bergman. Reprinted by permission of Simon & Schuster, Inc.

Arna Bontemps: "A Summer Tragedy," from *The Old South* by Arna Bontemps. Copyright 1933 by Arna Bontemps. Copyright renewed. Reprinted by permission of Dodd, Mead & Company, Inc.

Jackson Browne: "For a Dancer." Copyright © 1974 WB Music Corp. All rights reserved. Used by permission of Warner Bros. Music.

Paul Carus: "The Folly of Mourning," from *The Gospel of Buddha* by Paul Carus. Reprinted from *The Gospel of Buddha* by permission of The Open Court Publishing Company, La Salle, Illinois. Copyright 1894, 1915.

Miguel de Cervantes: "Don Quixote," excerpted from *Don Quixote* by Miguel de Cervantes. Translated by J. M. Cohen (Penguin Classics, 1950). Copyright 1950 by J. M. Cohen. Reprinted by permission of Penguin Books, Ltd.

Anton Chekhov: "Heartache," from *The Portable Chekhov,* edited by Avrahm Yarmolinsky. Copyright 1947 by The Viking Press, Inc. Copyright renewed © 1975 by The Viking Press, Inc. All rights reserved. Reprinted by permission of The Viking Press, Inc.

Mei Yao Ch'en: "I Remember the River at Wu Sung," from Kenneth Rexroth's *One Hundred Poems from the Chinese.* Copyright © 1971 by Kenneth Rexroth. All rights reserved. Reprinted by permission of New Directions Publishing Corp.

Margaret Craven: "I Heard the Owl Call My Name," excerpted from *I Heard the Owl Call My Name* by Margaret Craven. Copyright © 1973 by Margaret Craven. Reprinted by permission of Doubleday & Company, Inc.

Alphonse Daudet (1840–1897): "The Arlesian Girl," from *The Abnormal Personality Through Literature,* Alan A. Stone and Sue

Smart Stone, editors. Copyright © 1966. Reprinted by permission of Prentice-Hall, Inc., Englewood Cliffs, New Jersey.

Peter DeVries: "Blood of the Lamb," excerpted from *Blood of the Lamb* by Peter DeVries by permission of Little, Brown & Company. Copyright © 1961 by Peter DeVries.

Kahlil Gibran: "On Death," reprinted from *The Prophet* by Kahlil Gibran with permission of the publisher, Alfred A. Knopf, Inc. Copyright 1923 by Kahlil Gibran. Copyright renewed 1951 by the Administrators C.T.A. of the Kahlil Gibran Estate and Mary G. Gibran.

Ernest Hemingway: "For Whom the Bell Tolls," excerpted from *For Whom the Bell Tolls* by Ernest Hemingway. Reprinted by permission of Charles Scribner's Sons. Copyright 1940 by Ernest Hemingway.

Aldous Huxley: "Island," excerpted from *Island* by Aldous Huxley. Copyright © 1962 by Aldous Huxley. Reprinted by permission of Harper & Row, Publishers, Inc.

James Weldon Johnson: "Go Down Death," from *God's Trombones* by James Weldon Johnson. Copyright 1927 by The Viking Press, Inc. Copyright renewed © 1955 by Grace Nail Johnson. All rights reserved. Reprinted by permission of The Viking Press, Inc.

Nikos Kazantzakis: "Zorba the Greek," excerpted from *Zorba the Greek* by Nikos Kazantzakis. Copyright 1952 by Simon & Schuster, Inc. Reprinted by permission of the publisher.

Cevdet Kudret: "Feast of the Dead," by Cevdet Kudret, translated by Filiz Ofluoglu. Reprinted by permission of the author and translator.

C. S. Lewis: "A Grief Observed," excerpted from *A Grief Observed* by C. S. Lewis. Copyright © 1961 by N. W. Clerk. Used by permission of the publisher, The Seabury Press, Inc.

Doris Lund: "Eric," excerpted from *Eric* by Doris Lund. Copyright © 1974 by Doris Lund. Reprinted by permission of J. B. Lippincott Company.

Carson Smith McCullers: Excerpt from *The Heart Is a Lonely Hunter*. Copyright 1940 by Carson Smith McCullers. Reprinted by permission of Houghton Mifflin Company.

Yukio Mishima: "Patriotism," excerpted from "Patriotism" from *Death in Midsummer and Other Stories.* Translated by Geoffrey W. Sargent. Copyright © 1966 by New Directions Publishing Corp. Reprinted by permission of New Directions.

Micki Mulkern: "To My Godmother," from *Erin—Mourning Journey to Joy.* Copyright © 1976 by Micki Mulkern, 1530 West Calle Tiburon, Tucson, Ariz. 85704. Reprinted by permission of the author.

R. K. Narayan: Excerpts from *Grateful to Life and Death* by R. K. Narayan. Reprinted by permission of Michigan State University Press.

Dorothy Parker: "Resume," from *The Portable Dorothy Parker* by Dorothy Parker. Copyright 1926, 1954 by Dorothy Parker. All rights reserved. Reprinted by permission of The Viking Press, Inc.

Tom Paxton: "Forest Lawn." Copyright © 1969 by United Artists Music Co., Inc., New York, New York.

Padraic Pearse: "The Mother," from the *Penguin Book of Irish Verse* by Brendan Kennelly, Penguin Books, Ltd., publisher.

Luigi Pirandello: "War," from *The Medals and Other Stories* by Luigi Pirandello. Translated by Michael Pettinati. Copyright 1939 by E. P. Dutton & Co. Copyright renewed © 1967 by E. P. Dutton & Co., Inc. Reprinted with the publisher's permission.

Rainer Maria Rilke: "The Notebooks of Malte Laurids Brigge," excerpted from *The Notebooks of Malte Laurids Brigge* by Rainer Maria Rilke. Translated by M. D. Herter Norton. Copyright 1949 by W. W. Norton & Company, Inc. Reprinted by permission of W. W. Norton & Company, Inc.

Edwin Arlington Robinson: "Richard Cory." Reprinted by permission of Charles Scribner's Sons from *The Children of the Night* by Edwin Arlington Robinson.

Sandra Scoppettone: Excerpt from *Trying Hard to Hear You* by Sandra Scoppettone. Copyright © 1974 by Sandra Scoppettone. Reprinted by permission of Harper & Row, Publishers, Inc.

Eneriko Seruma: "Early Dawn," from *The Heart Seller*. Reprinted by permission of East African Publishing House, Nairobi, Kenya.

William Shakespeare: "Hamlet," from *Hamlet* by William Shakespeare. Edited by Willard Farnham, in *The Pelican Shakespeare*. General Editor: Alfred Harbage. Copyright © 1957, 1970 by Penguin Books, Inc. Reprinted by permission of Penguin Books, Inc.

Isaac Bashevis Singer: "Fool's Paradise," from *Zlateh the Goat and Other Stories* by Isaac Bashevis Singer. Copyright © 1966 by Isaac Bashevis Singer. Reprinted by permission of Harper & Row, Publishers, Inc.

Bruce Springsteen: "For You." Reprinted by permission of Laurel Canyon Music.

Barbara Stanford: "Accepting Death," from *Myths and Modern Man* by Barbara Stanford and Gene Stanford. Published by Pocket Books. Copyright © 1972 by Barbara Dodds Stanford and Gene Stanford. Reprinted by permission of the authors.

John Steinbeck: "The Grapes of Wrath," excerpt from *The Grapes of Wrath* by John Steinbeck. Copyright 1939 by John Steinbeck. Copyright renewed © 1967 by John Steinbeck. All rights reserved. Reprinted by permission of The Viking Press, Inc.

Arnold Toynbee: "Reflections on My Own Death." Reprinted by *The Rotarian* for May, 1972.

Alice Walker: "To Hell with Dying," by Alice Walker from *The Best Short Stories by Negro Writers*. Published by Little, Brown & Company, 1967. Copyright © 1967 by Alice Walker. Reprinted by permission of Jo Stewart, ICM.

Aurora White: "The Impartiality of Death," from *Literary Folklore of the Hispanic Southwest*. Published by The Naylor Company, 1953. Reprinted by permission of the publisher.

Hilma Wolitzer: "Ending," abridged by permission of William Morrow & Company, Inc., from *Ending* by Hilma Wolitzer. Copyright © 1974 by Hilma Wolitzer.

TO OUR PARENTS

PREFACE

"The new four-letter word of pornography is d-e-a-d," wrote Earl A. Grollman. Death seems to have replaced sex as the topic people are least willing to talk about, and dying is now considered by many to be an unnatural act. Ironically, the further back in history you go, the more comfortable people seem to have been with death. They did not find the concept any more pleasant, but somehow it seemed more familiar.

Why should this be? After all, despite wonder drugs and all the miracles of science, the odds of dying are still identical to what they were at the beginning of time: one hundred percent a certainty. So it's not that the death rate has decreased. In fact, considering the tremendous increase in world population, death is actually occurring in far greater numbers today. The probable cause for today's greater discomfort with death is that death has become less public. It has gone into hiding, and we have put it there. "Real" death is hidden in huge, uninviting hospitals, places that feel like home to no one and where children are often prohibited and families feel in the way. Simultaneously, fake death, with all the attendant fantasies and lack of sincere emotion, is broadcast hourly on the television screen.

Forty or fifty years ago young people grew up with death all around them. It came at an earlier age then: parents and grandparents died when a person was quite young; epidemics of measles and diphtheria often killed one's childhood friends. By the time a person reached adulthood, he or she had probably experienced the death of several close friends and numerous relatives. Today it's not unusual for someone to be thirty or forty before having any direct experience with death.

In the past death seemed to be a more open event, shared and expected, as much a part of the family as childbirth or holidays. Relatives died at home, surrounded by children as well as adults. But today most Americans do their dying in hospitals, surrounded by strangers and mechanical devices—with children kept away by hospital rules. We no longer grow up experiencing death as a natural part of life, and thus when it does come, when we are forced to confront it, it comes as a shock. It not only seems unwelcome (as it always was), but also unexpected and unnatural.

This lack of familiarity with death allows it to become a hidden and powerful tyrant. People who have not made some peace with the idea of their inevitable death rarely lead a fully contented life. They refuse to admit to themselves that their lives are not limitless, and hence they fail to choose carefully how they are going to use the limited time they've been given. By contrast, persons who have accepted death as natural and inevitable examine their lives more closely and evaluate the quality of their lives. They take life less for granted and live it to the fullest. The fear of death can also intrude upon a person's everyday affairs in disguised and disruptive ways. For example, a person who is not comfortable with death is less likely to be helpful to friends and relatives who are dying or who have just lost a loved one in death. Anxiety about death stimulates some people to engage in death-defying stunts to "prove" that they are more powerful than death. Often people will postpone getting a medical examination because they are so fearful of the idea of death that they can't face the possibility that they might be ill.

No age group is invulnerable to the problems resulting from today's lack of familiarity with death. Even adolescents have a generally high level of preoccupation with death, despite the fact that young people seem to be the very embodiment of life. Studies have shown that, at least on an unconscious level, most adolescents are extremely concerned about death. Their concern is nowhere better demonstrated than by the lengths many young people go to deny it. Dangerous and daredevil behavior is one form this denial takes. It's as though the person is saying, "I can drive my car as fast as I please and death will never catch me, because I'm invincible."

But the messages of this book are not aimed solely at youth. They apply to anyone who has a curiosity about the subject, feels a need to come to better terms with it, and enjoys reading good literature. Why literature as a vehicle for helping readers understand death, rather than psychological studies or sociological works? For one thing, literature is usually less ponderous than scholarly works in psychology, sociology, and philosophy. The average reader will find the stories, poems, and personal essays in this anthology easier to read then technical writing. But also literature can tap an awareness from the times when death was more familiar to people. It can portray events and feelings that defy analysis or lose all relevance in the translation. It reflects the observations of some of the keenest minds and sharpest eyes of the past five thousand years. It can make contact with the emotional and intuitive as well as the intellectual side of one's nature. And finally, an anthology such as this can provide a fine introduction to some of the world's best literature.

The selections have been divided into six parts. The first is an exploration of the various attitudes persons and societies could or do hold toward death. The underlying theme of this section is that death is a natural and necessary part of the life cycle, an awareness of which can make living more meaningful. The second part contains accounts of the process of dying. Selections deal with the psychological experience of facing death, the various ways that people approach death, and the ways people deal with feelings about dying and with dying persons.

Part III explores what happens after death. It presents a number of ideas about immortality, but does not imply that any one explanation is more valid than others. The fourth part examines the means various societies have devised to cope with death, particularly their funeral practices. The dominant theme of this section is that individuals and groups have certain needs that the funeral service, to a greater or lesser extent, fulfills. In Part V the ways people cope with the loss of someone they love is explored. Grief is presented as something to be confronted and worked through, rather than avoided.

The last part focuses on suicide, a serious problem today, particularly among young people. We have attempted to deal honestly with this topic, since it is our conviction that a thorough understanding of it can help to diminish rather than to promote its likelihood.

At long last some inroads against the death taboo are beginning to be made. Stimulated by the pioneering work of a warm and courageous psychiatrist, Dr. Elizabeth Kübler-Ross, whose book, *On Death and Dying*, helped both laymen and medical personnel change their view of dying, medical schools, universities, and even high schools are starting to offer courses on death to their students. We hope this book will be a contribution toward the establishment of death education as a standard part of American schooling. We also hope that the individual reader will gain a better view of death from reading these selections and that, as a result, he or she will have a richer and more meaningful life.

C.S.A.
G.S.
S.M.A.

CONTENTS

Introduction by Elisabeth Kübler-Ross, M.D.   xvii

I. "TO MELT INTO THE SUN": *Perceptions of Death*   1

"On Death" from *The Prophet* by Kahlil Gibran   6
"The Folly of Mourning" by Paul Carus   7
"Blind Date" by Conrad Aiken   9
"Reflections on My Own Death" by Arnold Toynbee   10
"Death Be Not Proud" by John Donne   12
"Go Down Death" by James Weldon Johnson   13
from *Gulliver's Travels* by Jonathan Swift   15
"If There Were No Death in Our World" by Nikolai Berdyaev   23
"For a Dancer" by Jackson Browne   24
"The Impartiality of Death" by Aurora White-Lea   25

II. "TO STAND AT THAT LAST MOMENT": *The Process of Dying*   27

from *Ending* by Hilma Wolitzer   35
from *The Notebook of Malte Laurids Brigge* by Rainer Maria Rilke   43
from *Island* by Aldous Huxley   45
from *Malone Dies* by Samuel Beckett   54
from "The Death of Ivan Ilych" by Leo Tolstoy   56
from *Don Quixote* by Miguel Cervantes   65
"Early Dawn" by Eneriko Seruma   71
from *Zorba the Greek* by Nikos Kazantzakis   73
"To Hell with Dying" by Alice Walker   80

III. "A CORPSE, A MEMORY, AND . . .
   A GHOST":
   What Comes After Death   87

from *Hamlet* by William Shakespeare   91
"Because I Could Not Stop for Death"
   by Emily Dickinson   95
"Man Chooses Death" Folktale   96
from *The Holy Bible*, Corinthians I, Chapter 15 97
from *A Grief Observed* by C. S. Lewis   98
from *Grateful to Life and Death*
   by R. K. Narayan   100
from *For Whom the Bell Tolls*
   by Ernest Hemingway   102
"Invocation" by Helene Johnson   114
"Fool's Paradise" by Isaac Bashevis Singer   114
from *Song of Myself* by Walt Whitman   120
from *The Seventh Seal* by Ingmar Bergman   120

IV. "PERFORMING THE RITES":
   Customs for Coping with Death   125

from *Trying Hard to Hear You*
   by Sandra Scoppettone   130
"Forest Lawn" by Tom Paxton   135
The Undertaker's Chat by Mark Twain   137
from *The Grapes of Wrath* by John Steinbeck   139
from *Eric* by Doris Lund   147
from *I Heard the Owl Call My Name*
   by Margaret Craven   154
from *Grateful to Life and Death*
   by R. K. Narayan   157
"Feast of the Dead" by Cevdet Kudret   160

V. "ON A JOURNEY WITHOUT ME": *Grief and Mourning*   169

"Heartache" by Anton Chekhov   174

"Sonnet 71" by William Shakespeare   180

from *Madame Bovary* by Gustave Flaubert   181

"I Remember the River at Wu Sung"
    by Mei Yao Ch'en   183

from *A Grief Observed* by C. S. Lewis   184

"The Mother" by Padraic Pearse   185

"War" by Luigi Pirandello   186

"To W. P., II" by Rudyard Kipling   190

from *Blood of the Lamb* by Peter DeVries   191

from "The Arlesian Girl" by Alphonse Daudet   198

"For You" by Bruce Springsteen   201

"Accepting Death" by Barbara Stanford with
    Gene Stanford   204

VI. "UNSPEAKABLE DARKNESS": *Suicide*   205

"Richard Cory" by Edwin Arlington Robinson   209

from *Madame Bovary* by Gustave Flaubert   210

"A Summer Tragedy" by Arna Bontemps   221

from *The Heart Is a Lonely Hunter*
    by Carson McCullers   231

"Résumé" by Dorothy Parker   237

from "Patriotism" by Yukio Mishima   238

Drawings and lithographs by Kathe Kollwitz
appear between pages 116 and 117.

INTRODUCTION
ELISABETH KÜBLER-ROSS, M.D.

"Every ending is a bright new beginning" was written in my guest book when I left my childhood country of Switzerland to emigrate to the United States almost two decades ago. This is perhaps the main message of this book, *We Are But a Moment's Sunlight,* which deals with death as a form of loss for those who fear it themselves, as well as those who observe the death or the loss of a loved one.

Dealing with death at an early age means opportunity to evaluate one's character, courage, values, and willingness to face the hurt that comes with growth. Doctors Adler and Stanford use literature from all over the world to familiarize us with the attitude toward death in ancient and more recent times throughout different cultures and religions. The excerpts are well chosen and range from the unforgettable Rilke; to Kazantzakis' *Zorba the Greek,* an example of loving care of the dying; to the touching passage from Steinbeck's *The Grapes of Wrath,* a funeral of migrating farmers on their way West; to a most revealing and humorous cure for laziness in Isaac B. Singer's *Fool's Paradise.* Selections like the one from Hilma Wolitzer's novel, *Ending,* will touch the heart of the reader because they are neither funny nor poetic—but simple, stern and grim, realistic sharings which will make us reflect on the real issues of life and transitions.

Perhaps Francine Klagsbrun's "Too Young to Die" and Micki Mulkern's "Erin: Mourning Journey to Joy," should be added to this colorful collection, simply to help the young reader understand two other forms of death that we often tend to ignore because of the seeming senselessness of it all. The former deals with young people's suicide—the third most frequent cause of death in teenagers in the United States at this time—and the latter is a moving story of a young mother who tried desperately to cope with many "little deaths"—first the realization of her baby's severe retardation and the child's mental inability to ever recognize her as a mother, followed by the ending of Micki's marriage and the new responsibility to now suddenly care for two, small, needy children. Ultimately, everything in life has a purpose and a meaning—even violent or self-imposed deaths do not happen by coincidence. What we all have to learn is to live in such a way that everything we touch and do is ultimately done with love and understanding realizing that we are accountable for all our actions and thoughts. They are the foundation stones of the future. Micki was able to work through her agony and see a purpose in the birth of such a brain-damaged child. Her poem speaks eloquently of this change.

TO MY GODMOTHER

What is a Godmother? I know you're special
You waited many months for my arrival
You were there and saw me when only minutes old
And changed my diapers when I had been here a few
    days

You had dreams for your first Godchild
She would be precocious like her sister
You'd see her off to school, college, and marry
How would I turn out, a credit to those who love me?

God had other plans for me, I am just me
No one ever used the word precocious about me
Something hasn't hooked up right in my mind
I'll be a child of God for all time

I am happy, I love everyone and they me
There aren't many words I can say
But I can communicate and understand
Affection, warmth, softness and love

There are special people in my life
Sometimes I see them smile and sometimes cry
I wonder why? I'm happy and loved by special
    friends
What more could I ask for?

I'll never go to college or marry
But do not be sad, God made me special
I can not hurt, only love, and maybe
God needs some children who simply love

When I was baptized you held me
Hoping I wouldn't cry and you wouldn't drop me
Neither happened and it was a happy day
Is that why you are my Godmother?

I know you're soft and warm and give me loves
But there's something special in your eyes
I see that look and feel that love from others
I must be special to have so many mothers

There are many things we won't be able to share
That's part of being Godmother to God's special child
But there is another who needs your love, too
Take my sister and let your dreams still come true

No, I will never be a success in the eyes of the world
But I promise you something few people can
Since all I know is love, goodness and innocence
Eternity will be ours to share, my Godmother.

Love,
Erin

And so, may I say to the readers of this book, take
time out—and travel through these pages, through history
and time—register the many ways man has attempted
to deal with the knowledge of his finiteness and re-evaluate
your own life while there is still time to change . . . to
grow . . . to make up for past errors . . . and to give
love, hope and faith to those around you. Remember
Richard Allen's famous ending of his poem about the life
of his father:

> . . . and if you have loved well
> then it will have been worth it
> and the joy of it
> will last you
> through the end . . .

May all of you who read these pages be able to say one day that your life has been worth it, and remember that "the joy of it will last you through the end."

Elisabeth Kübler-Ross, M.D.

I

"TO MELT INTO THE SUN":

Perceptions of Death

From the first dawn of consciousness, death has been a mystery to mankind. Without firsthand information from which to derive an explanation, we have all—from the most primitive tribes in distant lands to contemporary Americans—speculated about the meaning of death. For some people death is the enemy, a force to be struggled with and fought against with every resource available. For others death is the beginning of another form of existence, either similar to or different from life in this world. For still others death brings relief from the pain and hardship they must daily endure.

Perhaps the most basic way of viewing death is as a special form of loss. In this broad definition of death you will notice that people are not mentioned. This is not an oversight. A dream or a car battery can die just as a relationship can. This strange starting point is quite central to an understanding of total death in people. We are composed of parts. Our lives, our possessions, and our bodies are composed of different parts. These parts can individually die. We can lose our home in a fire. We can lose a leg in an accident. We can lose a sister through illness. We can lose a set of friends through graduation. We can lose an ability through aging. We can lose a kidney through infection. These are all partial deaths. The difference between these and total death is only one of degree.

Thus, when a close friend or relative dies, there are really two deaths. The dying person experiences a total death, which means the total loss of friends, possessions, and body, as they are represented in his or her mind. The person's friends, on the other hand, suffer a partial death. They are losing one part of their awareness, one friend, but are retaining the rest.

Paradoxically, growth itself involves losses (partial deaths), even when it involves constructive moves toward an adult goal. For example, if you choose to become a surgeon, you can't also be an engineer or a professional cellist or a racing-car driver. It's not merely what you are willing to become that must concern you, but also what you are willing to give up becoming, what future potentials and choices you are willing to lose. Plan-

3

ning for the future requires you to recognize a finite
number of years in which you are able to do only a finite
number of things. This realization is a form of death. What
dies is the possibility of doing or experiencing everything
that you might yearn to do now or in the future. Thus,
death is a form of loss. The loss can be of a thing, a part
of yourself, a wish, or a potential, as well as a person,
and all of these "deaths" need to be mourned, just as one
mourns for a dying person. Understanding death in this
sense has great relevance at all stages of life, not just at
its end.

Death can also be viewed as a separation. Imagine two
people on separate planets, with each planet moving in
an opposite direction. To the person on one planet it looks
like the other person is leaving. This is really the situation
that exists with the dying person and his/her surviving
friends. They face separation and both experience the
other as leaving.

In the view of many people death is an unspeakable
horror, the Grim Reaper, an enemy to be fought and
outwitted as long as possible. They see death as the bringer
of grief and heartache and the spoiler of their happiness.
But given the chance to live forever, how many of us
would really want immortality on this earth? How would
it feel to stay alive century after century while one's
friends came and went? Would it be boring to know that
one had an eternity to get done the things one wanted to?
What if no one or nothing on the earth ever died? Consider the problem of overpopulation, the strain on the
earth's resources. Little change and progress would be
likely to occur if older forms of life did not die, to be
replaced by newer, younger forms. Old forms of life must
constantly be renewed and replaced with better forms of
life if evolutionary progress is to take place. The individual human being must die so that humanity can change
and grow. Thus, death may not be the enemy after all,
but instead may be a positive force necessary so that
nature can fashion an evolving mankind.

Still another way of looking at death is that it provides
us with a particular identity in time. Human beings are
unique among the animals in their ability to span a vast
range of time with the mind, a range of time that far
exceeds an actual lifetime of seventy or eighty years. We
can hold in our minds the image of history from prehis-

toric times to a remote future. In fact, it is this very capacity to take the greater perspective, a perspective of ourselves from outside ourselves, moving from one point in time to another, that forces us to anticipate death and to fear it. But that same perspective expanded even further allows us to see life in the context of all people, of evolution, and of history. This sense of having a time identity, of belonging to a certain time period in the vast span of history, of our lifetime being part of a greater whole can also be reassuring. In the same way that we have a particular identity in terms of a place on earth where we live but yet comprehend ourselves as belonging to all humanity, we can have an identity of our allotted plot of time on earth and yet feel kinship with the ancient Greeks and the travelers in 2001.

We may also look at death as the event that gives meaning to life. If we were to live forever, time would have no importance. Because we have only a little time, time becomes the most valuable thing we own. Knowledge of our mortality gives meaning to life. If we could do anything over again that we wish to because we would be here forever, it wouldn't much matter what we did or how we did it. We'd be sure to get around to doing the rest sooner or later.

Death can also be viewed as a transition rather than as an end, the opening of a door to a new and better existence. Particularly people who are weary of a very arduous life or who have experienced oppression can have the conviction that whatever follows death must be better than their existence on earth. They may also see death as an opportunity for reunion with people who have died before them.

Finally, death can be perceived as an integral part of the cycle of nature, as natural as being born and growing to adulthood and becoming old. Rather than being something alien to our natures as humans, death can be seen as the last stage of our normal life cycle. Certain types of deaths, however, make it difficult for some people to accept this view. We have trouble seeing as "natural" the death of a child, for example. The loss of a parent is so serious an event to a child that he or she may understandably question how "natural" the death was. The fact that these are terribly tragic happenings, though, does not mean that they are unnatural. We would all like nature to be more kind at times, and we feel angry when it isn't. But kind or unkind, nature is always impartial and applies its unflinching laws to everyone and at all ages. Death comes, ultimately, to us all.

"ON DEATH"
from THE PROPHET
KAHLIL GIBRAN

The Prophet is a book of philosophical ideas in the form of poetry, giving the poet's views on many aspects of human existence, including love, marriage, children, work, teaching, friendship, and religion. Gibran, a Lebanese who spent the last twenty years of his life in the United States, was born in 1883 and died in 1931. In this selection he conveys a view that death need not be feared, because it merely marks the beginning of a new and more fulfilling relationship with God and nature.

Then Almitra spoke, saying, We would ask now of Death.

And he said:

You would know the secret of death.

But how shall you find it unless you seek it in the heart of life?

The owl whose night-bound eyes are blind unto the day cannot unveil the mystery of light.

If you would indeed behold the spirit of death, open your heart wide unto the body of life.

For life and death are one, even as the river and the sea are one.

In the depth of your hopes and desires lies your silent knowledge of the beyond;

And like seeds dreaming beneath the snow your heart dreams of spring.

Trust the dreams, for in them is hidden the gate to eternity.

Your fear of death is but the trembling of the shepherd when he stands before the king whose hand is to be laid upon him in honour.

Is the shepherd not joyful beneath his trembling, that he shall wear the mark of the king?

Yet is he not more mindful of his trembling?

For what is it to die but to stand naked in the wind and to melt into the sun?

And what is it to cease breathing, but to free the breath from its restless tides, that it may rise and expand and seek God unencumbered?

Only when you drink from the river of silence shall you indeed sing.

And when you have reached the mountain top, then you shall begin to climb.

And when the earth shall claim your limbs, then shall you truly dance.

THE FOLLY OF MOURNING
PAUL CARUS

This Buddhist parable retold by Paul Carus contains a basic truth about death that many persons fail to comprehend: death is inevitable. This simple truth finds expression in literature from many parts of the world, including the Book of Job in the Old Testament: "Man born of woman has a short life yet has his fill of sorrow. He blossoms and he withers like a flower; fleeting as a shadow, transient." The Buddhist view, as expressed in this parable, is that since death is inevitable, mourning for someone is wasteful. For most Westerners, a more characteristic response to loss, and one considered by many experts to be the most healthy, is to give open expression to their grief and to confront the pain of having lost someone they love.

Kisā Gotamī had an only son, and he died. In her grief she carried the dead child to all her neighbors, asking them for medicine, and the people said, "She has lost her senses. The boy is dead."

At length Kisā Gotamī met a man who replied to her request. "I cannot give thee medicine for thy child, but I know a physician who can."

And the girl said: "Pray tell me, sir, who is it?" And the man replied: "Go to Sakyamuni, the Buddha."

Kisā Gotamī repaired to the Buddha and cried, "Lord and Master, give me the medicine that will cure my boy."

The Buddha answered, "I want a handful of mustard seed." And when the girl in her joy promised to procure it, the Buddha added, "The mustard seed must be taken from a house where no one has lost a child, husband, parent, or friend."

Poor Kisā Gotamī now went from house to house, and the people pitied her and said, "Here is mustard seed; take it!" But when she asked, "Did a son or daughter, a father or mother, die in your family?" they answered her, "Alas! the living are few, but the dead are many. Do not remind us of our deepest grief." And there was no house but some beloved one had died in it.

Kisā Gotamī became weary and hopeless, and sat down at the wayside, watching the lights of the city, as they flickered up and were extinguished again. At last the darkness of the night reigned everywhere. And she considered the fate of men, that their lives flicker up and are extinguished. And she thought to herself: "How selfish am I in my grief! Death is common to all; yet in this valley of desolation there is a path that leads him to immortality who has surrendered all selfishness."

Putting away the selfishness of her affection for her child, Kisā Gotamī had the dead body buried in the forest. Returning to the Buddha, she took refuge in him and found comfort in the dharma which is a balm that will soothe all the pains of our troubled hearts.

The Buddha said, "The life of mortals in this world is troubled and brief and combined with pain. For there is not any means by which those that have been born can avoid dying. After reaching old age there is death; of such a nature are living beings.

"As ripe fruits are early in danger of falling, so mortals when born are always in danger of death.

"As all earthen vessels made by the potter end in being broken, so is the life of mortals.

"Both young and adult, both those who are fools and those who are wise, all fall into the power of death; all are subject to death.

"Of those who, overcome by death, depart from life, a father cannot save his son, nor kinsmen their relations.

"Mark! while relatives are looking on and lamenting deeply, one by one mortals are carried off, like an ox that is led to the slaughter.

"So the world is afflicted with death and decay; therefore the wise do not grieve, knowing the terms of the world.

"In whatever manner people think a thing will come to pass, it is often different when it happens, and great is the disappointment; see, such are the terms of the world.

"Not from weeping nor from grieving will anyone obtain peace of mind; on the contrary, his pain will be the greater and his body will suffer. He will make himself sick and pale, yet the dead are not saved by his lamentation.

"People pass away, and their fate after death will be according to their deeds.

"If a man live a hundred years, or even more, he will at last be separated from the company of his relatives, and leave the life of this world.

"He who seeks peace should draw out the arrow of lamentation, and complaint, and grief.

"He who has drawn out the arrow and has become composed will obtain peace of mind; he who has overcome all sorrow will become free from sorrow, and be blessed."

BLIND DATE
Conrad Aiken

To Conrad Aiken, a contemporary American poet, death is the ultimate "blind date," the eternal escort who waits in the parlor and will not be stood up. This image is thrown into bold relief by the poet, who sets it against an amusement park, the symbol of youth, vitality, and death-defying rides.

No more the swanboat on the artificial lake
its paddled path through neon light shall take;
the stars are turned out on the immortal ferris wheel,
dark and still are the cars of the Virginia Reel.
Baby, it is the last of all blind dates,
and this we keep with the keeper of the golden gates.

For the last time, my darling, the chute-the-chutes,
the Tunnel of Love, the cry 'all men are brutes,'
the sweaty dance-hall with the juke-box playing,
pretzels and beer, and our young love a-Maying:
baby, it is the last of all blind dates,
and this we keep with the keeper of the golden gates.

The radios in a thousand taxis die;
at last man's music fades from the inhuman sky;
as, short or long, fades out the impermanent wave
to find in the ether or the earth its grave.
Baby, it is the last of all blind dates,
and this we keep with the keeper of the golden gates.

Hold hands and kiss, it will never come again,
look in your own eyes and remember the deep pain,
how hollow the world is, like a bubble burst,
yes, and all beauty by some wretchedness accursed!
Baby, it is the last of all blind dates,
and this we keep with the keeper of the golden gates.

Love now the footworn grass, the trampled flowers,
and the divided man of crowds, for he is ours—
love him, yes, love him now, this sundered being,
who most himself seeks when himself most fleeing—
baby, it is the last of all blind dates,
and this we keep with the keeper of the golden gates.

But look—the scenic railway is flashed from red to
green—
and swiftly beneath our feet as this machine
our old star plunges down the precipitous sky,
down the hurrahs of space! So soon to die!—
But baby, it is the last of all blind dates;
and we shall keep it with the keeper of the golden
gates.

REFLECTIONS
ON MY OWN DEATH
Arnold Toynbee

*"Do not go gentle into that good night/Rage, rage against the
dying of the light," advises Dylan Thomas. In his opinion one
must struggle against death, the enemy. Edna St. Vincent Millay,
in the quatrain quoted below, also expresses her unwillingness to
accept death as inevitable. But the eminent British historian
Arnold Toynbee disagrees with the two poets, expressing in this
selection a perception of death somewhat similar to that contained
in the two previous selections—that death should be embraced
as part of the natural order.*

Down, down, down into the darkness of the grave,
Gently they go, the beautiful, the tender, the kind;
Quietly they go, the intelligent, the witty, the brave.
I know. But I do not approve. And I am not resigned.

EDNA ST. VINCENT MILLAY

"Gently," "quietly": In this quatrain, Edna St. Vincent
Millay is deploring, not her own mortality, but the deaths
of people who have died peacefully at a ripe age. I, too,
grieve over deaths like these. Surviving to be bereaved is
far worse than doing one's own dying. (Can I be sure of
this? Yes, I can be, because, two years ago, I had the experience of being at Death's door.)

Deeply though I grieve over such normal deaths, I am
resigned to death in this form, and I also do approve of it.
I should not like to see the Universe saddled with an un-
limited liability even for a Saint Francis or for a Buddha.
But I am not resigned to premature deaths from sickness
or in war. "The beautiful, the tender, the kind; the intelligent, the witty, the brave." I have seen them die before
their time in these monstrous ways, and in these cases I am
unreconciled and am indignant. For the deaths in war, I
indict my own species. Nonhuman animals, it is said, do
not fight to the death; they give quarter to a vanquished
opponent when he is an animal of their own kind. About
half of my dearest friends were killed in battle in 1915–16.
I do not forgive *homo sapiens* for that. An uncle, whose
namesake I am, died of meningitis at 30, and the son of
a schoolfellow of mine died at 32 of creeping paralysis
that was undiagnosable and incurable. If I believed in the
existence of an omnipotent creator god, I would bring him
to book for those two fiendish abuses of his power.

On my own death, my first reflection is that the prospect
of dying has always been familiar to me. Ever since I
have been aware of my name, I have known why I have
it and whose name it once was. I am called after my
Uncle Arnold, and, from the start, I knew that he had died
before I was born. Then, part of my education has been
the poetry of Lucretius, a Roman devotee of the two
Greek philosophers Democritus and Epicurus. Lucretius
was a dedicated missionary. His mission was to convince
his fellow human beings that Death is no evil. Besides being a disinterested philanthropist, Lucretius was an
eloquent writer. His argument has convinced me, and the

verses in which he expounds it have made a constant refrain for all my thoughts. And then, in the First World War, I suffered the cruel untimely deaths of my dear friends.

When I was 19, I was appalled at seeing my father's health break down. I was afflicted to the point of nearly losing my own zest for life. So I wrote, in Greek, a poem in which I defied the baneful demons of despair. "God," I declared, "had sworn that, having caused me to see the light of the Sun, I was not going to live for nothing; I was going to achieve something before going the way of all flesh." This declaration of faith was sincere, but it has not been confirmed by experience. I now know that it is only an accident that I have lived to my present age of 82. I might have been killed in a world war; my life might have been cut short by some disease. I have had time to achieve something through luck, and not by the fiat of a hypothetical omnipotent creator. If I were to wince from dying now, I should be utterly ashamed, considering how much better I have fared than my uncle and than so many of my contemporaries.

Why is Lucretius right in contending that Death is no evil, even though Life may be a boon? Every good thing has its price, and the price of being alive is to be separated temporarily from the rest of the Universe. The Universe is the self's true self; and Death will re-unite my fragment of the great reality with the whole of it. "Do not approve." "Am not resigned." Preposterous.

DEATH BE NOT PROUD
JOHN DONNE

This poem, one of the Holy Sonnets of the famous seventeenth-century English poet, John Donne, is a fearless, defiant statement addressed to death as though it were a person. Donne angrily and contemptuously mocks death, proclaiming that death is man's slave and not the mighty conqueror credited with controlling human existence.

Death, be not proud, though some have called thee
Mighty and dreadful, for thou art not so;
For those whom thou think'st thou dost overthrow
Die not, poor Death, nor yet canst thou kill me.

From rest and sleep, which but thy pictures be,
Much pleasure; then from thee much more must flow,
And soonest our best men with thee do go,
Rest of their bones, and soul's delivery.
Thou art slave to fate, chance, kings, and desperate
  men,
And dost with poison, war, and sickness dwell,
And poppy or charms can make us sleep as well
And better than thy stroke; why swell'st thou then?
One short sleep past, we wake eternally
And death shall be no more; Death, thou shalt die.

GO DOWN DEATH
JAMES WELDON JOHNSON

*This poem, written in the style of a Negro spiritual, portrays
death as mankind's exalted redeemer from pain. Death is seen
as a holy messenger who liberates people from their suffering
and unites them with a benevolent God. This deeply comforting
view recurs often in the folk literature of oppressed peoples.
James Weldon Johnson (1871–1938) was a lawyer as well as
a poet, and was the first black admitted to the Florida bar since
Reconstruction times.*

Weep not, weep not,
She is not dead;
She's resting in the bosom of Jesus.
Heart-broken husband—weep no more;
Grief-stricken son—weep no more;
Left-lonesome daughter—weep no more;
She's only just gone home.

Day before yesterday morning,
God was looking down from his great, high heaven,
Looking down on all his children,
And his eye fell on Sister Caroline,
Tossing on her bed of pain.
And God's big heart was touched with pity,
With the everlasting pity.

And God sat back on his throne,
And he commanded that tall, bright angel standing at
  his right hand:

Call me Death!
And that tall, bright angel cried in a voice
That broke like a clap of thunder:
Call Death!—Call Death!
And the echo sounded down the streets of heaven
Till it reached away back to that shadowy place,
Where Death waits with his pale, white horses.

And Death heard the summons,
And he leaped on his fastest horse,
Pale as a sheet in the moonlight.
Up the golden street Death galloped,
And the hoofs of his horse struck fire from the gold,
But they didn't make no sound.
Up Death rode to the Great White Throne,
And waited for God's command.

And God said: Go down, Death, go down,
Go down to Savannah, Georgia,
Down in Yamacraw,
And find Sister Caroline.
She's borne the burden and heat of the day,
She's labored long in my vineyard,
And she's tired—
She's weary—
Go down, Death, and bring her to me.

And Death didn't say a word,
But he loosed the reins on his pale, white horse,
And he clamped the spurs to his bloodless sides,
And out and down he rode,
Through heaven's pearly gates,
Past suns and moons and stars;
On Death rode,
And the foam from his horse was like a comet in the
    sky;
On Death rode,
Leaving the lightning's flash behind;
Straight on down he came.

While we were watching round her bed,
She turned her eyes and looked away,
She saw what we couldn't see;
She saw Old Death. She saw Old Death.

Coming like a falling star.
But Death didn't frighten Sister Caroline;
He looked to her like a welcome friend.
And she whispered to us: I'm going home,
And she smiled and closed her eyes.

And Death took her up like a baby,
And she lay in his icy arms,
But she didn't feel no chill.
And Death began to ride again—
Up beyond the evening star,
Out beyond the morning star,
Into the glittering light of glory,
On to the Great White Throne.
And there he laid Sister Caroline
On the loving breast of Jesus.

And Jesus took his own hand and wiped away her tears,
And he smoothed the furrows from her face,
And the angels sang a little song,
And Jesus rocked her in his arms,
And kept a-saying: Take your rest,
Take your rest, take your rest.

Weep not—weep not,
She is not dead;
She's resting in the bosom of Jesus.

from GULLIVER'S TRAVELS
JONATHAN SWIFT

*Written in 1725, Gulliver's Travels is the best-known work of
the great satirist, Jonathan Swift. Swift was an Irish church-
man and a pointed social critic. He wrote Gulliver's Travels to
protest the outrages of his day, and he intended it as a serious
work, hardly the child's adventure story it is marketed as today.
Gulliver travels to some marvelous lands (not to be found on
any maps), and encounters a number of bizarre customs which
are curiously similar to those in England that Swift wished
to criticize. In the excerpt below, Swift examines the problems
that might arise if human beings could live forever.*

One day in much good company I was asked by a person

of quality, whether I had seen any of their Struldbruggs or
Immortals. I said I had not, and desired he would explain
to me what he meant by such an appellation applied to a
mortal creature. He told me, that sometimes, though very
rarely, a child happened to be born in a family with a
red circular spot in the forehead, directly over the left eye-
brow, which was an infallible mark that it should never
die. The spot, as he described it, was about the compass
of a silver threepence, but in the course of time grew
larger, and changed its colour; for at twelve years old it
became green, so continued till five and twenty, then
turned to a deep blue; at five and forty it grew coal black,
and as large as an English shilling, but never admitted any
farther alteration. He said these births were so rare, that
he did not believe there could be above eleven hundred
Struldbruggs of both sexes in the whole kingdom, of
which he computed about fifty in the metropolis, and
among the rest a young girl born about three years ago.
That these productions were not peculiar to any family,
but a mere effect of chance, and the children of the Strul-
bruggs themselves, were equally mortal with the rest of
the people.

I freely own myself to have been struck with inexpres-
sible delight upon hearing this account: and the person
who gave it me happening to understand the Balnibarbian
language, which I spoke very well, I could not forbear
breaking out into expressions perhaps a little too extravagant. I cried out as in a rapture; Happy nation where
every child hath at least a chance for being immortal!
Happy people who enjoy so many living examples of ancient virtue, and have masters ready to instruct them in
the wisdom of all former ages! But, happiest beyond all
comparison are those excellent Struldbruggs, who being
born exempt from that universal calamity of human nature, have their minds free and disengaged, without the
weight and depression of spirits caused by the continual
apprehension of death. I discovered my admiration that
I had not observed any of these illustrious persons at
Court, the black spot on the forehead being so remarkable
a distinction, that I could not have easily overlooked it:
and it was impossible that his Majesty, a most judicious
Prince, should not provide himself with a good number of
such wise and able counsellors. Yet perhaps the virtue of
those reverend sages was too strict for the corrupt and

libertine manners of a Court. And we often find by experience that young men are too opinionative and volatile to be guided by the sober dictates of their seniors. However, since the King was pleased to allow me access to his royal person, I was resolved upon the very first occasion to deliver my opinion to him on this matter freely, and at large, by the help of my interpreter; and whether he would please to take my advice or no, yet in one thing I was determined, that his Majesty having frequently offered me an establishment in this country, I would with great thankfulness accept the favour, and pass my life here in the conversation of those superior beings the Struldbruggs, if they would please to admit me.

The gentleman to whom I addressed my discourse, because (as I have already observed) he spoke the language of Balnibarbi, said to me with a sort of a smile, which usually ariseth from pity to the ignorant, that he was glad of any occasion to keep me among them, and desired my permission to explain to the company what I had spoke. He did so, and they talked together for some time in their own language, whereof I understood not a syllable, neither could I observe by their countenances what impression my discourse had made on them. After a short silence the same person told me, that his friends and mine (so he thought fit to express himself) were very much pleased with the judicious remarks I had made on the great happiness and advantages of immortal life, and they were desirous to know in a particular manner, what scheme of living I should have formed to myself, if it had fallen to my lot to have been born a Struldbrugg.

I answered, it was easy to be eloquent on so copious and delightful a subject, especially to me who have been often apt to amuse myself with visions of what I should do if I were a King, a General, or a great Lord: and upon this very case I had frequently run over the whole system how I should employ myself, and pass the time if I were sure to live for ever.

That, if it had been my good fortune to come into the world a Struldbrugg, as soon as I could discover my own happiness by understanding the difference between life and death, I would first resolve by all arts and methods whatsoever to procure myself riches. In the pursuit of which by thrift and management, I might reasonably expect in about two hundred years, to be the wealthiest man in the kingdom. In the second place, I would from my earliest youth apply myself to the study of arts and sciences, by which I should arrive in time to excel all others in learning. Lastly I would carefully record every action and event of consequence that happened in the public, impartially draw the characters of the several successions of princes, and great ministers of state, with my own observations on every point. I would exactly set down the several changes in customs, language, fashions of dress, diet and diversions. By all which acquirements, I should be a living treasury of knowledge and wisdom, and certainly become the oracle of the nation.

I would never marry after threescore, but live in an hospitable manner, yet still on the saving side. I would entertain myself in forming and directing the minds of hopeful young men, by convincing them from my own remembrance, experience and observation, fortified by numerous examples, of the usefulness of virtue in public and private life. But, my choice and constant companions should be a set of my own immortal brotherhood, among whom I would elect a dozen from the most ancient down to my own contemporaries. Where any of these wanted fortunes, I would provide them with convenient lodges round my own estate, and have some of them always at my table, only mingling a few of the most valuable among you mortals, whom length of time would harden me to lose with little or no reluctance, and treat your posterity after the same manner, just as a man diverts himself with the annual succession of pinks and tulips in his garden, without regretting the loss of those which withered the preceding year.

These Struldbruggs and I would mutually communicate our observations and memorials through the course of time, remark the several gradations by which corruption steals into the world, and oppose it in every step, by giving perpetual warning and instruction to mankind; which, added to the strong influence of our own example, would probably prevent that continual degeneracy of human nature so justly complained of in all ages.

Add to all this, the pleasure of seeing the various revolutions of states and empires, the changes in the lower and upper world, ancient cities in ruins, and obscure villages become the seats of kings. Famous rivers lessening into shallow brooks, the ocean leaving one coast dry,

and overwhelming another: the discovery of many countries yet unknown. Barbarity overrunning the politest na-
tions, and the most barbarous becoming civilized. I should
then see the discovery of the *longitude*, the *perpetual
motion*, the *universal medicine*, and many other great
inventions brought to the utmost perfection.

What wonderful discoveries should we make in astron-
omy, by outliving and confirming our own predictions, by
observing the progress and returns of comets, with the
changes of motion in the sun, moon and stars.

I enlarged upon many other topics which the natural
desire of endless life and sublunary happiness could easily
furnish me with. When I had ended, and the sum of my
discourse had been interpreted as before, to the rest of
the company, there was a good deal of talk among them
in the language of the country, not without some laughter
at my expense. At last the same gentleman who had been
my interpreter said, he was desired by the rest to set me
right in a few mistakes, which I had fallen into through
the common imbecility of human nature, and upon that
allowance was less answerable for them. That, this breed
of Struldbruggs was peculiar to their country, for there
were no such people either in Balnibarbi or Japan, where
he had the honour to be ambassador from his Majesty,
and found the natives in both those kingdoms very hard
to believe that the fact was possible, and it appeared
from my astonishment when he first mentioned the matter
to me, that I received it as a thing wholly new, and
scarcely to be credited. That in the two kingdoms above-
mentioned, where during his residence he had conversed
very much, he observed long life to be the universal desire
and wish of mankind. That whoever had one foot in the
grave, was sure to hold back the other as strongly as he
could. That the oldest had still hopes of living one day
longer, and looked on death as the greatest evil, from
which Nature always prompted him to retreat; only in this
island of Luggnagg, the appetite for living was not so
eager, from the continual example of the Struldbruggs
before their eyes.

That the system of living contrived by me was unrea-
sonable and unjust, because it supposed a perpetuity of
youth, health, and vigour, which no man could be so foolish to hope, however extravagant he might be in his wishes.
That the question therefore was not whether a man would

choose to be always in the prime of youth, attended with
prosperity and health, but how he would pass a perpetual
life under all the usual disadvantages which old age brings
along with it. For although few men will avow their desires of being immortal upon such hard conditions, yet
in the two kingdoms before-mentioned of Balnibarbi and
Japan, he observed that every man desired to put off
death for some time longer, let it approach ever so late,
and he rarely heard of any man who died willingly, except
he were incited by the extremity of grief or torture. And
he appealed to me whether in those countries I had trav-
elled, as well as my own, I had not observed the same
general disposition.

After this preface he gave me a particular account of
the Struldbruggs among them. He said they commonly
acted like mortals, till about thirty years old, after which
by degrees they grew melancholy and dejected, increasing
in both till they came to fourscore. This he learned from
their own confession; for otherwise there not being above
two or three of that species born in an age, they were too
few to form a general observation by. When they came to
fourscore years, which is reckoned the extremity of living
in this country, they had not only all the follies and in-
firmities of other old men, but many more which arose
from the dreadful prospect of never dying. They were not
only opinionative, peevish, covetous, morose, vain, talka-
tive, but uncapable of friendship, and dead to all natural
affection, which never descended below their grandchildren. Envy and impotent desires are their prevailing
passions. But those objects against which their envy seems
principally directed, are the vices of the younger sort, and
the deaths of the old. By reflecting on the former, they
find themselves cut off from all possibility of pleasure;
and whenever they see a funeral, they lament and repine
that others are gone to an harbour of rest, to which they
themselves never can hope to arrive. They have no remembrance of anything but what they learned and observed in their youth and middle age, and even that is
very imperfect. And for the truth or particulars of any
fact, it is safer to depend on common traditions than upon
their best recollections. The least miserable among them
appear to be those who turn to dotage, and entirely lose
their memories; these meet with more pity and assistance,

because they want many bad qualities which abound in others.

If a Struldbrugg happen to marry one of his own kind, the marriage is dissolved of course by the courtesy of the kingdom, as soon as the younger of the two comes to be fourscore. For the law thinks it is a reasonable indulgence, that those who are condemned without any fault of their own to a perpetual continuance in the world, should not have their misery doubled by the load of a wife.

As soon as they have completed the term of eighty years, they are looked on as dead in law; their heirs immediately succeed to their estates, only a small pittance is reserved for their support, and the poor ones are maintained at the public charge. After that period they are held incapable of any employment of trust or profit, they cannot purchase lands or take leases, neither are they allowed to be witnesses in any cause, either civil or criminal, not even for the decision of meres and bounds.

At ninety they lose their teeth and hair, they have at that age no distinction of taste, but eat and drink whatever they can get, without relish or appetite. The diseases they were subject to, still continue without increasing or diminishing. In talking they forget the common appellation of things, and the names of persons, even of those who are their nearest friends and relations. For the same reason they never can amuse themselves with reading, because their memory will not serve to carry them from the beginning of a sentence to the end; and by this defect they are deprived of the only entertainment whereof they might otherwise be capable.

The language of this country being always upon the flux, the Struldbruggs of one age do not understand those of another, neither are they able after two hundred years to hold any conversation (farther than by a few general words) with their neighbours the mortals, and thus they lie under the disadvantage of living like foreigners in their own country.

This was the account given me of the Struldbruggs, as near as I can remember. I afterwards saw five or six of different ages, the youngest not above two hundred years old, who were brought to me at several times by some of my friends; but although they were told that I was a great traveller, and had seen all the world, they had not the least curiosity to ask me a question; only desired I would give them *slumskudask,* or a token of remembrance, which is a modest way of begging, to avoid the law that strictly forbids it, because they are provided for by the public, although indeed with a very scanty allowance.

They are despised and hated by all sorts of people; when one of them is born, it is reckoned ominous, and their birth is recorded very particularly; so that you may know their age by consulting the registry, which however hath not been kept above a thousand years past, or at least hath been destroyed by time or public disturbances. But the usual way of computing how old they are, is, by asking them what kings or great persons they can remember, and then consulting history, for infallibly the last Prince in their mind did not begin his reign after they were fourscore years old.

They were the most mortifying sight I ever beheld, and the women more horrible than the men. Besides the usual deformities in extreme old age, they acquired an additional ghastliness in proportion to their number of years, which is not to be described, and among half a dozen I soon distinguished which was the eldest, although there were not above a century or two between them.

The reader will easily believe, that from what I had heard and seen, my keen appetite for perpetuity of life was much abated. I grew heartily ashamed of the pleasing visions I had formed, and thought no tyrant could invent a death into which I would not run with pleasure from such a life. The King heard of all that had passed between me and my friends upon this occasion, and rallied me very pleasantly, wishing I would send a couple of Struldbruggs to my own country, to arm our people against the fear of death; but this it seems is forbidden by the fundamental laws of the kingdom or else I should have been well content with the trouble and expense of transporting them.

I could not but agree that the laws of this kingdom, relating to the Struldbruggs, were founded upon the strongest reasons, and such as any other country would be under the necessity of enacting in the like circumstances. Otherwise, as avarice is the necessary consequent of old age, those Immortals would in time become proprietors of the whole nation, and engross the civil power, which, for want of abilities to manage, must end in the ruin of the public.

IF THERE WERE NO DEATH
IN OUR WORLD
Nikolai Berdyaev

This poem expresses in a straightforward way the importance of death in the total life experience, emphasizing that if man were to live forever, life would become meaningless and empty. It is the threat of death, Berdyaev believes, that encourages mankind to value life and to live each day to its fullest.

Death is the most profound
   and significant fact of life:
it lifts the very last of mortals
   above the greyness
and banality of life.
   And only the fact of death
puts the question of life's meaning
   in all its depth.
Life in this world has meaning
   only because there is death:
if there were no death in our world,
   life would be deprived of meaning.
Meaning is linked with ending.
   And if there were no end,
if in our world there was evil
   and endlessness of life,
there would be no meaning to life whatever . . .
   The meaning of man's moral experience
throughout his whole life
   lies in putting him into a position
to comprehend death.

FOR A DANCER
JACKSON BROWNE

These lyrics by contemporary American songwriter Jackson Browne constitute an interesting statement of the complex mysteries of life and death. In a strongly positive message Browne advises mankind not to give up on life but to live fully with the disciplined grace and commitment of a dancer.

Keep a fire burning in your eye
Pay attention to the open sky
You never know what will be coming down
I don't remember losing track of you
You were always dancing in and out of view
I must have thought you'd always be around
Always keeping things real by playing the clown
Now you're nowhere to be found

I don't know what happens when people die
Can't seem to grasp it as hard as I try
It's like a song I can hear playing in my ear that
   I can't sing
I can't help listening
And I can't help feeling stupid standing 'round
Crying as they ease you down
'Cause I know that you'd rather we were dancing
Dancing our sorrow away (right on dancing)
No matter what fate chooses to play
(There's nothing you can do about it anyway)

Just do the steps that you've been shown
By everyone you've ever known
Until the dance becomes your very own
No matter how close to yours another's steps have grown
In the end there is one dance you'll do alone

Keep a fire for the human race
And let your prayers go drifting into space
You never know what will be coming down
Perhaps a better world is drawing near
And just as easily it could all disappear
Along with whatever meaning you might have found

Don't let the uncertainty turn you around
(The world keeps turnin' around and around)
Go on and make a joyful sound

Into a dancer you have grown
From a seed somebody else has thrown
Go on ahead and throw some seeds of your own
And somewhere between the time you arrive
And the time you go
May lie a reason you were alive
But you'll never know

THE IMPARTIALITY
OF DEATH
AURORA LUCERO WHITE-LEA

While death has often been viewed as an enemy by those in good circumstances, to the victim of lifelong discrimination death may be quite different. In this selection, a Southwestern folktale collected by Aurora Lucero White-Lea with the cooperation of the people in small towns and villages, death wears the mask of "the great equalizer" and bestows an ultimate sense of respect upon a man who has been shortchanged all his life.

An old man stole a rooster from a chicken coop because he was very hungry. He took it home, killed it, and put it to boil. Someone came to the door. The man did not want to go because he thought it was the owner of the bird, but the knocking continued and he could not ignore it. "Who are you and what do you want?" he asked the man standing there.

"I am God and I want something to eat."

"I am sorry but I cannot give you anything," said the man.

"Why," asked our Lord. "I smell food so I know you are not in want."

"No, I am not in want," said the man.

"Then what is the reason?" said the visitor.

"The reason is," said the man, "that I do not like to feed anyone who does not treat everyone alike. I notice that to some you give much; to others little."

"Yes, that is true," said the visitor, and departed.

Soon there came another knock at the door. A woman

stood there this time. "And who are you?" said the man.

"I am the Virgin," said the woman, "and I would like something to eat."

"I am sorry," said the man, "but I cannot share my food with you."

"Why?" asked the Virgin.

"Because," said the man, "you are one of those who does not treat everyone alike. To some you give much; to others little." The Virgin had nothing to say so she left.

And now the rooster was cooked and the man was ready to sit down and eat. Another knock was heard. "I wonder who it can be this time?" said the man. At the door stood Death. She said, "I smelled your rooster and I came along to help you eat it."

"And why not?" said the man. "Aren't you one who treats everyone alike?"

"That is so," said Death. "I have no favorites. The poor, the rich, the young, the old, the sick, the well—all look alike to me."

"That is the reason you may come in and share my food," said the man. Death entered and the two had a grand feast.

(Gathered by Juanita Gonzales, Pojouaque, New Mexico)

II

"TO STAND AT THAT LAST MOMENT":

The Process of Dying

Although our knowledge of death is essentially speculative, the scientist and artist have observed the process of dying for centuries, and we now know a considerable amount about it. We know that it is a voyage that must be taken alone. We also know that because of this, the prospect of dying brings up memories from the past of being alone, of departures, and of periods of loneliness—memories that may date as far back as early childhood.

Every voyage involves leaving someplace familiar and going to someplace that is unfamiliar. When the voyage is death, no travel agent can prepare us for that uncertain destination. No one can tell us with authority what it is like to be dead. In a poem by T. S. Eliot, one of his characters had the fantasy of rebelling against his passive, meaningless life by doing just that. He pictured his return: "I am Lazarus, come from the dead, come back to tell you all, and I shall tell you all." He would have been quite a crowd-getter if he had succeeded.

In Part III we will focus in more detail on this second aspect, the destination. However, at the time of dying, most people seem to be primarily concerned with the leaving, the separation. To a young child, separation and death are synonymous. To some extent, they always remain related because their effects upon people are so similar. Whether a classmate dies or moves to Australia, the result is the same: he or she is gone—gone from the playground and the schoolyard, and not likely to return. In the 1800's, when many persons emigrated from Ireland to the United States, families would hold what was known as an "American wake" for the children leaving for a new life abroad. (A wake is a traditional form of funeral service.) The leaving was treated as a death in which both parties underwent grief and mourning, as they never expected to see one another again.

To understand the experience of dying a little more personally, it might be helpful for you to think back to a time of significant loss and remember the feelings of that time. If you have no loss through death to remember, perhaps there was a move away from the city that had

29

been home for many years or leaving home to go to school or camp. What was that feeling like? Then try to imagine what it would be like if that feeling were magnified a hundred times. You may get some idea of what it feels like to know that you will soon be dead.

Like marriage, pregnancy, and mental illness, death is an intensely personal thing that brings out each person's characteristic defenses, strengths, habits, and perceptions. The variety of selections in this book, especially in this section, point out the broad range of reactions. No two people are ever quite alike and, as a result, we can witness as many different experiences of dying as there are individuals who die. Nevertheless, there are a number of frequently observed reactions to fatal illness that bear mentioning.

Many people develop a gradual awareness that "something is seriously wrong," and by the time they arrive at the doctor's office, it is as if they are half-expecting a confirmation of their worst fears and are not startled when it comes. In fact, it can be generally stated that most people with terminal illness suspect the seriousness of their condition long before their families—and, often, before their physicians—believe they do. Neither party wants to break the hard news to the other, and a conspiracy of silence often ensues, marked by an atmosphere of tense, insincere optimism.

Other patients, particularly those for whom there has been no gradual development of warning signals or to whom the news is broken abruptly, react for a period with shock, numbness, and disbelief. The person is stunned and, in all likelihood, relatively emotionless. Sometimes this lasts for minutes, sometimes for months. The news is so overwhelming that it simply doesn't get through to the person. This numbness can be viewed as a way that the individual defends himself against the devastating truth.

Another defense used against such an onslaught of intolerable news is the refusal to accept the facts. This is a psychological mechanism known as denial. The person may insist that there's been an error or that the condition can be easily "fixed" by drugs or surgery. Even when confronted with the facts about their illness, such persons manage to shield themselves from the truth and to hold to the belief that they will go on living.

Fear is another reaction to learning that one is dying.

Many people worry that dying will be painful, but their fear is not supported by what we know about the dying process. Naturally, certain types of illness may cause pain, but the death process itself need not be painful and may, in fact, bring relief from pain. According to Harvard professor Dr. Alfred Worchester, in his book, *The Care of the Aged, the Dying, and the Dead,* "Dying is always easy at the last. However great the previous suffering, there is always an interval of perfect peace and often of ecstasy before death. . . . All competent observers agree that except in the imagination, there is no such thing as 'death agony.' "

Other people may fear disability before death, with helplessness and dependency on others. Shame and loss of self-esteem may accompany dying if the patient has an illness that causes loss of the ability to take care of personal hygiene and appearance or if the patient suffers disfigurement. The patient may feel, "This isn't how I want to be remembered." For particular individuals, especially those who have placed a great value on self-reliance, dependency may be an even greater blow than the fear of death itself. Friends and family can be especially helpful to the dying person by showing that they don't view these bodily changes negatively.

Anger is another way some people react to the news that they are dying. They accuse Fate or God or even the doctors of being unfair. These persons demand to know "Why me?" and lash out at everyone around them, even those they love most. To the person who is dying, it is understandably infuriating to be continually surrounded by healthy people who will probably live out normal lifespans and do not face the imminent loss of their whole world.

Somewhat related to anger is bargaining, a reaction characteristic of some dying persons. They may bargain with God or even with the doctor: "Just give me one or two good years, and I'll lead a good productive life." Or, "I'll go, but only let me live until I can see my daughter grown into a young woman." They seem unaware that death makes no deals and grants no special exceptions.

For most dying persons, the predominant emotional reaction is depression. Since they are, in effect, mourning the loss of their self and their entire world, these persons feel profoundly sad about their impending deaths. They may cry frequently and show little interest in normal everyday activities.

At the very end, many dying patients come to accept the fact that they are dying and assume an attitude of resignation to the inevitable. This does not mean that they necessarily approve of what is happening to them, but that they at last realize the futility of fighting. This acceptance of one's imminent death is not a painful state, but rather a willing resignation to the inevitable course of nature. As the patient becomes resigned to death, he or she often begins to withdraw from the world and the people in it. Since death means irreversible separation from the things of the earth, the person stops looking at what he or she is leaving and often starts to look ahead to where he or she is going.

People's reactions to the news of impending death is often determined to a great extent by the setting in which their dying takes place. In the twentieth century, home and family have been replaced by nursing home and hospital as the site where most people die. The fear that death will be unnatural and alien is surely accentuated when sickness is accompanied by removal to an unnatural and unfamiliar place, where accomplishments, acquisitions, and identity must be left behind. Likewise, the patient's family is also removed from the setting in which it has developed the means for providing support. One simple example is that they can't make the patient's favorite food in the hospital. The tendencies toward depression and anger are also aggravated by the fact that in many hospitals the dying patient is unintentionally segregated, and he or she receives progressively less attention from the staff due to their own discomfort with patients to whom they can offer no tangible hope of cure. It is unfortunate that the educational focus in the health professions is chiefly on how to prolong life, and that it often fails to provide instruction in how to help a person die with grace and dignity. Thus, graduates of this system may feel unprepared and guilty when confronted with a patient's inevitable death.

But dying need not be painful nor meaningless nor shameful nor desperate, if the proper setting is provided. For example, at a center devoted exclusively to the care of terminally ill patients in England, it has been found that wholesome attitudes on the part of the staff lead to wholesome and optimistic outlooks on the part of the patients, and many of the gloomy reactions seen in our typical hospitals simply do not occur. By focusing only on the horror of impending death, we interfere with a person's chance to die with courage and dignity. Put another way, if we can't see beyond the fact that we would not choose to die, we become paralyzed and unable to choose anything about how we will die. Dr. Victor Frankl, a psychiatrist who survived the death camp at Auschwitz, realized during his experience there that "when everything else is taken from us, our last freedom is our ability to decide what attitude we will take towards what is happening to us." Regardless of the setting or the disease, this is the opportunity that any dying person and his family have the choice to retain.

Death, according to Shakespeare, is a voyage to "that undiscovered country from whose bourne no traveler returns." Those of us who remain behind may often be called upon to give comfort and support to that traveler, but it's not always easy to know how to be most helpful. We wonder whether the best thing is to try to distract the dying person with talk about the future or to tell jokes and stories. Many times, because we aren't completely at ease with the idea of death, we may be tempted to stay away from the person altogether, to spare ourselves pain. Yet somehow we must set aside our own discomfort and harness the natural capacity for empathy which each of us has. The dying person needs this warmth and caring most to be able to face the crisis of dying. We can help by simply being there.

At some point, most—though not all—people with terminal illness wish to talk about it to someone of their choosing. If it's unclear how much the person desires to talk about the future, it can be very helpful to leave an opening in the conversation that can be either taken or ignored. An example of such a statement would be, "The doctor certainly seems to be running quite a few tests on you." The person can then either reply with, "Yes, I wonder what she's looking for" (or something similar that indicates his desire to talk about it) or he can ignore the comment or change the subject. If the comment is subtle enough, it will give an indication that the visitor is willing to talk about the illness if the patient wants to.

Patients will frequently reveal their knowledge of and

feelings about their illnesses by nonverbal cues and symbolic talk. For example, they may talk about the future in ways that indicate recognition that they might not be around to participate. Sometimes, it's easiest to communicate with them in symbolic ways, also. In particular, touching often says far more than words. Touching can be a deep communication for both parties when words are hard to come by. People with terminal illness often look to others to find clues as to how they should regard their new self with its disordered structure and function—in particular, whether or not they should be ashamed of it. Touching is one simple way to indicate that they are cared for in whatever state—that their body is not viewed as something horrible or shameful. At times, it is helpful to divert attention from a hopeless, distant future and to refer to comforting things in the present or near future and to focus on functions that are retained.

Another very positive activity to share with a dying person is constructive reminiscing—a retrospective ordering of the events in that person's life. This "life review" helps them consolidate their views of themselves and their past, perhaps to see it as a unified structure with meaning and beauty. It serves an equally important purpose for the survivor, who simultaneously can mourn and consolidate those same shared memories. Comments that remind people of a sense of continuity, such as "Eleanor wants your recipe for pound cake," or "Charlie is taking your old drafting tools off to college," also serve this same purpose.

In the initial stages of fatal illness, it is important to instill a reasonable sense of hope, and this can usually be done without encouraging the person to deny reality. However, toward the end of the illness, if patients reach the stage of acceptance and feel the need to withdraw, it's important to allow them to give up hope and to let go of the people and things of the world. This can be extremely difficult for friends and relatives since, in some ways, it amounts to giving them permission to die. Nevertheless, even to the end, it is important to be present in spirit and reality, but to have the courage not to demand that the patient "be there" also.

from ENDING
HILMA WOLITZER

This selection is an excerpt from a novel by Hilma Wolitzer, a wife and mother of two daughters, who presently lives in Syosset, New York. The book tells of the struggle against cancer by a young husband, Jay Kaufman; the narrator is his wife Sandy. Jay, confined to the hospital since the beginning of his illness, has not been told that he is dying. This selection begins with Sandy's decision to tell him the truth.

I wanted to do it while he was still able to walk. It seemed *immoral* somehow to tell a dying man the miserable and imminent truth when he was helpless, lying down in the very path of the words. Maybe I expected him to be able to run, believed that I could give him a fighting chance. Driving to the hospital I remembered old movies where the girl came to the hideout and warned the rotten but lovable crook that the law was coming. Sometimes she said, Give yourself up, sweetheart. They'll get you in the end. Other times she said, Run for it. You still have a chance.

I was supposed to tell Jay that too. There's always a chance. It seemed like the most terrible of lies. He could look in the mirror, couldn't he? He could see the truth in the wasting of himself, in the way he *felt*. How do you feel? Fine. How do *you* feel? I'm dying.

My hands and feet were cold, even though the heater blasted away. Maybe Jay would make it easier for me. He knows already, I told myself. How could he not know? It was just a matter of acknowledgment now. I know that you know that I know. That sort of crap. Oh Jesus. I had read it somewhere once. *They* always know. They. An unfortunate exclusive club of mortals. He was like his father, would be like his father, would be dust. . . .

It was old home week in the hospital room. Martin and his parents were there, a man from the television studio was visiting Jay, and in the corner of the room two strangers in coveralls wrestled with the vent of the heating unit. "Be out of here in a minute, folks," one of them said, and he knocked on metal with a hammer, as if for emphasis.

Into that chaos I smiled at Jay, who winked back. Does a dying man who *knows* wink at his wife, smile at his friends, endure hammering and visitors, the whole selfish business of the surviving world? It didn't seem possible. Jay wasn't such a good actor. It was hard for us to hide anything from each other. Without thinking about it, we always sent out signals and clues of what we were feeling. Yet there we were. The man from the studio relinquished his seat to me, still laughing about something Jay had said to him. Potted plants languished on the windowsills, Martin's father filed away at my brain with his voice.

"How do you feel?" I said idiotically to Jay, and then I kissed him, forestalling an answer.

"Not so hot," he admitted, as we separated.

The man from the studio found his coat on a low shelf and said that he was leaving. I envied him his freedom to go and at the same time I wished that he would stay. I couldn't speak to Jay in front of anyone else and now that it had to be done, now that I had decided to just *do* it, I wanted more time, delays, distractions. But I couldn't remember the man's name, even as I thought of seductive words to keep him in the room. I noticed with sharp attention a shiny place on the lapel of his suit jacket and I said, "Please don't go yet. It's early." But it sounded only courteous, the perfunctory remark of a hostess who really wants to do the dishes and go to bed.

"We'll walk you to the elevator," I said, and Jay lifted himself from the bed and put his robe and slippers on. Doing those simple things seemed to require a real and deliberate effort on his part that made me want to hurry him along, to push his arms through the sleeves, the way you do to a small child with whom you've lost patience. The other man watched too, with a certain fascination, but none of us said anything.

We walked down the hall at Jay's new slow pace and when we came to the elevator I changed my mind again. I wanted the man to go quickly, to make his escape taking with him his small, inconsequential talk, his shiny lapels that made me feel so sad.

When he was gone and Jay turned again in the direction of his room, I put my hand on his arm. "Wait," I said. "Let's not go back there yet."

His look was questioning and I tried to explain. "I want to be alone with you."

"Oh, yeah?" Jay said, out of the corner of his mouth, but it was a small weak joke that didn't seem to help either of us.

"Let's try the other end of the hall, the solarium," I said. All the way there I was terribly aware of the people everywhere: patients, visitors, aides, nurses. It was a goddam circus. Maybe I should put it off, I thought, and try to get permission to come up during the day when no one else was around. How could I say something like that without privacy? How could I say it anyway?

There was a cramp in my chest as if I had been running instead of trying to walk very slowly and not get there ahead of Jay. "Well, here we are," I said, when we were indeed there, in the large room at the end of the hall. It wasn't very busy that night, and there were two empty couches at the farthest corner of the room. Here? I thought. Now? Us? What if he screamed, or made a terrible scene? What if he cried, fainted, bellowed? What if I did? Oh God, what if?

We sat down, sharing one cushion of the smaller couch. The other people seemed far away and out of focus, like people in the background of a photograph. He knows, I told myself, with one last desperate surge of hope, and then I looked up and saw his eyes. They seemed strange, like the eyes of someone I had never met. There was no meaning, no message in their expression. He looked merely quizzical, expectant.

Maybe it's the drugs, I thought. Personality changes happen. Everybody knows that. Maybe the drugs had dulled his senses a little, and it wouldn't have the same horrendous meaning. Maybe I was crazy.

"Jay," I said. Our hands joined, automatically finding one another in my lap. I took a deep difficult breath, sending out signals wildly like a sailor on a doomed ship.

But Jay just sat there, not willing to cooperate at all.

"Jay," I said again. "I saw Doctor Block."

Still he waited, silent.

"He *asked* me to come in. Jay?"

His hand was passive in mine, but his eyes were beginning to change, the pupils contracting to black points. It was a retreat. Run for it, sweetheart. You still have a chance.

His head tilted slightly now as if he found it difficult to hear me.

"We talked about the tests," I said. Oh help me.

But he seemed to draw slightly away from me, from this unsolicited news.

"It's not so good, darling." Please.

He started, like someone jolted from a dream. "What in hell are you *saying*, Sandy?"

"It's not *good*," I said again.

He looked quickly around the room, his eyes darting like those of a schoolboy ready to cheat on an exam.

I followed his glance. No one was looking at us. People were leaving the solarium. We were going to be alone.

Jay looked back at me again, his face full of terrible belief. "He *told* you that? Block told you that?"

I nodded, gripping his hand against the trembling that had begun. "Jay, listen, darling. He said there's research going on this very minute. There are remissions, you know . . ."

"Oh God. Oh shit," he said. "Where is it? Is it everywhere?" He was terrified, terrifying.

I put my other hand against the pain in my chest. "Marrow," I whispered.

His eyes widened, shut for a moment and then fastened me down again. "So this is the whole thing," he said, and he dropped my hand, as if *that* was what had betrayed him.

"Please, darling. Don't," I said, not even knowing what I meant. Don't what? Don't mourn for yourself? Don't rage or grieve? How did I dare tell him what to do? Give yourself up, sweetheart. They'll get you in the end.

I thought that the other questions would come then: How long do I have? Have you told anyone? What about pain? Will it be very bad? I braced myself, but he didn't say anything at all. And he didn't touch me again then, not even absently.

I felt even worse than I had before. It was as if I had killed him myself, or tried to, only inflicting a terrible wound. Bang bang, you're almost dead. My love, my dearest.

I didn't know what to do now in this reversal of roles. It was always Jay who had wrung whatever goodness there was out of me at the same time that he protected me from the worst of myself with the fierce concentration

THE PROCESS OF DYING   39

of his love. Now *I* had to protect *him,* save him at least
from the monster of this fear, if I couldn't save him from
death itself.

"Jay," I said. "I *love* you, darling." As if that mattered. As if anything mattered.

But it did. We turned at the same moment, colliding
painfully in the desperate need to hold and to be held.
We made sounds against one another, small anguished
sounds that I would always remember.

When it was possible to be quiet again we stood together, and now it seemed *natural* for me to move
slowly, as if I had become a part of Jay, of his cancer,
his knowledge, his very being.

"Don't come back now," he whispered, at the elevator.
"Go home."

"All right," I said, feeling all the unsaid words, crowding around us. I *had* to do it. Forgive me. Love me. Don't
give up the ship. Remember faith and hope and charity.
Remember.

The elevator came. Someone in a wheelchair waited
inside it, looked up at us with saintly patience. So we
kissed briefly, a peck really, and I took the last of his
innocence and went home.

Jay slept so much that I became used to it, to the long
bedside vigils where I would sit drooped in thought, or
nonthought, suffering instant lapses of memory. What day
was it? What time? What had I been thinking only a few
minutes before?

But then there were times when he came sharply and
suddenly awake, emerging from one of those long and
enervating dreams. He would continue conversations
begun in the dream, fix me with his eyes, and demand a
response. He was there again, but he was not quite himself. Drugged, drained, pummeled into hopelessness. It
scared me because I never knew what to expect, and I
was ashamed, because this was the only contact possible,
the only thing left between us, and I wanted to avoid it.

"The policies," he began one day while his eyes were
still closed.

I was startled out of my slouch. "Sweetheart," I said.
"We talked about that. Don't you remember? I spoke to
Murray. We took care of everything."

"Yeah," he said. "It comes back. Do they call?"

"Who?"

"I don't know. Everybody. The crew. Murray. Jerry."

"Yes yes, they all do." Sick with guilt, I knew that I wanted him to sleep again. He had interrupted that strange new state of nothingness I had been clever enough to discover, and he was leading me back to reality. If we talked anymore it would become painful, real, catastrophic. "Do you want some water, darling?" That was a safe topic—the diminishing needs of a diminishing man.

But he didn't even bother to answer. "There are things you have to do, Sandy," he said.

"What things?"

"Take care of some of my stuff. You could sell some of the equipment, the cameras."

"I gave the Rolleiflex to Martin. You told me," I said, worried that he had forgotten and would feel betrayed.

But he only nodded, shutting his eyes again.

Just sleep, I thought. Sweet nothing sleep. I could do it myself right now if there was some place to lie down.

"I keep thinking about the book," Jay said.

The book! I felt an instant throb of jealousy. Why did he think about that? Why didn't he think about the children, about me? But I recognized my own lack of fairness and reason. After all the book was an extension of himself. When he was gone the book would be the real and final proof of himself. As far back as I could remember it was the thing he most looked forward to. Not to its completion, perhaps, but to its growth, to the very act of doing it.

"I wish I could have finished it," he said, and he might have been talking about anything, even his own life.

"I know," I said.

"I took my own sweet time."

"There's a lot there," I said. "You did a lot."

He sighed. "Would you look through it for me, Sandy? Would you see if you can get it into any order, make some sense of it?"

"Sure," I said. "I can do that. I have anyway. I do."

"What?"

"Look through it sometimes when I go home." I felt shy, embarrassed, as if I had been discovered in some naive and romantic practice.

"Maybe you can show it to somebody someday," he said.

"You mean try and get it published, Jay? Is that what you mean?"

"I don't know."

"That's a *good* idea," I said, trying to force some excitement into the monotone of my voice. "It's a beautiful book, Jay. I'm going to do it this week. Look through the folder, get things going for you."

"It wouldn't have much of a chance," he said. "It needs work."

"Who knows? Listen, what do you want to call it? Something simple and right to the point, I think. New York, a Photographic Essay. Or New York City, A Life Story. Is that corny? What do you think?"

"I don't know." He turned his head away, as if he were bored, weary of the subject.

But I felt compelled to continue, desperately chatty, like a woman being eased out of a love affair. I said positive things, things that implied the future. What was wrong with me? I couldn't stop.

"Ah, who gives a damn," he said then, into the wall. "Who gives a damn about anything."

And I found myself sinking back into the chair, the new false energy instantly spent. He was right. Who gives a damn. Who cares. "Darling," I said. "Do you think you can sleep? Will you try to sleep?"

His voice came with a muffled resonance, his face still turned away. "I'm not tired," he said, and fell instantly asleep.

He died in his sleep, in my sleep, as I nodded, dozing in the waiting room. My shoes were off and my skirt twisted around so that the zipper was in the front. The nurse woke me, called my name. I could not, would not remember where I was. I chose to be dreaming or back in childhood, wakened by my mother for school, or anywhere that was not here. "No," I said, sealing out the invasion of light with my heavy eyelids. I shoved against her, pushing away the reality of her presence, her inevitable news. Oh, I wanted to sleep, sleep.

They woke me after Harry was born. I had gone out in that last moment of creation. "It's a boy! Look, Sandy, it's a boy. He's fine. It's all over." I came awake to astonishment and pleasure. Jay, inflated with joy, my mother and father, transformed into grandparents. Plants, flowers, greeting cards that celebrated life.

"I won't," I said to this nurse, but she would not allow it. Her urging became less gentle and I had to open my eyes. The two brothers were there, huddled together in a corner, and the woman in the gray coat was asleep in her chair. Wake *her*, I thought. Let it be *their* news. Why did she pick on me?

I sat up and rubbed my eyes. The nurse sat next to me on the couch and she took my hand. "He's gone," she said. "In his sleep."

Gone. But she meant dead. Gone was someone gone from a room, someone escaped from a prison. Dead was no breath, no pain, no pleasure. It was nothing.

"Do you want something?" she asked. "A sedative?"

But I shook my head. I had been asleep, sedated when Harry was born, so that I would not feel the final and earthshaking thrust of his head. "Give me something. Hurry up!" I had ordered. Who wanted to be a martyr to the birth of a stranger? The mask came and I rose to meet it, grateful and greedy.

But now it was necessary to be alert, to know everything. The others in the room stared at me, their eyes like the watchful eyes of small animals in a forest.

"Did he say anything?" I asked the nurse, thinking of an urgent message, last words that would unravel the mystery.

But she said, "No, quietly, in his sleep. I was with him."

Not me, ear cocked for final sounds, but this strange and gentle woman, who was there because it was her job. At the end of the week she would get a paycheck, with deductions, for sitting with my husband while he died. It was the strangest thing to think about, as if I were trying to understand the mores of another culture.

"Would you like to see him?" she asked, and I drew away from her for a moment. Of course not. Of course I didn't want to see him. All the terrible death words rushed into my head. Corpse, body, remains. God. But I had promised myself that I would know everything. The ritual would be completed. I stood, light-headed and uncertain. The tiled floor was cold under my stockinged feet, and she led me, holding my elbow, like a mother leading a child to the bathroom during the night.

The room had been emptied of all the paraphernalia:

the tubes, trays, the machines that defied this terrible and natural process of life. I hoped for a moment that he would appear to be sleeping, that I could be comforted by all the American phrases of solace. He is just away. He is only asleep. He is out of it now. At least his suffering is over. See how peaceful he looks.

But he didn't even look like Jay anymore. It was the right room. There was the yellow water stain under the windowsill, the familiar whorls in the wood of the door. And there on the bed was a dead body, nothing more. The nurse was right. Gone was the right word after all. The force of life, gone. The miracle of emotion, gone. Nothing.

I left the room, padding silently down the hall to get my shoes and coat. I wanted to go home and get on with the real business of mourning. But it wouldn't wait. The others in the waiting room made the first ovations. "Sorry. Out of pain now. At peace. So sorry." They murmured, fluttered and flapped near me until tears burned in my throat. Don't, I warned myself. What did those stock phrases have to do with Jay, with me, with our real lives? I would not let them enter me and take hold. And yet the texture of that gray coat against my skin, the whispering chorus of their voices, the real and human smell and warmth of their breath invaded me and I passed among them weeping.

I went home and I let myself into the apartment, going quickly past the dumb, expectant faces of my parents and the children. I went into the bedroom and I shut the door. They called timidly. "Sandy? Are you all right? Sandy?" They knocked on the door. But I would not answer. I lay down on the bed, the only place where it was possible to begin.

from THE NOTEBOOK
OF MALTE LAURIDS BRIGGE
RAINER MARIA RILKE

Rilke lived from 1875 to 1926 and is probably best known as one of Germany's leading poets. In this excerpt from an autobiographical novel, he remembers the awesome power of his grandfather's death. The concept of a unique death that we each carry within us like our individual personalities is nowhere more succinctly expressed.

Christoph Detlev's death had been living at Ulsgaard for many, many days now and he had spoken to everyone and demanded: demanded to be carried, demanded the blue room, demanded the little salon, demanded the large hall. Demanded the dogs, demanded that people should laugh, talk, play and be quiet and all at the same time. Demanded to see friends, women, and people who were dead, and demanded to die itself: demanded. Demanded and shouted.

For when night had fallen and those of the overwearied domestics who were not on watch tried to go to sleep, then Christoph Detlev's death would shout, shout and groan, roar so long and so constantly that the dogs, at first howling along with him, were silent and did not dare lie down, but stood on their long, slender, trembling legs, and were afraid. And when they heard it in the village roaring through the spacious, silvery, Danish summer night, they rose from their beds as if there were a thunderstorm, put on their clothes and remained sitting round the lamp without a word until it was over. And women near their time were laid in the most remote rooms and in the most impenetrable closets; but they heard it, they heard it, as if it were in their own bodies, and they pled to be allowed to get up too, and came, white and wide, and sat among the others with their blurred faces. And the cows that were calving at that time were helpless and bound, and from the body of one they tore the dead fruit with all the entrails, as it would not come at all. And everyone did their daily work badly and forgot to bring in the hay, because they spent the day dreading the night and because they were so fagged out by all their continuous watchings and terrified arisings, that they could not remember anything. And when they went on Sundays to the white, peaceful church, they prayed that there might no longer be a master at Ulsgaard: for this was a dreadful master. And what they all thought and prayed the pastor said aloud from the height of his pulpit; for he also had no nights any more and could not understand God. And the bell said it, having found a terrible rival that boomed the whole night through, and against which, even though it took to sounding with all its metal, it could do nothing.

Indeed, they all said it; and there was one among the young men who dreamed that he had gone to the manor-house and killed the master with his pitch-fork; and they were so exasperated, so done, so overwrought, that they all listened as he told his dream, and, quite unconsciously, looked at him to see if he were really equal to such a deed. Thus did they feel and speak throughout the whole district where, only a few weeks before, the chamberlain had been loved and pitied. But though they talked thus, nothing changed. Christoph Detlev's death, which dwelt at Ulsgaard, was not to be hurried. It had come to stay for ten weeks, and for ten weeks it stayed. And during that time it was more master than ever Christoph Detlev Brigge had been; it was like a king who, afterward and forever, is called the Terrible.

That was not the death of just any dropsical person; it was the wicked, princely death which the chamberlain had carried within him and nourished on himself his whole life long. All excess of pride, will and lordly vigor that he himself had not been able to consume in his quiet days, had passed into his death, that death which now sat, dissipating, at Ulsgaard.

How the chamberlain would have looked at anyone who asked of him that he should die any other death than this. He was dying his own hard death.

And when I think of the others whom I have seen or about whom I have heard: it is always the same. They all have had a death of their own.

(Translated by M. D. Herter Norton)

from ISLAND
ALDOUS HUXLEY

The tendency to fight and bitterly resent death is not common to all cultures, despite its prevalence in urban America. This selection includes a portrayal of a peaceful, unhindered death, in which both the dying person (Lakshmi) and those present (including Susila, Lakshmi's daughter-in-law; Will, Lakshmi's son; and Dr. Robert, her husband) confront with grace and dignity the reality of death. Lakshmi's comfortable death is

*juxtaposed for the purpose of contrast with a previous death
that Will remembers, that of his Aunt Mary, who did not
possess the serenity of Lakshmi. The selection makes reference
to a number of phenomena, such as the patient experiencing an
intense light at the time of death and having the sensation of
being outside her body looking at herself, which recent scientific
inquiries have found to be common among persons revived
after being pronounced dead in the hospital. The author,
Aldous Huxley, was born in England in 1894, but moved to
the United States in the late 1930's. His most famous work,
Brave New World, was published in 1932. He died in 1963.*

"This way," said the nurse, and held open a swing door.

Will stepped forward. The conditioned reflex of polite-
ness clicked automatically into action. "Thank you," he
said, and smiled. But it was with a dull, sick feeling in
the pit of the stomach that he went hobbling towards the
apprehended future.

"The last door on the left," said the nurse. But now she
had to get back to her desk in the lobby. "So I'll leave
you to go on alone," she added as the door closed behind
her.

Alone, he repeated to himself, alone—and the apprehended future was identical with the haunting past, the
Essential Horror was timeless and ubiquitous. This long
corridor with its green-painted walls was the very same
corridor along which, a year ago, he had walked to the
little room where Molly lay dying. The nightmare was re-
current. Foredoomed and conscious, he moved on towards
its horrible consummation. Death, yet another vision of
death.

Thirty-two, thirty-three, thirty-four . . . He knocked
and waited, listening to the beating of his heart. The door
opened and he found himself face to face with little
Radha.

"Susila was expecting you," she whispered.

Will followed her into the room. Rounding a screen, he
caught a glimpse of Susila's profile silhouetted against a
lamp, of a high bed, of a dark emaciated face on the pillow, of arms that were no more than parchment-covered
bones, of clawlike hands. Once again the Essential Horror.
With a shudder he turned away. Radha motioned him to
a chair near the open window. He sat down and closed
his eyes—closed them physically against the present, but,

by that very act, opened them inwardly upon that hateful past of which the present had reminded him. He was there in that other room, with Aunt Mary. Or rather with the person who had once been Aunt Mary, but was now this hardly recognizable somebody else—somebody who had never so much as heard of the charity and courage which had been the very essence of Aunt Mary's being; somebody who was filled with an indiscriminate hatred for all who came near her, loathing them, whoever they might be, simply because they didn't have cancer, because they weren't in pain, had not been sentenced to die before their time. And along with this malignant envy of other people's health and happiness had gone a bitterly querulous self-pity, an abject despair.

"Why to me? Why should this thing have happened to me?"

He could hear the shrill complaining voice, could see that tearstained and distorted face. The only person he had ever really loved or wholeheartedly admired. And yet, in her degradation, he had caught himself despising her—despising, positively hating.

To escape from the past, he reopened his eyes. Radha, he saw, was sitting on the floor, cross-legged and upright, in the posture of meditation. In her chair beside the bed Susila seemed to be holding the same kind of focused still-ness. He looked at the face on the pillow. That too was still, still with a serenity that might almost have been the frozen calm of death. Outside, in the leafy darkness, a peacock suddenly screamed. Deepened by contrast, the ensuing silence seemed to grow pregnant with mysterious and appalling meanings.

"Lakshmi." Susila laid a hand on the old woman's wasted arm. "Lakshmi," she said again more loudly. The death-calm face remained impassive. "You mustn't go to sleep."

Not go to sleep? But for Aunt Mary, sleep—the arti-ficial sleep that followed the injections—had been the only respite from the self-lacerations of self-pity and brooding fear.

"Lakshmi!"

The face came to life.

"I wasn't really asleep," the old woman whispered. "It's just my being so weak. I seem to float away."

"But you've got to be here," said Susila. "You've got to

know you're here. All the time." She slipped an additional pillow under the sick woman's shoulders and reached for a bottle of smelling salts that stood on the bed table.

Lakshmi sniffed, opened her eyes, and looked up into Susila's face. "I'd forgotten how beautiful you were," she said. "But then Dugald always did have good taste." The ghost of a mischievous smile appeared for a moment on the fleshless face. "What do you think, Susila?" she added after a moment and in another tone. "Shall we see him again? I mean, over there?"

In silence Susila stroked the old woman's hand. Then, suddenly smiling, "How would the Old Raja have asked that question?" she said. *"Do you think 'we' (quote, unquote) shall see 'him' (quote, unquote) 'over there' (quote, unquote)?"*

"But what do *you* think?"

"I think we've all come out of the same light, and we're all going back into the same light."

Words, Will was thinking, words, words, words. With an effort, Lakshmi lifted a hand and pointed accusingly at the lamp on the bed table.

"It glares in my eyes," she whispered.

Susila untied the red silk handkerchief knotted around her throat and draped it over the lamp's parchment shade. From white and mercilessly revealing, the light became as dimly, warmly rosy as the flush, Will found himself thinking, on Babs's rumpled bed, whenever Porter's Gin proclaimed itself in crimson.

"That's much better," said Lakshmi. She shut her eyes. Then, after a long silence, "The light," she broke out, "the light. It's here again." Then after another pause, "Oh, how wonderful," she whispered at last, "how wonderful!" Suddenly she winced and bit her lip.

Susila took the old woman's hand in both of hers. "Is the pain bad?" she asked.

"It would be bad," Lakshmi explained, "if it were really *my* pain. But somehow it isn't. The pain's here; but I'm somewhere else. It's like what you discover with the *moksha*-medicine. Nothing really belongs to you. Not even your pain."

"Is the light still there?"

Lakshmi shook her head. "And looking back, I can tell you exactly when it went away. It went away when I started talking about the pain not being really mine."

"And yet what you were saying was good."

"I know—but I was *saying* it." The ghost of an old habit of irreverent mischief flitted once across Lakshmi's face.

"What are you thinking of?" Susila asked.

"Socrates."

"Socrates?"

"Gibber, gibber, gibber—even when he'd actuallly swallowed the stuff. Don't let me talk, Susila. Help me to get out of my own light."

"Do you remember that time last year," Susila began after a silence, "when we all went up to the old Shiva temple above the High Altitude Station? You and Robert and Dugald and me and the two children—do you remember?"

Lakshmi smiled with pleasure at the recollection.

"I'm thinking specially of that view from the west side of the temple—the view out over the sea. Blue, green, purple—and the shadows of the clouds were like ink. And the clouds themselves—snow, lead, charcoal, satin. And while we were looking, you asked a question. Do you remember, Lakshmi?"

"You mean, about the Clear Light?"

"About the Clear Light," Susila confirmed. "Why do people speak of Mind in terms of Light? Is it because they've seen the sunshine and found it so beautiful that it seems only natural to identify the Buddha Nature with the clearest of all possible Clear Lights? Or do they find the sunshine beautiful because, consciously or unconsciously, they've been having revelations of Mind in the form of Light ever since they were born? I was the first to answer," said Susila, smiling to herself. "And as I'd just been reading something by some American behaviorist, I didn't stop to think—I just gave you the (quote, unquote) 'scientific point of view.' People equate Mind (whatever *that* may be) with hallucinations of light, because they've looked at a lot of sunsets and found them very impressive. But Robert and Dugald would have none of it. The Clear Light, they insisted, comes first. You go mad about sunsets because sunsets remind you of what's always been going on, whether you knew it or not, inside your skull and outside space and time. You agreed with them, Lakshmi—do you remember? You said, 'I'd like to be on your side, Susila, if only because it isn't good for these men of ours to be right *all* the time. But in this case—surely it's pretty obvious—in this case they *are* right.' Of course they were right, and of course I was hopelessly wrong. And, needless to say, you had known the right answer before you asked the question."

"I never *knew* anything," Lakshmi whispered. "I could only *see*."

"I remember your telling me about seeing the Clear Light," said Susila. "Would you like me to remind you of it?"

The sick woman nodded her head.

"When you were eight years old," said Susila. "That was the first time. An orange butterfly on a leaf, opening and shutting its wings in the sunshine—and suddenly there was the Clear Light of pure Suchness blazing through it, like another sun."

"Much brighter than the sun," Lakshmi whispered.

"But much gentler. You can look into the Clear Light and not be blinded. And now remember it. A butterfly on a green leaf, opening and shutting its wings—and it's the Buddha Nature totally present, it's the Clear Light outshining the sun. And you were only eight years old."

"What had I done to deserve it?"

Will found himself remembering that evening, a week or so before her death, when Aunt Mary had talked about the wonderful times they had had together in her little Regency house near Arundel where he had spent the better part of all his holidays. Smoking out the wasps' nests with fire and brimstone, having picnics on the downs or under the beeches. And then the sausage rolls at Bognor, the gypsy fortuneteller who had prophesied that he would end up as Chancellor of the Exchequer, the black-robed, red-nosed verger who had chased them out of Chichester Cathedral because they had laughed too much. "Laughed too much," Aunt Mary had repeated bitterly. *"Laughed too much . . ."*

"And now," Susila was saying, "think of that view from the Shiva temple. Think of those lights and shadows on the sea, those blue spaces between the clouds. Think of them, and then let go of your thinking. Let go of it, so that the not-Thought can come through. Things into Emptiness. Emptiness into Suchness. Suchness into things again, into your own mind. Remember what it says in the Sutra. 'Your own consciousness shining, void, inseparable from the great Body of Radiance, is subject neither to birth nor death, but is the same as the immutable Light, Buddha Amitabha.' "

"The same as the light," Lakshmi repeated. "And yet it's all dark again."

"It's dark because you're trying too hard," said Susila. "Dark because you want it to be light. Remember what you used to tell me when I was a little girl. 'Lightly, child, lightly, act lightly, feel lightly. Yes, feel lightly, even through you're feeling deeply. Just lightly let things happen and lightly cope with them.' I was so preposterously serious in those days, such a humorless little prig. Lightly, lightly—it was the best advice ever given me. Well, now I'm going to say the same thing to you, Lakshmi . . . Lightly, my darling, lightly. Even when it comes to dying. Nothing ponderous, or portentous, or emphatic. No rhetoric, no tremolos, no self-conscious persona putting on its celebrated imitation of Christ or Goethe or Little Nell. And, of course, no theology, no metaphysics. Just the fact of dying and the fact of the Clear Light. So throw away all your baggage and go forward. There are quicksands all about you, sucking at your feet, trying to suck you down into fear and self-pity and despair. That's why you must walk so lightly. Lightly, my darling. On tiptoes; and no luggage, not even a sponge bag. Completely unencumbered."

Completely unencumbered . . . Will thought of poor Aunt Mary sinking deeper and deeper with every step into the quicksands. Deeper and deeper until, struggling and protesting to the last, she had gone down, completely and forever, into the Essential Horror. He looked again at the fleshless face on the pillow and saw that it was smiling.

"The Light," came the hoarse whisper, "the Clear Light. It's here—along with the pain, in spite of the pain."

"And where are *you?*" Susila asked.

"Over there, in the corner." Lakshmi tried to point, but the raised hand faltered and fell back, inert, on the coverlet. "I can see myself there. And she can see my body on the bed."

"Can she see the Light?"

"No. The Light's here, where my body is."

The door of the sickroom was quietly opened. Will turned his head and was in time to see Dr. Robert's small spare figure emerging from behind the screen into the rosy twilight.

Susila rose and motioned him to her place beside the bed. Dr. Robert sat down and, leaning forward, took his wife's hand in one of his and laid the other on her forehead.

"It's me," he whispered.

"At last . . ."

A tree, he explained, had fallen across the telephone line. No communication with the High Altitude Station except by road. They had sent a messenger in a car, and the car had broken down. More than two hours had been lost. "But thank goodness," Dr. Robert concluded, "here I finally am."

The dying woman sighed profoundly, opened her eyes for a moment and looked up at him with a smile, then closed them again. "I knew you'd come."

"Lakshmi," he said very softly. "Lakshmi." He drew the tips of his fingers across the wrinkled forehead, again and again. "My little love." There were tears on his cheeks; but his voice was firm and he spoke with the tenderness not of weakness, but of power.

"I'm not over there any more," Lakshmi whispered.

"She was over there in the corner," Susila explained to her father-in-law. "Looking at her body here on the bed."

"But now I've come back. Me and the pain, me and the Light, me and you—all together."

The peacock screamed again and, through the insect noises that in this tropical night were the equivalent of silence, far off but clear came the sound of gay music, flutes and plucked strings and the steady throbbing of drums.

"Listen," said Dr. Robert. "Can you hear it? They're dancing."

"Dancing," Lakshmi repeated. "Dancing."

"Dancing so lightly," Susila whispered. "As though they had wings."

The music swelled up again into audibility.

"It's the Courting Dance," Susila went on.

"The Courting Dance. Robert, do you remember?"

"Could I ever forget?"

Yes, Will said to himself, could one ever forget? Could one ever forget that other distant music and, nearby, unnaturally quick and shallow, the sound of dying breath in a boy's ears? In the house across the street somebody was practicing one of those Brahms Waltzes that Aunt Mary had loved to play. One-two and three and One-two and three and O-o-o-ne two three, One- and One and Two-Three and One and . . . The odious stranger who had once been Aunt Mary stirred out of her artificial stupor and opened her eyes. An expression of the most intense malignity had appeared on the yellow, wasted face. "Go and tell them to stop," the harsh, unrecognizable voice had almost screamed. And then the lines of malignity had changed into the lines of despair, and the stranger, the pitiable odious stranger started to sob uncontrollably. Those Brahms Waltzes—they were the pieces, out of all her repertory, that Frank had loved best.

Another gust of cool air brought with it a louder strain of the gay, bright music.

"All those young people dancing together," said Dr. Robert. "All that laughter and desire, all that uncomplicated happiness! It's all here, like an atmosphere, like a field of force. Their joy and our love—Susila's love, my love—all working together, all reinforcing one another. Love and joy enveloping you, my darling; love and joy carrying you up into the peace of the Clear Light. Listen to the music. Can you still hear it, Lakshmi?"

"She's drifted away again," said Susila. "Try to bring her back."

Dr. Robert slipped an arm under the emaciated body and lifted it into a sitting posture. The head drooped sideways onto his shoulder.

"My little love," he kept whispering. "My little love . . ."

Her eyelids fluttered open for a moment. "Brighter," came the barely audible whisper, "brighter." And a smile of happiness intense almost to the point of elation transfigured her face.

Through his tears Dr. Robert smiled back at her. "So now you can let go, my darling." He stroked her gray hair. "Now you can let go. Let go," he insisted. "Let go of this poor old body. You don't need it any more. Let it fall away from you. Leave it lying here like a pile of worn-out clothes."

In the fleshless face the mouth had fallen cavernously open, and suddenly the breathing became stertorous.

"My love, my little love . . ." Dr. Robert held her

more closely. "Let go now, let go. Leave it here, your old worn-out body, and go on. Go on, my darling, go on into the Light, into the peace, into the living peace of the Clear Light . . ."

Susila picked up one of the limp hands and kissed it, then turned to little Radha.

"Time to go," she whispered, touching the girl's shoulder.

Interrupted in her meditation, Radha opened her eyes, nodded and, scrambling to her feet, tiptoed silently towards the door. Susila beckoned to Will and, together, they followed her. In silence the three of them walked along the corridor. At the swing door Radha took her leave.

"Thank you for letting me be with you," she whispered.

Susila kissed her. "Thank *you* for helping to make it easier for Lakshmi."

from MALONE DIES
SAMUEL BECKETT

Samuel Beckett, an Irish writer of the twentieth century, won the Nobel Prize for Literature. In this selection, Malone is an aged, intelligent gentleman, abandoned for his last days in a room in what could be a nursing home. Beckett obviously understands that life continues when the flame of will can be fanned and ceases when that flame goes out. Malone is fully aware of his approaching death but he is dissociated from it, even objective toward his progressive failure of physiological and mental functioning. While his future seems inevitable, he does not forgive the lack of kindness toward him in life that allowed his spirit to reach such a hopeless state.

I shall soon be quite dead at last in spite of all. Perhaps next month. Then it will be the month of April or of May. For the year is still young, a thousand little signs tell me so. Perhaps I am wrong, perhaps I shall survive Saint John the Baptist's Day and even the Fourteenth of July, festival of freedom. Indeed I would not put it past me to pant on to the Transfiguration, not to speak of the Assumption. But I do not think so, I do not think I am wrong in saying that these rejoicings will take place in my absence, this year. I have that feeling, I have had it now for some days, and I credit it. But in what does it differ from those that have abused me ever since I was born? No, that is the kind of bait I do not rise to any more, my need for prettiness is gone. I could die today, if I wished, merely by making a little effort, if I could wish, if I could make an effort. But it is just as well to let myself die, quietly, without rushing things. Something must have changed. I will not weigh upon the balance any more, one way or the other. I shall be neutral and inert. No difficulty there. Throes are the only trouble, I must be on my guard against throes. But I am less given to them now, since coming here. Of course I still have my little fits of impatience, from time to time, I must be on my guard against them, for the next fortnight or three weeks. Without exaggeration to be sure, quietly crying and laughing, without working myself up into a state. Yes, I shall be natural at last, I shall suffer more, then less, without drawing any conclusions, I shall pay less heed to myself, I shall be neither hot nor cold any more, I shall be tepid, I shall die tepid, without enthusiasm. I shall not watch myself die, that would spoil everything. Have I watched myself live? Have I ever complained? Then why rejoice now? I am content, necessarily, but not to the point of clapping my hands. I was always content, knowing I would be repaid. There he is now, my old debtor. Shall I then fall on his neck? I shall not answer any more questions. I shall even try not to ask myself any more. While waiting I shall tell myself stories, if I can. They will not be the same kind of stories as hitherto, that is all. They will be neither beautiful nor ugly, they will be calm, there will be no ugliness or beauty or fever in them any more, they will be almost lifeless, like the teller. What was that I said? It does not matter. I look forward to their giving me great satisfaction, some satisfaction. I am satisfied, there, I have enough, I am repaid, I need nothing more. Let me say before I go any further that I forgive nobody. I wish them all an atrocious life and then the fires and ice of hell and in the execrable generations to come an honoured name. Enough for this evening.

from THE DEATH
OF IVAN ILYCH
LEO TOLSTOY

Count Leo Tolstoy, the author of War and Peace, *lived in
Russia from 1828 to 1910. His story, "The Death of Ivan
Ilych," is one of the most instructive portrayals of death in all
of literature. It shows us that the process of dying can be an act
of personal growth and enlightenment, despite physical deteriora-
tion. The approach of death stimulates Ivan Ilych to review
his life and assess its meaning. In his death torment, Ilych
alienates those around him, and in his confusion he appears
out of contact with them. Yet, it is the final act of kindness
by his son that allows him to break through and find peace—
a reminder to us all of the deep need of the dying for loving
companions in the final ·stages of serious illness. In his last
moments, Ilych comes to accept the pain that has plagued him
and resigns himself for the first time to death. As Ilych takes
his last breaths, he sees a bright light and experiences ecstasy,
phenomena actually reported by many patients revived after
being pronounced dead.*

. . . His wife returned late at night. She came in on tip-
toe, but he heard her, opened his eyes, and made haste to
close them again. She wished to send Gerasim away and
to sit with him herself, but he opened his eyes and said:
"No, go away."

"Are you in great pain?"

"Always the same."

"Take some opium."

He agreed and took some. She went away.

Till about three in the morning he was in a state of
stupefied misery. It seemed to him that he and his pain
were being thrust into a narrow, deep black sack, but
though they were pushed further and further in they
could not be pushed to the bottom. And this, terrible
enough in itself, was accompanied by suffering. He was
frightened yet wanted to fall through the sack, he struggled but yet cooperated. And suddenly he broke through,
fell, and regained consciousness. Gerasim was sitting at the
foot of the bed dozing quietly and patiently, while he
himself lay with his emaciated stockinged legs resting on

Gerasim's shoulders; the same shaded candle was there and the same unceasing pain.

"Go away, Gerasim," he whispered.

"It's all right, sir. I'll stay a while."

"No. Go away."

He removed his legs from Gerasim's shoulders, turned sideways onto his arm, and felt sorry for himself. He only waited till Gerasim had gone into the next room and then restrained himself no longer but wept like a child. He wept on account of his helplessness, his terrible loneliness, the cruelty of man, the cruelty of God, and the absence of God.

"Why hast Thou done all this? Why hast Thou brought me here? Why, why dost Thou torment me so terribly?"

He did not expect an answer and yet wept because there was no answer and could be none. The pain again grew more acute, but he did not stir and did not call. He said to himself: "Go on! Strike me! But what is it for? What have I done to Thee? What is it for?"

Then he grew quiet and not only ceased weeping but even held his breath and became all attention. It was as though he were listening not to an audible voice but to the voice of his soul, to the current of thoughts arising within him.

"What is it you want?" was the first clear conception capable of expression in words, that he heard.

"What do you want? What do you want?" he repeated to himself.

"What do I want? To live and not to suffer," he answered.

And again he listened with such concentrated attention that even his pain did not distract him.

"To live? How?" asked his inner voice.

"Why, to live as I used to—well and pleasantly."

"As you lived before, well and pleasantly?" the voice repeated.

And in imagination he began to recall the best moments of his pleasant life. But strange to say none of those best moments of his pleasant life now seemed at all what they had then seemed—none of them except the first recollections of childhood. There, in childhood, there had been something really pleasant with which it would be possible to live if it could return. But the child who had experienced that happiness existed no longer, it was like a reminiscence of somebody else.

As soon as the period began which had produced the present Ivan Ilych, all that had then seemed joys now melted before his sight and turned into something trivial and often nasty.

And the further he departed from childhood and the nearer he came to the present the more worthless and doubtful were the joys. This began with the School of Law. A little that was really good was still found there—there was light-heartedness, friendship, and hope. But in the upper classes there had already been fewer of such good moments. Then during the first years of his official career, when he was in the service of the Governor, some pleasant moments again occurred: they were the memories of love for a woman. Then all became confused and there was still less of what was good; later on again there was still less that was good, and the further he went the less there was. His marriage, a mere accident, then the disenchantment that followed it, his wife's bad breath and the sensuality and hypocrisy: then that deadly official life and those preoccupations about money, a year of it, and two, and ten, and twenty, and always the same thing. And the longer it lasted the more deadly it became. "It is as if I had been going downhill while I imagined I was going up. And that is really what it was. I was going up in public opinion, but to the same extent life was ebbing away from me. And now it is all done and there is only death."

"Then what does it mean? Why? It can't be that life is so senseless and horrible. But if it really has been so horrible and senseless, why must I die and die in agony? There is something wrong!"

"Maybe I did not live as I ought to have done," it suddenly occurred to him. "But how could that be, when I did everything properly?" he replied, and immediately dismissed from his mind this, the sole solution of all the riddles of life and death, as something quite impossible.

"Then what do you want now? To live? Live how? Live as you lived in the law courts when the usher proclaimed 'The judge is coming!' The judge is coming, the judge!" he repeated to himself. "Here he is, the judge. But I am not guilty!" he exclaimed angrily. "What is it for?" And he ceased crying, but turning his face to the wall continued to ponder on the same question: Why, and for what purpose, is there all this horror? But however much he pondered he found no answer. And whenever the thought occurred to him, as if often did, that it all resulted from his not having lived as he ought to have done, he at once recalled the correctness of his whole life and dismissed so strange an idea.

Another fortnight passed. Ivan Ilych now no longer left his sofa. He would not lie in bed but lay on the sofa, facing the wall nearly all the time. He suffered ever the same unceasing agonies and in his loneliness pondered always on the same insoluble question: "What is this? Can it be that it is Death?" And the inner voice answered: "Yes, it is Death."

"Why these sufferings?" And the voice answered, "For no reason—they just are so." Beyond and besides this there was nothing.

From the very beginning of his illness, ever since he had first been to see the doctor, Ivan Ilych's life had been divided between two contrary and alternating moods: now it was despair and the expectation of this uncomprehended and terrible death, and now hope and an intently interested observation of the functioning of his organs. Now before his eyes there was only a kidney or an intestine that temporarily evaded its duty, and now only that incomprehensible and dreadful death from which it was impossible to escape.

These two states of mind had alternated from the very beginning of his illness, but the further it progressed the more doubtful and fantastic became the conception of the kidney, and the more real the sense of impending death.

He had but to call to mind what he had been three months before and what he was now, to call to mind with what regularity he had been going downhill, for every possibility of hope to be shattered.

Latterly during that loneliness in which he found himself as he lay facing the back of the sofa, a loneliness in the midst of a populous town and surrounded by numerous acquaintances and relations but that yet could not have been more complete anywhere—either at the bottom of the sea or under the earth—during that terrible loneliness Ivan Ilych had lived only in memories of the past. Pictures of his past rose before him one after another.

They always began with what was nearest in time and then went back to what was most remote—to his childhood—and rested there. If he thought of the stewed prunes that had been offered him that day, his mind went back to the raw shrivelled French plums of his childhood, their peculiar flavour and the flow of saliva when he sucked their stones, and along with the memory of that taste came a whole series of memories of those days: his nurse, his brother, and their toys. "No, I mustn't think of that. . . . It is too painful," Ivan Ilych said to himself, and brought himself back to the present—to the button on the back of the sofa and the creases in its morocco. "Morocco is expensive, but it does not wear well: there had been a quarrel about it. It was a different kind of quarrel and a different kind of morocco that time when we tore father's portfolio and were punished, and mamma brought us some tarts. . . ." And again his thoughts dwelt on his childhood, and again it was painful and he tried to banish them and fix his mind on something else.

Then again together with that chain of memories another series passed through his mind—of how his illness had progressed and grown worse. There also the further back he looked the more life there had been. There had been more of what was good in life and more of life itself. The two merged together. "Just as the pain went on getting worse and worse, so my life grew worse and worse," he thought. "There is one bright spot there at the back, at the beginning of life, and afterwards all becomes blacker and blacker and proceeds more and more rapidly—in inverse ratio to the square of the distance from death," thought Ivan Ilych. And the example of a stone falling downwards with increasing velocity entered his mind. Life, a series of increasing sufferings, flies further and further towards its end—the most terrible suffering. "I am flying. . . ." He shuddered, shifted himself, and tried to resist, but was already aware that resistance was impossible, and again with eyes weary of gazing but unable to cease seeing what was before them, he stared at the back of the sofa and waited—awaiting that dreadful fall and shock and destruction.

"Resistance is impossible!" he said to himself. "If I could only understand what it is all for! But that too is impossible. An explanation would be possible if it could be said that I have not lived as I ought to. But it is impossible to say that," and he remembered all the legality, correctitude, and propriety of his life. "That at any rate can certainly not be admitted," he thought, and his lips smiled ironically as if someone could see that smile and be taken in by it. "There is no explanation! Agony, death . . . What for?"

Another two weeks went by in this way and during that fortnight an event occurred that Ivan Ilych and his wife had desired. Petrishchev formally proposed. It happened in the evening. The next day Praskovya Fëdorovna came into her husband's room considering how best to inform him of it, but that very night there had been a fresh change for the worse in his condition. She found him still lying on the sofa but in a different position. He lay on his back, groaning and staring fixedly straight in front of him.

She began to remind him of his medicines, but he turned his eyes towards her with such a look that she did not finish what she was saying; so great an animosity, to her in particular, did that look express.

"For Christ's sake let me die in peace!" he said.

She would have gone away, but just then their daughter came in and went up to say good morning. He looked at her as he had done at his wife, and in reply to her inquiry about his health said dryly that he would soon free them all of himself. They were both silent and after sitting with him for a while went away.

"Is it our fault?" Lisa said to her mother. "It's as if we were to blame! I am sorry for papa, but why should we be tortured?"

The doctor came at his usual time. Ivan Ilych answered "Yes" and "No," never taking his angry eyes from him, and at last said: "You know you can do nothing for me, so leave me alone."

"We can ease your sufferings."

"You can't even do that. Let me be."

The doctor went into the drawing-room and told Praskovya Fëdorovna that the case was very serious and that the only resource left was opium to allay her husband's sufferings, which must be terrible.

It was true, as the doctor said, that Ivan Ilych's physical sufferings were terrible, but worse than the physical sufferings were his mental sufferings, which were his chief torture.

His mental sufferings were due to the fact that that night, as he looked at Gerasim's sleepy, good-natured face with its prominent cheekbones, the question suddenly occurred to him: "What if my whole life has really been wrong?"

It occurred to him that what had appeared perfectly impossible before, namely that he had not spent his life as he should have done, might after all be true. It occurred to him that his scarcely perceptible attempts to struggle against what was considered good by the most highly placed people, those scarcely noticeable impulses which he had immediately suppressed, might have been the real thing, and all the rest false. And his professional duties and the whole arrangement of his life and of his family, and all his social and official interests, might all have been false. He tried to defend all those things to himself and suddenly felt the weakness of what he was defending. There was nothing to defend.

"But if that is so," he said to himself, "and I am leaving this life with the consciousness that I have lost all that was given me and it is impossible to rectify it—what then?"

He lay on his back and began to pass his life in review in quite a new way. In the morning when he saw first his footman, then his wife, then his daughter, and then the doctor, their every word and movement confirmed to him the awful truth that had been revealed to him during the night. In them he saw himself—all that for which he had lived—and saw clearly that it was not real at all, but a terrible and huge deception which had hidden both life and death. This consciousness intensified his physical suffering tenfold. He groaned and tossed about, and pulled at his clothing which choked and stifled him. And he hated them on that account.

He was given a large dose of opium and became unconscious, but at noon his sufferings began again. He drove everybody away and tossed from side to side.

His wife came to him and said:

"Jean, my dear, do this for me. It can't do any harm and often helps. Healthy people often do it."

He opened his eyes wide.

"What? Take communion? Why? It's unnecessary! However . . ."

She began to cry.

"Yes, do, my dear. I'll send for our priest. He is such a nice man."

"All right. Very well," he muttered.

When the priest came and heard his confession, Ivan Ilych was softened and seemed to feel a relief from his doubts and consequently from his sufferings, and for a moment there came a ray of hope. He again began to think of the vermiform appendix and the possibility of correcting it. He received the sacrament with tears in his eyes.

When they laid him down again afterwards he felt a moment's ease, and the hope that he might live awoke in him again. He began to think of the operation that had been suggested to him. "To live! I want to live!" he said to himself.

His wife came in to congratulate him after his communion, and when uttering the usual conventional words she added:

"You feel better, don't you?"

Without looking at her he said "Yes."

Her dress, her figure, the expression of her face, the tone of her voice, all revealed the same thing. "This is wrong, it is not as it should be. All you have lived for and still live for is falsehood and deception, hiding life and death from you." And as soon as he admitted that thought, his hatred and his agonizing physical suffering again sprang up, and with that suffering a consciousness of the unavoidable, approaching end. And to this was added a new sensation of grinding shooting pain and a feeling of suffocation.

The expression of his face when he uttered that "yes" was dreadful. Having uttered it, he looked her straight in the eyes, turned on his face with a rapidity extraordinary in his weak state and shouted:

"Go away! Go away and leave me alone!"

From that moment the screaming began that continued for three days, and was so terrible that one could not hear it through two closed doors without horror. At the moment he answered his wife he realized that he was lost, that there was no return, that the end had come, the very end, and his doubts were still unsolved and remained doubts.

"Oh! Oh! Oh!" he cried in various intonations. He had

begun by screaming "I won't" and continued screaming on the letter *O*.

For three whole days, during which time did not exist for him, he struggled in that black sack into which he was being thrust by an invisible, resistless force. He struggled as a man condemned to death struggles in the hands of the executioner, knowing that he cannot save himself. And every moment he felt that despite all his efforts he was drawing nearer and nearer to what terrified him. He felt that his agony was due to his being thrust into that black hole and still more to his not being able to get right into it. He was hindered from getting into it by his conviction that his life had been a good one. That very justification of his life held him fast and prevented his moving forward, and it caused him most torment of all.

Suddenly some force struck him in the chest and side, making it still harder to breathe, and he fell through the hole and there at the bottom was a light. What had happened to him was like the sensation one sometimes experiences in a railway carriage when one thinks one is going backwards while one is really going forwards and suddenly becomes aware of the real direction.

"Yes, it was all not the right thing," he said to himself, "but that's no matter. It can be done. But what *is* the right thing?" he asked himself, and suddenly grew quiet.

This occurred at the end of the third day, two hours before his death. Just then his schoolboy son had crept softly in and gone up to the bedside. The dying man was still screaming desperately and waving his arms. His hand fell on the boy's head, and the boy caught it, pressed it to his lips, and began to cry.

At that very moment Ivan Ilych fell through and caught sight of the light, and it was revealed to him that though his life had not been what it should have been, this could still be rectified. He asked himself, "What *is* the right thing?" and grew still, listening. Then he felt that someone was kissing his hand. He opened his eyes, looked at his son, and felt sorry for him. His wife came up to him and he glanced at her. She was gazing at him open-mouthed, with undried tears on her nose and cheek and a despairing look on her face. He felt sorry for her too.

"Yes, I am making them wretched," he thought. "They are sorry, but it will be better for them when I die." He wished to say this but had not the strength to utter it. "Besides, why speak? I must act," he thought. With a look at his wife he indicated his son and said: "Take him away . . . sorry for him . . . sorry for you too. . . ." He tried to add, "forgive me," but said "forgo" and waved his hand, knowing that He whose understanding mattered would understand.

And suddenly it grew clear to him that what had been oppressing him and would not leave him was all dropping away at once from two sides, from ten sides, and from all sides. He was sorry for them, he must act so as not to hurt them: release them and free himself from these sufferings. "How good and how simple!" he thought. "And the pain?" he asked himself. "What has become of it? Where are you, pain?"

He turned his attention to it.

"Yes, here it is. Well, what of it? Let the pain be."

"And death . . . where is it?"

He sought his former accustomed fear of death and did not find it. "Where is it? What death?" There was no fear because there was no death.

In place of death there was light.

"So that's what it is!" he suddenly exclaimed aloud. "What joy!"

To him all this happened in a single instant, and the meaning of that instant did not change. For those present his agony continued for another two hours. Something rattled in his throat, his emaciated body twitched, then the gasping and rattle became less and less frequent.

"It is finished!" said someone near him.

He heard those words and repeated them in his soul.

"Death is finished," he said to himself. "It is no more!"

He drew in a breath, stopped in the midst of a sigh, stretched out, and died.

(Translated by Rosemary Edmunds)

from DON QUIXOTE
MIGUEL CERVANTES

In his youth Miguel Cervantes served in the Spanish navy, where he was seriously wounded and subsequently captured by pirates. Despite his injuries, he later petitioned to serve in America, which, in 1590, showed that he had himself the plucky

spirit with which he endowed the hero of his best-known work.
Don Quixote. In the novel, set at the end of the sixteenth cen-
tury in Spain, a man named Alonso Quixano mounts a rickety
horse and—with his trusty though simple companion, Sancho
Panza—rides off to perform noble deeds under the assumed
name of Don Quixote de la Mancha. One of literature's most
memorable characters, he rides through a thousand pages of
hilarious adventure and misfortune. In this excerpt, we meet
him and his companions at the end of their journey, as Don
Quixote seems at peace, able to accept the necessity of his
departure and concerned only that his affairs be in order for
his survivors. The need to grant a person in such a state
permission to die is apparent here, as is the difficulty survivors
have in granting it.

As all human things, especially the lives of men, are
transitory, being ever on the decline from their beginnings
till they reach their final end, and as Don Quixote had no
privilege from Heaven exempting him from the common
fate, his dissolution and end came when he least expected
it. Whether that event was brought on by melancholy
occasioned by the contemplation of his defeat or whether
it was by divine ordination, a fever seized him and kept
him to his bed for six days, during which time he was
frequently visited by his friends, the priest, the Bachelor
and the barber, and his good squire Sancho Panza never
left his bedside.

All of them believed that grief at his overthrow and the
disappointment of his hopes for Dulcinea's deliverance
and disenchantment had brought him to this state, and
tried to cheer him in every possible way. The Bachelor
bade him be of good heart, and get up and begin on his
pastoral life, for which he had already composed an
eclogue, which would knock out every one Sannazaro
had ever written. He said that he had bought a couple of
fine dogs with his own money from a herdsman from
Quintanar to guard the flock, one called Barcino and the
other Butron. But Don Quixote's dejection persisted all
the same. His friends called in a doctor, who took his
pulse and did not offer much comfort, saying that he
should certainly attend to the salvation of his soul, for his
body's was in danger. Don Quixote heard this with a quiet
mind, but not so his housekeeper, his niece and his squire,
who began to weep piteously, as if he already lay dead

before their eyes. It was the doctor's opinion that melancholy and despondency were bringing him to his end. Don Quixote begged to be left alone, for he wanted to sleep a little. They obeyed him, and he slept for more than six hours, at a stretch as they say, so long, in fact, that his housekeeper and his niece thought that he would pass away in his sleep. But at the end of that time he woke and cried out loudly: "Blessed be Almighty God, who has vouchsafed me this great blessing! Indeed his mercies are boundless, nor can the sins of men limit or hinder them."

His niece was listening to her uncle, and these words seeming to her more rational than his general speech, at least during that illness, she asked him: "What is it you say, sir? Is there anything new? What mercies are these, or what sins of men?"

"The mercies, niece," answered Don Quixote, "are those which God has shown me at this moment, mercies to which, as I have said, my sins are no impediment. My judgment is now clear and free from the misty shadows of ignorance with which my ill-starred and continuous reading of those detestable books of chivalry had obscured it. Now I know their absurdities and their deceits, and the only thing that grieves me is that this discovery has come too late, and leaves me no time to make amends by reading other books, which might enlighten my soul. I feel, niece, that I am on the point of death, and I should like to meet it in such a manner as to convince the world that my life has not been so bad as to leave me the character of a madman; for though I have been one, I would not confirm the fact in my death. Call my good friends, my dear, the priest, Bachelor Sampson Carrasco and Master Nicholas the barber, for I want to confess and make my will."

But his niece was excused this task by the entrance of the three. And the moment Don Quixote saw them he exclaimed: "Congratulate me, good sirs, for I am Don Quixote de la Mancha no longer, but Alonso Quixano, called for my way of life the Good. Now I am the enemy of Amadis of Gaul and of all the infinite brood of his progeny. Now all profane histories of knight errantry are odious to me. I know my folly now, and the peril I have incurred from the reading of them. Now, by God's mercy, I have learnt from my own bitter experience and I abominate them."

When the three heard his words they believed some fresh madness had certainly seized him, and Sampson said to him: "Must you come out with that, Don Quixote, just now when we have news that the Lady Dulcinea is disenchanted? Now that we are just on the point of turning shepherds to spend our lives singing like any princes, do you want to turn hermit? No more of that, I pray you. Return to your senses and cease your idle tales."

"Tales?" replied Don Quixote. "Up to now they have been only too real, to my cost. But, with Heaven's aid, my death shall turn them to my profit. I feel, sirs, that I am rapidly dying. Stop your fooling, and bring me a priest to confess me and a clerk to make my will, for in such extremities as this a man must not jest with his soul. So send for a clerk, I beg of you, while my friend the priest confesses me."

They looked at one another in amazement at Don Quixote's words and, though in doubt, were inclined to believe him. And one of the signs by which they concluded that he was dying was the ease with which he changed from mad to sane; for he said much more in the vein of his last utterances, so well spoken, so Christian and so connected, that they were finally resolved of all their doubts and convinced that his mind was sound. The priest made everyone leave the room, remained alone with him and confessed him. The Bachelor went for the clerk, and in a short time came back with him and with Sancho Panza, who had had news from Carrasco of his master's state and, finding the housekeeper and the niece in tears, began to blubber and weep himself. When the confession was ended the priest came out, saying: "Truly he is dying and truly he is sane, Alonso Quixano the Good. We had better go in so that he can make his will." This news gave a terrible start to the brimming eyes of his housekeeper, his niece and his good squire, Sancho Panza, causing them to break out into fresh tears and groans. For in truth, as has been said before, whether he was plain Alonso Quixano the Good, or Don Quixote de la Mancha, he was always of an amiable disposition and kind in his behavior, so that he was well beloved, not only by his own household but by everyone who knew him.

The clerk went in with the others and, after he had drawn up the heads of the will, Don Quixote disposed of his soul with all the requisite Christian formalities and came to the bequests, saying:

"Item, this is my will regarding certain moneys which Sancho Panza, whom in my madness I made my squire, retains, there having been between him and me certain accounts, receipts and disbursements. I wish him not to be charged with them, nor asked to account for them, but if there should be any surplus after he has paid himself what I owe him, the residue is to be his. It will be very little, and may it do him much good. And if when I was mad I was party to giving him the governorship of an isle, now that I am sane I would give him a kingdom, were I able, for the simplicity of his nature and the fidelity of his conduct deserve it."

Then, turning to Sancho, he said: "Pardon me, friend, that I caused you to appear mad, like me, making you fall into the same sort of error as myself, the belief that there were and still are knights errant in the world."

"Oh, don't die, dear master!" answered Sancho in tears. "Take my advice and live many years. For the maddest thing a man can do in this life is to let himself die just like that, without anybody killing him, but just finished off by his own melancholy. Don't be lazy, look you, but get out of bed, and let's go out into the fields dressed as shepherds, as we decided to. Perhaps we shall find the lady Dulcinea behind some hedge, disenchanted and as pretty as a picture. If it's from grief at being beaten you're dying, put the blame on me and say you were tumbled off because I girthed Rocinante badly. For your worship must have seen in your books of chivalries that it's a common thing for one knight to overthrow another, and the one that's conquered to-day may be the conqueror to-morrow."

"That's right," said Sampson. "Honest Sancho has hit the truth of the matter."

"Let us go gently, gentlemen," said Don Quixote, "for there are no birds this year in last year's nests. I was mad, but I am sane now. I was Don Quixote de la Mancha, but to-day, as I have said, I am Alonso Quixano the Good. May my sincere repentance restore your former esteem for me. Now let the clerk go on.

"Item, I bequeath all my estate, without reserve, to Antonia Quixana, my niece, here present, there being first deducted from it in the most convenient way all that is

necessary for the fulfilment of my bequests. And the first payment to be made I desire to be the wages due to my housekeeper for the time she has been in my service, and twenty ducats besides for a dress. I leave as my executors Master Priest and Master Sampson Carrasco, here present. Item, it is my wish that, should my niece Antonia Quixana be inclined to wed, she should marry a man of whom she has first had evidence that he does not even know what books of chivalry are; and in case it shall be discovered that he does know, and my niece shall yet wish to marry him, and shall marry him, she shall lose all I have bequeathed her, which my executors may distribute in pious works as they think fit. Item, I beseech the said gentlemen, my executors, that if by good fortune they should come to know the alleged author of a history circulating hereabouts under the title of The Second Part of the Exploits of Don Quixote de la Mancha, *they shall beg him on my behalf, with the greatest earnestness, to forgive the occasion I unwittingly gave him of publishing so many gross absurdities as are therein written; for I quit this life with an uneasy conscience at having given him an excuse for writing them."*

With this he concluded his testament and, falling into a faint, lay stretched at full length on the bed. Everyone was alarmed and ran to his assistance, and during the three days that he lived after making his will he fainted very frequently. The house was in a turmoil. However his niece ate, his housekeeper drank and Sancho Panza was cheerful; for legacies tend to dull or moderate in the inheritor the grief that nature claims for the deceased.

At last Don Quixote's end came, after he had received all the sacraments and expressed his horror of books of chivalry in strong and moving terms. The clerk, who happened to be present, said that he had never read in any book of chivalries of a knight errant dying in his bed in so calm and Christian a manner as Don Quixote, who amidst the compassionate tears of all present gave up the ghost—that is to say, died.

(Translated by J. M. Cohen)

EARLY DAWN
Eneriko Seruma

*Eneriko Seruma is a contemporary African writer, whose
stories are generally set in his native Uganda. The young man
in this story finds that the death of his brother brings about a
temporary reshuffling of the roles in the family. Previously de-
pendent on his parents, he must now provide emotional support
for them and meet the crisis with fortitude. Stoicism is often a
necessary temporary measure, but if it provides an excuse to
permanently delay grieving, there will eventually be negative
consequences to the individual's emotional well-being.*

Father and Mother were poor peasants who lived in
Buloba village, about twelve miles from Kampala. They
had an uncemented five-room house with mud-and-reed
walls, the roof covered with corrugated iron. They had
only one other child besides me. His name was Jonathan,
and he was two years younger than me.

At the age of five Jonathan was very sick, lying on his
homemade cot in Father's room. He had been taken sick
seven days previously, seven days that seemed like years
to me. Each day he was getting worse and worse; each day
all of us were getting more and more oppressed by the
shadow of Death.

I was the last person in the dining room that evening,
sitting all alone with the heap of food that had been left
untouched by my parents, trying to create an appetite—
attempting something my parents had failed to do. They
got up abruptly and went to their respective rooms, leaving the food staring at me, as if it was accusing me of
having the nerve to eat when the more-hardened parents
could not eat anything. I ignored the accusation—I was
hungry—and went on swallowing the food that somehow was too rough for my throat.

Finally I gave up trying to eat. I collected the dishes
quietly, stored them away, and put the food in the cupboard to be eaten tomorrow, God willing. I did not go to
say good-night to Jonathan in Father's room, which was
opposite my own room. I did not have the courage to go
there. Instead, I tiptoed to my bed where I lay staring at
the darkness that was everywhere.

In the darkness in this house, I felt, lurked Death. I just could not lie to myself about his presence, not when I could feel him around me and could smell him in the sickroom. Not when my mother sometimes wept helplessly, not when my father was most of the time a defeated figure, head bent between hands to hide his fears. We all were aware that Death was serious about winning this struggle, for we had tried all sorts of doctors without success.

I guess I went off to sleep somewhere around ten o'clock, when sleep finally snatched me away from a world of agony, fear, and murmured prayers, like a friendly eagle swooping down to rescue a rabbit from a bushfire.

In the early hours of the morning, the eagle was getting rid of the rabbit, as if it was too much of a burden to carry over the spreading fire. Through the mysterious world of half-awareness, my mind was flying back to the reality it had left some hours ago. I tried to remain clinging onto the wings of the eagle, but kept losing my hold. Whatever had changed the eagle's mind was very persuasive: I was waking up. For a moment my eyes stared at the darkness, uncomprehending, still sleepy. Gradually I became aware of a hand on my shoulder. Someone was shaking me awake.

"Dear son," a voice said: so strange out of the darkness. It was my father, but I had never known him to call either of us "Dear son." I wondered why he was turning sentimental, all of a sudden. What was he waking me up for so early in the morning?

"Dear son, wake up," Father's voice said again.

"Yes, sir?"

"Please do wake up. You've got to help me."

Something was *very* wrong with Father. He had always been my image of a tough man: strong voice and a commanding personality. When he wanted a thing, he got it, without saying "please." But now—his voice was unsteady and he sounded as if he was pleading with me.

I got up and started looking for the box of matches. I applied a light to the kerosene lamp. The light spread out, chasing the darkness from the room and showing me a very much-changed Father. Forty years old, he had always been steady and confident, with determination showing plainly on his face. Father now was a broken man, utterly defeated and uncertain. When his eyes looked at me they were clouded, but looking at me as if they were seeing me for the first time and were happy for my being alive.

Father must have noticed the way I was looking at him in puzzlement. He turned his head the other way and said, in a voice I could not help hating: "Your brother is dead. . . . Please come and help me tend to the body before we wake up your mother."

Neither I nor my father acted like people who had lived with Death for a whole week. I had thought that perhaps we would all go steadily about it if the end was fatal. *How* could my own brother possibly die and leave me to grow up alone, without anyone to play with, anyway?

Now it had happened. There were just us, the two men in the family, to tend to the body before the neighbours were summoned by my mother's screaming.

I was now a grown-up; I was going to go through an experience not all adults have been through.

I was shaking; it was hard to stand on my own two legs. Yet somewhere in me I felt strong. I felt I was needed to be strong. Young as I was, I was stronger emotionally than my father; he needed me to assure him that all was not lost. . . . All the same, I was surprised when no tears flowed down my face.

from ZORBA THE GREEK
NIKOS KAZANTZAKIS

In this excerpt from the novel Zorba the Greek, *Zorba's wife of recent times, Madame Hortense, is dying of tuberculosis. Zorba comforts her merely by being with her and by accepting her return in memory to earlier and happier times. He does not deny his own anguish, nor does he parade it in front of her. Despite his grief, his commitment to loving her allows him to stay with her and gently hold her hand until death has claimed her.*

The large bed . . . had been put in the middle of her little room and nearly filled it. Above her head there bent over the singer her devoted privy councillor, the parrot—with his green crown, yellow bonnet and round, evil eye. He was gazing down at his mistress as she lay groaning. And he leaned his almost human head to one side to listen.

. . . The beads of ice-cold sweat running down his mistress's face, her hair like tow—unwashed, uncombed —sticking to her temples, the convulsive movements in the bed, these the parrot saw for the first time, and he was uneasy. He wanted to shout: "Canavaro! Canavaro!" but his voice stuck in his throat.

His poor mistress was groaning; she kept lifting up the sheets with her wilting, flabby arms; she was suffocating. She had no make-up on her face and her cheeks were swollen; she smelled of stale sweat and of flesh which is beginning to decompose. Her down-at-heel, out-of-shape court shoes were poking out from under the bed. It wrung your heart to see them. Those shoes were more moving than the sight of their owner herself.

Zorba sat at her bedside, looking at the shoes. He could not take his eyes off them. He was biting his lips to keep back the tears. I went in and sat behind Zorba, but he did not hear me.

The poor woman was finding it difficult to breathe; she was choking. Zorba took down a hat decorated with artificial roses and fanned her with it. He waved his big hand up and down very quickly and clumsily as though he were trying to light some damp coal.

She opened her eyes in terror and looked around her. It was dark and she could see no one, not even Zorba fanning her with the flowered hat.

Everything was dark and disturbing about her; blue vapors were rising from the ground and changing shape. They formed sneering mouths, claw-like feet, black wings.

She dug her nails into her pillow, which was stained with tears, saliva and sweat, and she cried out.

"I don't want to die! I don't want to!"

But the two mourners from the village had heard of the condition she was in and had just arrived. They slipped into the room, sat on the floor and leaned against the wall.

The parrot saw them, with his round staring eyes, and was angry. He stretched out his head and cried: "Canav . . ." but Zorba savagely shot his hand out at the cage and silenced the bird.

Again the cry of despair rang out.

"I don't want to die! I don't want to!"

Two beardless youths, tanned by the sun, poked their heads round the door, looked carefully at the sick woman. Satisfied, they winked at each other and disappeared.

Soon afterwards we heard a terrified clucking and beating of wings coming from the yard; someone was chasing the hens.

The first dirge singer, old Malamatenia, turned to her companion.

"Did you see them, auntie Lenio, did you see them? They're in a hurry, the hungry wretches; they're going to wring the hens' necks and eat them. All the good-for-nothings of the village have collected in the yard; it'll not be long before they plunder the place!"

Then, turning to the dying woman's bed:

"Hurry up and die, my friend," she muttered impatiently; "give up the ghost as quick as you can so that we get a chance as well as the others."

"To tell you God's own truth," said aunt Lenio, creasing her little toothless mouth, "mother Malamatenia, they're doing right, those boys. 'If you want to eat something, pilfer; if you want to own something, steal. . . .' That's what my old mother used to say to me. We've only got to rattle off our *mirologues* as fast as we can, lay our hands on a couple of handfuls of rice, some sugar, and a saucepan, and then we can bless her memory. She had neither parents nor children, did she, so who's going to eat her hens and her rabbits? Who'll drink her wine? Who'll inherit all those cottons and combs and sweets and things? Ha, what d'you expect, mother Malamatenia? God forgive me, but that's the way the world is . . . and I'd like to pick up a few things myself!"

"Wait a bit, dear, don't be in too much of a hurry," said mother Malamatenia, seizing her arm. "I had the same idea myself, I don't mind admitting, but just wait till she's given up the ghost."

Meanwhile the dying woman was fumbling frantically beneath her pillow. As soon as she thought she was in danger she had taken out of her trunk a crucifix in gleaming white bone and thrust it under her pillow. For years she had entirely forgotten it and it had lain among her tattered chemises and bits of velvet and rags at the bottom of the trunk. As if Christ were a medicine to be taken only when gravely ill, and of no use so long as you can have a good time, eat, drink and make love.

At last her groping hand found the crucifix and she pressed it to her bosom, which was damp with sweat.

"Dear Jesus, my dear Jesus . . ." she uttered passionately, clasping her last lover to her breast.

Her words, which were half-French, half-Greek, but full of tenderness and passion, were very confused. The parrot heard her. He sensed that the tone of voice had changed, remembered the former long sleepless nights and livened up immediately.

"Canavaro! Canavaro!" he shouted hoarsely, like a cock crowing at the sun.

Zorba this time did not try to silence him. He looked at the woman as she wept and kissed the crucified image whilst an unexpected sweetness spread over her ravaged face.

The door opened, old Anagnosti came in quietly, cap in hand. He came up to the sick woman, bowed and knelt down.

"Forgive me, dear lady," he said to her, "forgive me, and may God forgive you. If sometimes I spoke a harsh word, we're only men . . . Forgive me."

But the dear soul was now lying quietly, sunk in an unspeakable felicity, and she did not hear what old Anagnosti said. All her torments were gone—unhappy old age, all the sneers and hard words she had endured, the sad evenings she had spent alone in her doorway, knitting thick woollen socks. This elegant Parisienne, this tantalizing woman men could not resist and who, in her time, had bounced the four great Powers on her knee, and had been saluted by four naval squadrons!

The sea was azure blue, the waves were flecked with foam, the sea-going fortresses were dancing in the harbor, and flags of many colors were flapping from every mast. You could smell the partridges roasting and the red mullet on the grill, glacé fruits were carried to the table in bowls of cut crystal and the champagne corks flew up to the ceiling.

Black and fair beards, red and grey beards, four sorts of perfume—violet, eau-de-Cologne, musk, patchouli; the doors of the metal cabin were closed, the heavy curtains drawn to, the lights were lit. Madame Hortense closed her eyes. All her life of love, all her life of torment—ah, almighty God! it had lasted no more than a second. . . .

She goes from knee to knee, clasps in her arms gold-braided uniforms, buries her fingers in thick-scented beards. She cannot remember their names, any more than her parrot can. She can only remember Canavaro, because he was the youngest of them all and his name was the only one the parrot could pronounce. The others were complicated and difficult to pronounce, and so were forgotten.

Madame Hortense sighed deeply and hugged the crucifix passionately to her.

"My Canavaro, my little Canavaro . . ." she murmured in her delirium, pressing it to her flabby breasts.

"She's beginning not to know what she's saying," murmured aunt Lenio. "She must have seen her guardian angel and had a scare. . . . We'll loosen our kerchiefs and go nearer."

"What! Haven't you any fear of God, then?" said mother Malamatenia. "D'you want us to begin singing while she's still alive?"

"Ha, mother Malamatenia," grumbled aunt Lenio under her breath, "instead of thinking about her trunk and her clothes and all the things she has outside in the shop, and the hens and rabbits in the yard, there are you telling me we ought to wait till she's breathed her last! No! First come first served, I say!"

And as she spoke she stood up, and the other followed her angrily. They undid their black kerchiefs, let down their thin white hair and gripped the edges of the bed.

Aunt Lenio gave the signal by letting out a long piercing cry enough to make a cold shiver go down your spine.

"Eeeee!"

Zorba leaped up, seized the two old women by the hair and dragged them back.

"Shut your traps, you old magpies!" he shouted. "Can't you see she's still alive? Go to hell!"

"Doddering old idiot!" grumbled mother Malamatenia, fastening her kerchief again. "Where's he sprung from, I'd like to know, the interfering fool!"

Dame Hortense, the sorely tried old siren, heard the strident cry beside her bed. Her sweet vision faded; the admiral's vessel sank, the roast pheasants, champagne and perfumed beards disappeared and she fell back on to that stinking deathbed, at the end of the world. She made an effort to raise herself, as though trying to escape, but she fell back again and cried softly and plaintively.

"I don't want to die! I don't want to. . . ."

Zorba leaned forward and touched her forehead with his great horny hand, and brushed away the hair which was sticking to her face; his bird-like eyes filled with tears.

"Quiet, my dear, quiet," he murmured. "I'm here; this is Zorba. Don't be afraid."

And suddenly the vision returned, like an enormous sea-green butterfly and spread its wings over the whole bed. The dying woman seized Zorba's big hand, slowly stretched out her arm and put it round his neck as he bent over her. Her lips moved . . .

"My Canavaro, my little Canavaro. . . ."

The crucifix slipped off the pillow, fell to the floor and broke into little pieces. A man's voice rang out in the yard:

"Come on! Pop the hen in now, the water's boiling!"

I was sitting in a corner of the room and from time to time my eyes filled with tears. That is life, I thought— checkered, incoherent, indifferent, perverse . . . pitiless. These primitive Cretan peasants surround this old cabaret singer come from the other end of the earth and with inhuman joy watch her die, as if she were not also a human being. As though a huge exotic bird had fallen from the sky, its wings broken, and they had gathered on the seashore by their village to watch it die. An old pea fowl, an old angora cat, a sick old seal. . . .

Zorba gently removed Dame Hortense's arm from round his neck and stood up, white-faced. He wiped his eyes with the back of his hand, looked at the sick woman but could see nothing. He wiped his eyes again and could just see her moving her swollen helpless feet in the bed and twisting her mouth in terror. She shook herself once, twice, the bedclothes slipped to the floor and she appeared, half-naked, covered with sweat, swollen, a greenish-yellow color. She uttered a strident, piercing cry like a fowl when its throat is cut, then she remained motionless, her eyes wide open, terrified, glassy.

The parrot jumped down to the bottom of its cage, clutched the bars and watched as Zorba reached out his huge hand and, with indescribable tenderness, closed his mistress's eyelids.

"Quick, all of you! She's gone!" yelped the dirge singers, rushing to the bed. They uttered a prolonged cry, rocking backwards and forwards, clenching their fists and beating their breasts. Little by little the monotony of this lugubrious oscillation produced in them a slight state of hypnosis, old griefs of their own invaded their minds like poison, their hearts were opened and the *mirologue* burst forth.

"It was not meet for thee, to lie beneath the earth. . . ."

Zorba went out into the yard. He wanted to weep, but he was ashamed to do so in front of the women. I remember he said to me once: "I'm not ashamed to cry, if it's in front of men. Between men there's some unity, isn't there? It's no disgrace. But in front of women a man always has to prove that he's courageous. Because if we started crying our eyes out, too, what'd happen to these poor creatures? It would be the end!"

They washed her with wine; the old woman who was laying her out opened the trunk, took out clean clothes and changed her, pouring over her a bottle of eau-de-Cologne. From the nearby gardens came the blow flies and laid their eggs in her nostrils, round her eyes and in the corners of her lips.

Night was falling. The sky to the west was beautifully serene. Small, fleecy red clouds edged with gold were sailing slowly across the dark-purple evening sky, looking one moment like ships, the next like swans, then like fantastic monsters made of cotton wool and frayed silk. Between the reeds in the yard could be seen the gleaming waves of the choppy sea.

Two well-fed crows flew from a fig tree close by and walked up and down the yard. Zorba angrily picked up a pebble and made them fly away.

(Translated by Carl Wildman)

TO HELL WITH DYING
ALICE WALKER

One of America's promising young black authors, Alice Walker graduated from Sarah Lawrence College in 1966. In this short story she portrays death as a social and psychological phenomenon as well as a medical one. The story illustrates well the view that, as the poet Richard Shelton has said, "Death will arrive when we have nothing left to use to get what we want, or when we no longer want anything, whichever comes first."

"To hell with dying," my father would say, "these children want Mr. Sweet!"

Mr. Sweet was a diabetic and an alcoholic and a guitar player and lived down the road from us on a neglected cotton farm. My older brothers and sisters got the most benefit from Mr. Sweet, for when they were growing up he had quite a few years ahead of him and so was capable of being called back from the brink of death any number of times—whenever the voice of my father reached him as he lay expiring. . . . "To hell with dying, man," my father would say, pushing the wife away from the bedside (in tears although she knew the death was not necessarily the last one unless Mr. Sweet really wanted it to be), "the children want Mr. Sweet!" And they did want him, for at a signal from Father they would come crowding around the bed and throw themselves on the covers and whoever was the smallest at the time would kiss him all over his wrinkled brown face and begin to tickle him so that he would laugh all down in his stomach, and his moustache which was long and sort of straggly, would shake like Spanish moss and was also that color.

Mr. Sweet had been ambitious as a boy, wanted to be a doctor or lawyer or sailor, only to find that black men fare better if they are not. Since he could be none of those things he turned to fishing as his only earnest career and playing the guitar as his only claim to doing anything extraordinarily well. His son, the only one that he and his wife, Miss Mary, had, was shiftless as the day is long

and spent money as if he were trying to see the bottom
of the mint, which Mr. Sweet would tell him was the
clean brown palm of his hand. Miss Mary loved her
"baby," however, and worked hard to get him the "li'l
necessaries" of life, which turned out mostly to be women.

Mr. Sweet was a tall, thinnish man with thick kinky
hair going dead white. He was dark brown, his eyes were
very squinty and sort of bluish, and he chewed Brown
Mule tobacco. He was constantly on the verge of being
blind drunk, for he brewed his own liquor and was not in
the least a stingy sort of man, and was always very melancholy and sad, though frequently when he was "feelin'
good" he'd dance around the yard with us, usually keeling
over just as my mother came to see what the commotion
was.

Toward all of us children he was very kind, and had
the grace to be shy with us, which is unusual in grown-
ups. He had great respect for my mother for she never
held his drunkenness against him and would let us play
with him even when he was about to fall in the fireplace
from drink. Although Mr. Sweet would sometimes lose
complete or nearly complete control of his head and neck
so that he would loll in his chair, his mind remained
strangely acute and his speech not too affected. His ability
to be drunk and sober at the same time made him an
ideal playmate, for he was as weak as we were and we
could usually best him in wrestling, all the while keeping
a fairly coherent conversation going.

We never felt anything of Mr. Sweet's age when we
played with him. We loved his wrinkles and would draw
some on our brows to be like him, and his white hair was
my special treasure and he knew it and would never come
to visit us just after he had had his hair cut off at the
barbershop. Once he came to our house for something,
probably to see my father about fertilizer for his crops,
for although he never paid the slightest attention to his
crops he liked to know what things would be best to use
on them if he ever did. Anyhow, he had not come with
his hair since he had just had it shaved off at the barbershop. He wore a huge straw hat to keep off the sun and
also to keep his head away from me. But as soon as I
saw him I ran up and demanded that he take me up
and kiss me, with his funny beard which smelled so
strongly of tobacco. Looking forward to burying my small

fingers into his woolly hair I threw away his hat only to find he had done something to his hair, that it was no longer there! I let out a squall which made my mother think that Mr. Sweet had finally dropped me in the well or something and from that day I've been wary of men in hats. However, not long after, Mr. Sweet showed up with his hair grown out and just as white and kinky and impenetrable as it ever was.

Mr. Sweet used to call me his princess, and I believed it. He made me feel pretty at five and six, and simply outrageously devastating at the blazing age of eight and a half. When he came to our house with his guitar the whole family would stop whatever they were doing to sit around him and listen to him play. He liked to play "Sweet Georgia Brown," that was what he called me sometimes, and also he liked to play "Caldonia" and all sorts of sweet, sad, wonderful songs which he sometimes made up. It was from one of these songs that I learned that he had to marry Miss Mary when he had in fact loved somebody else (now living in Chi'-ca-go, or De-stroy, Michigan). He was not sure that Joe Lee, her "baby," was also his baby. Sometimes he would cry and that was an indication that he was about to die again. And so we would all get prepared, for we were sure to be called upon.

I was seven the first time I remember actually participating in one of Mr. Sweet's "revivals"—my parents told me I had participated before. I had been the one chosen to kiss him and tickle him long before I knew the rite of Mr. Sweet's rehabilitation. He had come to our house, it was a few years after his wife's death, and he was very sad, and also, typically, very drunk. He sat on the floor next to me and my older brother, the rest of the children were grown-up and lived elsewhere, and began to play his guitar and cry. I held his woolly head in my arms and wished I could have been old enough to have been the woman he loved so much and that I had not been lost years and years ago.

When he was leaving my mother said to us that we'd better sleep light that night for we'd probably have to go over to Mr. Sweet's before daylight. And we did. For soon after we had gone to bed one of the neighbors knocked on our door and called my father and said that Mr. Sweet was sinking fast and if he wanted to get in a word before the crossover he'd better shake a leg and get over to Mr. Sweet's house. All the neighbors knew to come to our house if something was wrong with Mr. Sweet, but they did not know how we always managed to make him well, or at least stop him from dying, when he was often so near death. As soon as we heard the cry we got up, my brother and I and my mother and father, and put on our clothes. We hurried out of the house and down the road for we were always afraid that we might someday be too late and Mr. Sweet would get tired of dallying.

When we got to the house, a very poor shack really, we found the front room full of neighbors and relatives and someone met us at the door and said that it was all very sad that old Mr. Sweet Little (for Little was his family name although we mostly ignored it) was about to kick the bucket. My parents were advised not to take my brother and me into the "death-room" seeing we were so young and all, but we were so much more accustomed to the death-room than he that we ignored him and dashed in without giving his warning a second thought. I was almost in tears, for these deaths upset me fearfully, and the thought of how much depended on me and my brother (who was such a ham most of the time) made me very nervous.

The doctor was bending over the bed and turned back to tell us for at least the tenth time in the history of my family that alas, old Mr. Sweet Little was dying and that the children had best not see the face of implacable death (I didn't know what "implacable" was, but whatever it was, Mr. Sweet was not!). My father pushed him rather abruptly out of the way saying as he always did and very loudly for he was saying it to Mr. Sweet, "To hell with dying, man, these children want Mr. Sweet!" which was my cue to throw myself upon the bed and kiss Mr. Sweet all around the whiskers and under the eyes and around the collar of his nightshirt where he smelled so strongly of all sorts of things, mostly liniment.

I was very good at bringing him around, for as soon as I saw that he was struggling to open his eyes I knew he was going to be all right and so could finish my revival sure of success. As soon as his eyes were open he would begin to smile and that way I knew that I had surely won. Once though I got a tremendous scare for he could not open his eyes and later I learned that he had had a stroke and that one side of his face was stiff and hard to get into motion. When he began to smile I could tickle him in earnest for I was sure that nothing would get in the way of his laughter, although once he began to cough so hard that he almost threw me off his stomach, but that was when I was very small, little more than a baby, and my bushy hair had gotten in his nose.

When we were sure he would listen to us we would ask him why he was in bed and when he was coming to see us again and could we play with his guitar which more than likely would be leaning against the bed. His eyes would get all misty and he would sometimes cry out loud, but we never let it embarrass us for he knew that we loved him and that we sometimes cried too for no reason. My parents would leave the room to just the three of us; Mr. Sweet, by that time, would be propped up in bed with a number of pillows behind his head and with me sitting and lying on his shoulder and along his chest. Even when he had trouble breathing he would not ask me to get down. Looking into my eyes he would shake his white head and run a rather scratchy old finger all around my hairline, which was rather low down nearly to my eyebrows and for which some people said I looked like a baby monkey.

My brother was very generous in all this, he let me do all the revivaling—he had done it for years before I was born and so was glad to be able to pass it on to some-one new. What he would do while I talked to Mr. Sweet was pretend to play the guitar, in fact pretend that he was a young version of Mr. Sweet, and it always made Mr. Sweet glad to think that someone wanted to be like him —of course we did not know this then, we played the thing by ear, and whatever he seemed to like, we did. We were desperately afraid that he was just going to take off one day and leave us.

It did not occur to us that we were doing anything special; we had not learned that death was final when it did come. We thought nothing of triumphing over it so many times, and in fact became a trifle contemptuous of people who let themselves be carried away. It did not occur to us that if our own father had been dying we could not have stopped it, that Mr. Sweet was the only person over whom we had power.

When Mr. Sweet was in his eighties I was a young lady studying away in a university many miles from home. I saw him whenever I went home, but he was never on

the verge of dying that I could tell and I began to feel
that my anxiety for his health and psychological well-
being was unnecessary. By this time he not only had a
moustache but a long flowing snow-white beard which I
loved and combed and braided for hours. He was still a
very heavy drinker and was like an old Chinese opium-
user, very peaceful, fragile, gentle, and the only jarring
note about him was his old steel guitar which he still
played in the old sad, sweet, downhome blues way.

On Mr. Sweet's ninetieth birthday I was finishing my
doctorate in Massachusetts and had been making arrangements to go home for several weeks' rest. That morning I
got a telegram telling me that Mr. Sweet was dying again
and could I please drop everything and come home. Of
course I could. My dissertation could wait and my teachers
would understand when I explained to them when I got
back. I ran to the phone, called the airport, and within
four hours I was speeding along the dusty road to Mr.
Sweet's.

The house was more dilapidated than when I was last
there, barely a shack, but it was overgrown with yellow
roses which my family had planted many years ago. The
air was heavy and sweet and very peaceful. I felt strange
walking through the gate and up the old rickety steps. But
the strangeness left me as I caught sight of the long white
beard I loved so well flowing down the thin body over the
familiar quilt coverlet. Mr. Sweet!

His eyes were closed tight and his hands, crossed over
his stomach, were thin and delicate, no longer rough and
scratchy. I remembered how always before I had run and
jumped up on him just anywhere; now I knew he would
not be able to support my weight. I looked around at my
parents, and was surprised to see that my father and
mother also looked old and frail. My father, his own hair
very gray, leaned over the quietly sleeping old man who,
incidentally, smelled still of wine and tobacco, and said
as he'd done so many times, "To hell with dying, man!
My daughter is home to see Mr. Sweet!" My brother had
not been able to come as he was in the war in Asia. I
bent down and gently stroked the closed eyes and gradually they began to open. The closed, wine-stained lips
twitched a little, then parted in a warm, slightly embarrassed smile. Mr. Sweet could see me and he recognized
me and his eyes looked very spry and twinkly for a mo-

ment. I put my head down on the pillow next to his and
we just looked at each other for a long time. Then he
began to trace my peculiar hairline with a thin, smooth
finger. I closed my eyes when his finger halted above my
ear (he used to rejoice at the dirt in my ears when I was
little), his hand stayed cupped around my cheek. When
I opened my eyes, sure I had reached him in time, his
were closed.

Even at twenty-four how could I believe that I had
failed? that Mr. Sweet was really gone? He had never
gone before. But when I looked up at my parents I saw
that they were holding back tears. They had loved him
dearly. He was like a piece of rare and delicate china
which was always being saved from breaking and which
finally fell. I looked long at the old face, the wrinkled
forehead, the red lips, the hands that still reached out to
me. Soon I felt my father pushing something cool into my
hands. It was Mr. Sweet's guitar. He had asked them
months before to give it to me, he had known that even if
I came next time he would not be able to respond in the
old way. He did not want me to feel that my trip had
been for nothing.

The old guitar! I plucked the strings, hummed "Sweet
Georgia Brown." The magic of Mr. Sweet lingered still in
the cool steel box. Through the window I could catch the
fragrant delicate scent of tender yellow roses. The man on
the high old-fashioned bed with the quilt coverlet and the
flowing white beard had been my first love.

III

"A CORPSE, A MEMORY, AND ... A GHOST"

What Comes After Death

For most people the major mystery associated with death is not what it feels like to die, but what comes *after* death. We wonder whether it is simply the end of our existence, or whether life continues in some form even after the physical body has stopped functioning. Throughout the history of humanity people have sought answers to these questions, but the answers have never been conclusive. Although some scientists claim to have photographed a "soul" escaping from someone's body at the moment of death, science has done nothing to clear up conclusively the mysteries about life after death. Religion has supplied answers for many people, but religious explanations must be accepted on faith without regard for their compatibility with scientific knowledge. Some people have had personal experiences, such as the feeling that a dead loved one was present with them, that have convinced them that life continues after death. But not having shared that experience, others of us remain skeptical.

The selections in this section explore a number of answers to the question, "Is death the end?" Since entire books could be written on even a single answer to the question, we will not be able to examine more than a few views of immortality and the hereafter. Our purpose is not really to provide a comprehensive survey, but to raise possibilities. If we are successful, you will start to formulate individual conclusions, which may become further modified as years bring increased knowledge and maturity. A familiarity with a number of previous attempts to deal with this question can encourage you to be more open to serious consideration of all points of view. But in the end, we must each arrive at a personal point of view and live with the implications of that philosophy.

Certainly the most obvious and immediate—and, to some, perhaps most frightening—possibility is that what happens after death is nothing more than what seems to happen: the physical body dies and is reabsorbed into the earth. In this view awareness does not continue in any form, and "immortality" exists only in the fact that memories of the dead person, his or her works, and the effects

of his or her deeds continue for a while after the death of
the person. This is not atheism; deeply religious people
who believe in the existence of a God may hold this view.
And, alternately, atheists may believe in an afterlife.
The two subjects should not be confused with each other.
Although scientists have found little evidence for an afterlife, lack of confirmation is not refutation. Belief in science
can be compatible with belief in an afterlife. Einstein, for
example, embraced both beliefs strongly, as did Mendel,
a Catholic monk noted for his work in genetics.

In the most prevalent belief of what happens after
death, the person makes a transition from one place (or
state) to another one. For some societies, ancient Egypt,
for example, the actual body makes the transition. This
explains why great efforts are made by people in these
societies to preserve the bodies of the dead and to equip
the dead person for the journey with food and other pro-
visions. In other societies, the transition is made by the
person's spirit or "soul." People in these societies acknowledge that the physical body is left behind, and hence
they have no qualms about disposing of the body in ways
that destroy it. For them the essence of the person moves
somewhere else to begin a different kind of existence.
Among the destinations that various groups have concep-
tualized are limbo, hell, purgatory, heaven, hades, the
Elysian fields, paradise, and the happy hunting ground. In
some religions only certain people are thought to achieve
immortality, the chosen ones being either predetermined
by God or earning this place as a result of their deeds
while living on earth.

Some of the great religions of the Orient hold still another view of what happens after death. They view God
as the Universe; the Universe and its laws are God. Dead
or alive, we are one portion of the universe, of God; our
task is to become aware of this, aware that in this essential respect there is no change from living to dead. Stoic
philosophers of ancient Greece held similar views. Another
concept that is frequently a part of Eastern religions di-
vides our existence into an apparent physical self, which
is mortal, and residing in it, a spiritual self comprised of
energy, the essence of "life." If the body could be thought
of as a flute, the energy self would be the sound and the
wind that makes it. The energy self is immortal and
through "reincarnation" lives again and again, reborn into

different existences. It evolves and grows in its enlightenment during each successive existence.

Another way in which we continue to exist after death is through the things we leave behind: our works, our thoughts, our deeds, our children. Many people are able to achieve a sense of transcendence through creative efforts that will endure even after the person is gone—books, plays, music, works of art. For others immortality comes through their children. This view is clearly expressed in the African folktale, "Man Chooses Death," in which the first man and woman on earth choose to gain immortality through their offspring rather than themselves living forever. Even when people do not have children, they can achieve a type of immortality through the persons who survive them. In the excerpt from *For Whom the Bell Tolls* that appears in this section, Robert Jordan creates a form of immortality for himself by staying behind to face certain death in order to make it possible for Maria to escape. "I go with thee," he tells her. "As long as there is one of us there is both of us." He apparently believes, and attempts to convey to her, that although he will die if left behind to face the enemy, he will in a sense live through her if she escapes.

Finally, for some people—particularly those who feel especially close to nature—immortality lies in the fact that our bodies return to the soil and that the individual molecules become rearranged into life of a different form. If matter can be neither created nor destroyed, then human beings never really end their existence; they just reunite with nature and become something else. And perhaps this view is ultimately reassuring—that when we die we become one with Mother Earth.

from HAMLET
WILLIAM SHAKESPEARE

Visiting a cemetery with his friend Horatio, Hamlet sees a gravedigger tossing up skulls and muses on what happens to a person after death. He concludes that everyone, including Alexander the Great and Caesar, returns to dust when he dies —a none too glorious end.

Enter Hamlet and Horatio [as Clown digs and sings].

Song.

In youth when I did love, did love,
  Methought it was very sweet
To contract—O—the time for—a—my behove,
  O' methought there—a—was nothing—a—meet.

HAMLET Has this fellow no feeling of his business, that 'a
  sings at grave-making?
HORATIO Custom hath made it in him a property of easi-
  ness.
HAMLET 'Tis e'en so. The hand of little employment hath
  the daintier sense.
CLOWN   *Song*
        But age with his stealing steps
          Hath clawed me in his clutch,
        And hath shipped me intil the land,
          As if I had never been such.

[Throws up a skull.]

HAMLET That skull had a tongue in it, and could sing
  once. How the knave jowls it to the ground, as if 'twere
  Cain's jawbone, that did the first murder! This might be
  the pate of a politician, which this ass now o'erreaches;
  one that would circumvent God, might it not?
HORATIO It might, my lord.
HAMLET Or of a courtier, which could say 'Good morrow,
  sweet lord! How dost thou, sweet lord?' This might be
  my Lord Such-a-one, that praised my Lord Such-a-
  one's horse when 'a meant to beg it, might it not?
HORATIO Ay, my lord.
HAMLET Why, e'en so, and now my Lady Worm's, chap-
  less, and knocked about the mazzard with a sexton's
  spade. Here's fine revolution, an we had the trick to
  see't. Did these bones cost no more the breeding but to
  play at loggets with 'em? Mine ache to think on't.
CLOWN   *Song*
        A pickaxe and a spade, a spade,
          For and a shrouding sheet;
        O, a pit of clay for to be made
          For such a guest is meet.

[*Throws up another skull.*]

HAMLET There's another. Why may not that be the skull of a lawyer? Where be his quiddities now, his quillities, his cases, his tenures, and his tricks? Why does he suffer this mad knave now to knock him about the sconce with a dirty shovel, and will not tell him of his action of battery? Hum! This fellow might be in's time a great buyer of land, with his statutes, his recognizances, his fines, his double vouchers, his recoveries. [Is this the fine of his fines, and the recovery of his recoveries,] to have his fine pate full of fine dirt? Will his vouchers vouch him no more of his purchases, and double ones too, than the length and breadth of a pair of indentures? The very conveyances of his lands will scarcely lie in this box, and must th' inheritor himself have no more, ha?

HORATIO Not a jot more, my lord.

HAMLET Is not parchment made of sheepskins?

HORATIO Ay, my lord, and of calveskins too.

HAMLET They are sheep and calves which seek out assurance in that. I will speak to this fellow. Whose grave's this, sirrah?

CLOWN Mine, sir.

[*Sings*]   O, a pit of clay for to be made
          For such a guest is meet.

HAMLET I think it be thine indeed, for thou liest in't.

CLOWN You lie out on't, sir, and therefore 'tis not yours. For my part, I do not lie in't, yet it is mine.

HAMLET Thou dost lie in't, to be in't and say it is thine. 'Tis for the dead, not for the quick; therefore thou liest.

CLOWN 'Tis a quick lie, sir; 'twill away again from me to you.

HAMLET What man dost thou dig it for?

CLOWN For no man, sir.

HAMLET What woman then?

CLOWN For none neither.

HAMLET Who is to be buried in't?

CLOWN One that was a woman, sir; but, rest her soul, she's dead.

HAMLET How absolute the knave is! We must speak by the card, or equivocation will undo us. By the Lord, Horatio, this three years I have taken note of it, the age is grown so picked that the toe of the peasant comes so near the heel of the courtier he galls his kibe—How long hast thou been a grave-maker?

CLOWN Of all the days i' th' year, I came to't that day that our last king Hamlet overcame Fortinbras.

HAMLET How long is that since?

CLOWN Cannot you tell that? Every fool can tell that. It was the very day that young Hamlet was born—he that is mad, and sent into England.

HAMLET Ay, marry, why was he sent into England?

CLOWN Why, because 'a was mad. 'A shall recover his wits there; or if 'a do not, 'tis no great matter there.

HAMLET Why?

CLOWN 'Twill not be seen in him there. There the men are as mad as he.

HAMLET How came he mad?

CLOWN Very strangely, they say.

HAMLET How strangely?

CLOWN Faith, e'en with losing his wits.

HAMLET Upon what ground?

CLOWN Why, here in Denmark. I have been sexton here, man and boy, thirty years.

HAMLET How long will a man lie i' th' earth ere he rot?

CLOWN Faith, if 'a be not rotten before 'a die (as we have many pocky corses now-ad-days that will scarce hold the layin in), 'a will last you some eight year or nine year. A tanner will last you nine year.

HAMLET Why he more than another?

CLOWN Why, sir, his hide is so tanned with his trade that 'a will keep out water a great while, and your water is a sore decayer of your whoreson dead body. Here's a skull now hath lien you i' th' earth three-and-twenty years.

HAMLET Whose was it?

CLOWN A whoreson mad fellow's it was. Whose do you think it was?

HAMLET Nay, I know not.

CLOWN A pestilence on him for a mad rogue! 'A poured a flagon of Rhenish on my head once. This same skull, sir, was—sir—Yorick's skull, the king's jester.

HAMLET This?

CLOWN E'en that.

HAMLET Let me see. [*Takes the skull.*] Alas, poor Yorick! I knew him, Horatio, a fellow of infinite jest, of most excellent fancy. He hath borne me on his back a thousand times. And now how abhorred in my imagination it is! My gorge rises at it. Here hung those lips that I have kissed I know not how oft. Where be your gibes now? Your gambols, your songs, your flashes of merriment that were wont to set the table on a roar? Not one now to mock your own grinning? Quite chapfall'n? Now get you to my lady's chamber, and tell her, let her paint an inch thick, to this favor she must come. Make her laugh at that. Prithee, Horatio, tell me one thing.

HORATIO What's that, my lord?

HAMLET Dost thou think Alexander looked o' this fashion i' th' earth?

HORATIO E'en so.

HAMLET And smelt so? Pah!
[*Puts down the skull.*]

HORATIO E'en so, my lord.

HAMLET To what base uses we may return, Horatio! Why may not imagination trace the noble dust of Alexander till 'a find it stopping a bunghole?

HORATIO 'Twere to consider too curiously, to consider so.

HAMLET No, faith, not a jot, but to follow him thither with modesty enough, and likelihood to lead it; as thus: Alexander died, Alexander was buried, Alexander returneth to dust; the dust is earth; of earth we make loam; and why of that loam whereto he was converted might they not stop a beer barrel?
Imperious Caesar, dead and turned to clay,
Might stop a hole to keep the wind away.
O, that that earth which kept the world in awe
Should patch a wall t' expel the winter's flaw!

BECAUSE I COULD NOT STOP FOR DEATH
EMILY DICKINSON

A nineteenth-century American poet, Emily Dickinson produced a very substantial collection of poems which deal exclusively with death and dying. "Because I Could Not Stop Death" is a fine example of Dickinson's perception of life after death. She creates a positive, inviting scene of the soul of a dead woman and the courteous gentleman, Mr. Death, as they advance in their carriage toward eternity.

Because I could not stop for Death,
He kindly stopped for me;
The carriage held but just ourselves
And Immortality.

We slowly drove, he knew no haste,
And I had put away
My labor, and my leisure too,
For his civility.

We passed the school where children played
At wrestling in a ring;
We passed the fields of gazing grain,
We passed the setting sun.

We paused before a house that seemed
A swelling of the ground;
The roof was scarcely visible,
The cornice but a mound.

Since then 'tis centuries; but each
Feels shorter than the day
I first surmised the horses' heads
Were toward eternity.

MAN CHOOSES DEATH
FOLKTALE

The source of this fable is Madagascar, a large island off the coast of Africa. The fable attempts to explain how death came into the world, and indicates that the first couple chose to achieve immortality through their children rather than living forever themselves.

One day God asked the first human couple who then lived in heaven what kind of death they wanted, that of the moon or that of the banana. Because the couple wondered in dismay about the implications of the two modes of death, God explained to them: the banana puts forth shoots which take its place and the moon itself comes back to life. The couple considered for a long time before they made their choice. If they elected to be childless, they would avoid death, but they would also be very lonely, would themselves be forced to carry out all the work, and would not have anybody to work and strive for. Therefore they prayed to God for children, well aware of the consequences of their choice. And their prayer was granted. Since that time man's sojourn is short on this earth.

from THE HOLY BIBLE,
CORINTHIANS I, CHAPTER 15

This passage is taken from a letter which Paul, a disciple of Jesus, wrote to the early Christians living in Corinth. It expresses the traditional Christian view that a person's life continues after death.

Behold, I show you a mystery;
We shall not all sleep, but we shall all be changed, in a moment, in the twinkling of an eye, at the last trump:
For the trumpet shall sound, and the dead shall be raised incorruptible, and we shall be changed.
For this corruptible must put on incorruption,
And this mortal must put on immortality,
So when this corruptible shall have put on incorruption,
And this mortal shall have put on immortality,
Then shall be brought to pass the saying that is written,
"Death is swallowed up in victory.
O death, where is thy sting?
O grave, where is thy victory?"
The sting of death is sin; and the strength of sin is the law.
But thanks be to God,
Which giveth us the victory through our Lord Jesus Christ.
Therefore, my beloved brethen, be ye steadfast, unmovable.
Always abounding in the work of the Lord,
Forasmuch as ye know that your labour is not in vain in the Lord.

from A GRIEF OBSERVED
C. S. LEWIS

Written by C. S. Lewis (1898–1963), distinguished scholar, author, and teacher, A Grief Observed is a diary of Lewis's grieving process over the death of his wife, poet Joy Davidman. In this excerpt Lewis considers the issue of immortality. He does not allow himself to indulge in comforting delusions about life after death and of a happy reunion with his deceased wife. Instead, he gives a brutally practical account, not so much of what life after death is, but what it is not and cannot ever be.

What pitiable cant to say "She will live forever in my memory!" *Live?* That is exactly what she won't do. You might as well think like the old Egyptians that you can keep the dead by embalming them. Will nothing persuade us that they are gone? What's left? A corpse, a memory, and (in some versions) a ghost. All mockeries or horrors. Three more ways of spelling the word *dead*. It was H. I loved. As if I wanted to fall in love with my memory of her, an image in my own mind! It would be a sort of incest. . . .

But there are other difficulties. "Where is she now?" That is, *in what place* is she *at the present time*. But if H. is not a body—and the body I loved is certainly no longer she—she is in no place at all. And "the present time" is a date or point in our time series. It is as if she were on a journey without me and I said, looking at my watch, "I wonder is she at Euston now." But unless she is proceeding at sixty seconds a minute along this same time-line that all we living people travel by, what does *now* mean? If the dead are not in time, or not in our sort of time, is there any clear difference, when we speak of them, between *was* and *is* and *will be?*

Kind people have said to me "She is with God." In one sense that is most certain. She is, like God, incomprehensible and unimaginable.

But I find that this question, however important it may be in itself, is not after all very important in relation to grief. Suppose that the earthly lives she and I shared for a few years are in reality only the basis for, or prelude to, or earthly appearance of, two unimaginable, super-cosmic, eternal somethings. Those somethings could be pictured as spheres or globes. Where the plane of Nature cuts through them—that is, in earthly life—they appear as two circles (circles are slices of spheres). Two circles that touched. But those two circles, above all the point at which they touched, are the very thing I am mourning for, homesick for, famished for. You tell me "she goes on." But my heart and body are crying out, come back, come back. Be a circle, touching my circle on the plane of Nature. But I know this is impossible. I know that the thing I want is exactly the thing I can never get. The old life, the jokes, the drinks, the arguments, the lovemaking, the tiny, heartbreaking commonplace. On any view whatever, to say "H. is dead," is to say "All that is gone." It is a part of the past. And the past is the past and that is what time means, and time itself is one more name for death, and Heaven itself is a state where "the former things have passed away."

Talk to me about the truth of religion and I'll listen gladly. Talk to me about the duty of religion and I'll listen submissively. But don't come talking to me about the consolations of religion or I shall suspect that you don't understand.

Unless, of course, you can literally believe all that stuff about family reunions "on the further shore," pictured in entirely earthly terms. But that is all unscriptural, all out of bad hymns and lithographs. There's not a word of it in the Bible. And it rings false. We *know* it couldn't be like that. Reality never repeats. The exact same thing is never taken away and given back. How well the Spiritualists bait their hook! "Things on this side are not so different after all." There are cigars in Heaven. For that is what we should all like. The happy past restored.

And that, just that, is what I cry out for, with mad, midnight endearments and entreaties spoken into the empty air.

from GRATEFUL TO LIFE AND DEATH

R. K. NARAYAN

Whether the spirit of a person lives on after death and whether these spirits can communicate with the living has been widely debated for centuries. This excerpt from a novel by R. K. Narayan, one of the outstanding writers of contemporary India, deals with a man's encounter with the spirit of his dead wife. Whether this meeting is merely a figment of his imagination or an actual spiritual visitation is left to the reader to decide. Either way, this scene presents a powerful moment when life and death fuse into a timeless dimension in which immortality seems totally possible.

I was walking down our lone street late at night, enveloped in the fragrance of the jasmine and rose garland, slung on my arm. "For whom am I carrying this jasmine home?" I asked myself. Susila would treasure a garland for two whole days, cutting up and sticking masses of it in her hair morning and evening. "Carrying a garland to a lonely house—a dreadful job," I told myself.

I fumbled with the key in the dark, opened the door and switched on the light. I hung up the garland on a nail and kicked up the roll of bedding. The fragrance permeated the whole house. I sprinkled a little water on the flowers to keep them fresh, put out the light and lay down to sleep.

The garland hung by the nail right over my head. The few drops of water which I sprinkled on the flowers seemed to have quickened in them a new life. Their essences came forth into the dark night as I lay in bed, bringing a new vigour with them. The atmosphere became surcharged with strange spiritual forces. Their delicate aroma filled every particle of the air, and as I let my mind float in the ecstasy, gradually perceptions and senses deepened. Oblivion crept over me like a cloud. The past, present and the future welded into one.

I had been thinking of the day's activities and meetings and associations. But they seemed to have no place now. I checked my mind. Bits of memory came floating—a gesture of Brown's, the toy house in the dentist's front room, Rangappa with a garland, and the ring of many speeches and voices—all this was gently overwhelmed and swept aside, till one's mind became clean and bare and a mere chamber of fragrance. It was a superb, noble intoxication. And I had no choice but to let my mind and memories drown in it. I softly called "Susila! Susila, my wife . . ." with all my being. It sounded as if it were a hypnotic melody. "My wife . . . my wife, my wife . . ." My mind trembled with this rhythm, I forgot myself and my own existence. I fell into a drowse, whispering, "My wife, wife." How long? How could I say? When I opened my eyes again she was sitting on my bed looking at me with an extraordinary smile in her eyes.

"Susila! Susila!" I cried. "You here!" "Yes, I'm here, have always been here." I sat up leaning on my pillow. "Why do you disturb yourself?" she asked.

"I am making a place for you," I said, edging away a little. I looked her up and down and said: "How well you look!" Her complexion had a golden glow, her eyes sparkled with a new light, her saree shimmered with blue interwoven with "light" as she had termed it. . . . "How beautiful!" I said looking at it. "Yes, I always wear this when I come to you. I know you like it very much," she said. I gazed on her face. There was an overwhelming fragrance of jasmine surrounding her. "Still jasmine-scented!" I commented.

"Oh wait," I said and got up. I picked up the garland from the nail and returned to bed. I held it to her. "For you as ever. I somehow feared you wouldn't take it. . . ." She received it with a smile, cut off a piece of it and stuck it in a curve on the back of her head. She turned her head and asked: "Is this all right?"

"Wonderful," I said, smelling it.

A cock crew. The first purple of the dawn came through our window, and faintly touched the walls of our room. "Dawn!" she whispered and rose to her feet.

We stood at the window, gazing on a slender, red streak over the eastern rim of the earth. A cool breeze lapped our faces. The boundaries of our personalities suddenly dissolved. It was a moment of rare, immutable joy—a moment for which one feels grateful to Life and Death.

from FOR WHOM THE BELL TOLLS
ERNEST HEMINGWAY

*In considering whether death signals the end of a person's
existence, many people—even if they reject the idea of life
after death—recognize our ability to live on in the hearts,
minds, and memories of others. The anticipation of this form
of immortality can lessen the pain of separation for both the
dying person and the survivor. A beautiful example of this
is contained in the following excerpt from* For Whom the
Bell Tolls, *one of the finest novels by Ernest Hemingway, a
twentieth-century American writer. Robert Jordan is an American who has gone to Spain to fight fascism (as Hemingway
himself did) as a member of Pablo's guerrilla band, and the
band has just dynamited a crucial bridge and is trying to
escape. Although Robert Jordan has known Maria for only a
few days, they have fallen deeply in love. Jordan chooses
to stay behind to face the enemy, and certain death, alone
in order to make it possible for Maria to escape. In what is
surely one of the most poignant farewells in all of literature,
Jordan reassures Maria that he will live on as part of her.
The title of this novel is derived from a passage in the essay,
"Devotions upon Emergent Occasions," by John Donne, a
seventeenth-century English writer:*

> No man is an island, entire of itself;
> Every man is a piece of the continent,
> a part of the main;
> If a clod be washed away by the sea, Europe is
> the less,
> As well as if a promontory were,
> As well as if a manor of thy friend or of thine
> own were;
> Any man's death diminishes me,
> because I am involved in mankind;
> And therefore never send to know for whom the
> bell tolls;
> It tolls for thee.

Robert Jordan rode thirty yards farther up the road; beyond that the bank was too steep. The gun was firing now

with the rocket whish and the cracking, dirt-spouting boom. "Come on, you big gray fascist bastard," Robert Jordan said to the horse and put him down the slope in a sliding plunge. Then he was out in the open, over the road that was so hard under the hooves he felt the pound of it come up all the way to his shoulders, his neck and his teeth, onto the smooth of the slope, the hooves finding it, cutting it, pounding it, reaching, throwing, going, and he looked down across the slope to where the bridge showed now at a new angle he had never seen. It crossed in profile now without foreshortening and in the center was the broken place and behind it on the road was the little tank and behind the little tank was a big tank with a gun that flashed now yellow-bright as a mirror and the screech as the air ripped apart seemed almost over the gray neck that stretched ahead of him, and he turned his head as the dirt fountained up the hillside. The pack-horse was ahead of him swinging too far to the right and slowing down and Robert Jordan, galloping, his head turned a little toward the bridge, saw the line of trucks halted behind the turn that showed now clearly as he was gaining height, and he saw the bright yellow flash that signalled the instant whish and boom, and the shell fell short, but he heard the metal sailing from where the dirt rose.

He saw them all ahead in the edge of the timber watching him and he said, "*Arre caballo!* Go on, horse!" and felt his big horse's chest surging with the steepening of the slope and saw the gray neck stretching and the gray ears ahead and he reached and patted the wet gray neck, and he looked back at the bridge and saw the bright flash from the heavy, squat, mud-colored tank there on the road and then he did not hear any whish but only a banging acrid smelling clang like a boiler being ripped apart and he was under the gray horse and the gray horse was kicking and he was trying to pull out from under the weight.

He could move all right. He could move toward the right. But his left leg stayed perfectly flat under the horse as he moved to the right. It was as though there was a new joint in it; not the hip joint but another one that went sideways like a hinge. Then he knew what it was all right and just then the gray horse knee-ed himself up and Robert Jordan's right leg, that had kicked the stirrup loose just as it should, slipped clear over the saddle and came down beside him and he felt with his two hands of his thigh bone where the left leg lay flat against the ground and his hands both felt the sharp bone and where it pressed against the skin.

The gray horse was standing almost over him and he could see his ribs heaving. The grass was green where he sat and there were meadow flowers in it and he looked down the slope across to the road and the bridge and the gorge and the road and saw the tank and waited for the next flash. It came almost at once with again no whish and in the burst of it, with the smell of the high explosive, the dirt clods scattering and the steel whirring off, he saw the big gray horse sit quietly down beside him as though it were a horse in a circus. And then, looking at the horse sitting there, he heard the sound the horse was making.

Then Primitivo and Agustín had him under the arm-pits and were dragging him up the last slope and the new joint in his leg let it swing any way the ground swung it. Once a shell whished close over them and they dropped him and fell flat, but the dirt scattered over them and the metal sung off and they picked him up again. And then they had him up to the shelter of the long draw in the timber where the horses were, and Maria, Pilar and Pablo were standing over him.

Maria was kneeling by him and saying, "Roberto, what hast thou?"

He said, sweating heavily, "The left leg is broken, *guapa.*"

"We will bind it up," Pilar said. "Thou canst ride that." She pointed to one of the horses that was packed. "Cut off the load."

Robert Jordan saw Pablo shake his head and he nodded at him.

"Get along," he said. Then he said, "Listen, Pablo. Come here."

The sweat-streaked, bristly face bent down by him and Robert Jordan smelt the full smell of Pablo.

"Let us speak," he said to Pilar and Maria. "I have to speak to Pablo."

"Does it hurt much?" Pablo asked. He was bending close over Robert Jordan.

"No. I think the nerve is crushed. Listen. Get along. I am mucked, see? I will talk to the girl for a moment.

When I say to take her, take her. She will want to stay. I will only speak to her for a moment."

"Clearly, there is not much time," Pablo said.

"Clearly.

"I think you would do better in the Republic," Robert Jordan said.

"Nay. I am for Gredos."

"Use thy head."

"Talk to her now," Pablo said. "There is little time. I am sorry thou hast this, *Inglés*."

"Since I have it—" Robert Jordan said. "Let us not speak of it. But use thy head. Thou hast much head. Use it."

"Why would I not?" said Pablo. "Talk now fast, *Inglés*. There is no time."

Pablo went over to the nearest tree and watched down the slope, across the slope and up the road across the gorge. Pablo was looking at the gray horse on the slope with true regret on his face and Pilar and Maria were with Robert Jordan where he sat against the tree trunk.

"Slit the trouser, will thee?" he said to Pilar. Maria crouched by him and did not speak. The sun was on her hair and her face was twisted as a child's contorts before it cries. But she was not crying.

Pilar took her knife and slit his trouser leg down below the left-hand pocket. Robert Jordan spread the cloth with his hands and looked at the stretch of his thigh. Ten inches below the hip joint there was a pointed, purple swelling like a sharp-peaked little tent and as he touched it with his fingers he could feel the snapped-off thigh bone tight against the skin. His leg was lying at an odd angle. He looked up at Pilar. Her face had the same expression as Maria's.

"*Anda,*" he said to her. "Go."

She went away with her head down without saying anything nor looking back and Robert Jordan could see her shoulders shaking.

"*Guapa,*" he said to Maria and took hold of her two hands. "Listen. We will not be going to Madrid—"

Then she started to cry.

"No, *guapa,* don't," he said. "Listen. We will not go to Madrid now but I go always with thee wherever thou goest. Understand?"

She said nothing and pushed her head against his cheek with her arms around him.

"Listen to this well, rabbit," he said. He knew there was a great hurry and he was sweating very much, but this had to be said and understood. "Thou wilt go now, rabbit. But I go with thee. As long as there is one of us there is both of us. Do you understand?"

"Nay, I stay with thee."

"Nay, rabbit. What I do now I do alone. I could not do it well with thee. If thou goest then I go, too. Do you not see how it is? Whichever one there is, is both."

"I will stay with thee."

"Nay, rabbit. Listen. That people cannot do together. Each one must do it alone. But if thou goest then I go with thee. It is in that way that I go too. Thou wilt go now, I know. For thou art good and kind. Thou wilt go now for us both."

"But it is easier if I stay with thee," she said. "It is better for me."

"Yes. Therefore go for a favor. Do it for me since it is what thou canst do."

"But you don't understand, Roberto. What about *me*? It is worse for me to go."

"Surely," he said. "It is harder for thee. But I am thee also now."

She said nothing.

He looked at her and he was sweating heavily and he spoke now, trying harder to do something than he had ever tried in all his life.

"Now you will go for us both," he said. "You must not be selfish, rabbit. You must do your duty now."

She shook her head.

"You are me now," he said. "Surely thou must feel it, rabbit.

"Rabbit, listen," he said. "Truly thus I go too. I swear it to thee."

She said nothing.

"Now you see it," he said. "Now I see it is clear. Now thou wilt go. Good. Now you are going. Now you have said you will go."

She had said nothing.

"Now I thank thee for it. Now you are going well and fast and far and we both go in thee. Now put thy hand here. Now put thy head down. Nay, put it down. That is right. Now I put my hand there. Good. Thou art so good. Now do not think more. Now art thou doing what thou should. Now thou art obeying. Not me but us both. The me in thee. Now you go for us both. Truly. We both go in thee now. This I have promised thee. Thou art very good to go and very kind."

He jerked his head at Pablo, who was half-looking at him from the tree and Pablo started over. He motioned with his thumb to Pilar.

"We will go to Madrid another time, rabbit," he said. "Truly. Now stand up and go and we both go. Stand up. See?"

"No," she said and held him tight around the neck.

He spoke now still calmly and reasonably but with great authority.

"Stand up," he said. "Thou art me too now. Thou art all there will be of me. Stand up."

She stood up slowly, crying, and with her head down. Then she dropped quickly beside him and then stood up again, slowly and tiredly, as he said, "Stand up, *guapa.*"

Pilar was holding her by the arm and she was standing there.

"*Vamonos,*" Pilar said. "Dost lack anything, *Inglés?*" She looked at him and shook her head.

"No," he said and went on talking to Maria.

"There is no good-by, *guapa,* because we are not apart. That it should be good in the Gredos. Go now. Go good. Nay." He spoke now still calmly and reasonably as Pilar walked the girl along. "Do not turn around. Put thy foot in. Yes. Thy foot in. Help her up," he said to Pilar. "Get her in the saddle. Swing up now."

He turned his head, sweating, and looked down the slope, then back toward where the girl was in the saddle with Pilar by her and Pablo just behind. "Now go," he said. "Go."

She started to look around. "Don't look around," Robert Jordan said. "Go." And Pablo hit the horse across the crupper with a hobbling strap and it looked as though Maria tried to slip from the saddle but Pilar and Pablo were riding close up against her and Pilar was holding her and the three horses were going up the draw.

"Roberto," Maria turned and shouted. "Let me stay! Let me stay!"

"I am with thee," Robert Jordan shouted. "I am with

thee now. We are both there. Go!" Then they were out of sight around the corner of the draw and he was soaking wet with sweat and looking at nothing.

Agustín was standing by him.

"Do you want me to shoot thee, *Inglés?*" he asked, leaning down close. "*Quieres?* It is nothing."

"*No hace falta,*" Robert Jordan said. "Get along. I am very well here."

"*Me cago en la leche que me han dado!*" Agustín said. He was crying so he could not see Robert Jordan clearly. "*Salud, Inglés.*"

"*Salud,* old one," Robert Jordan said. He was looking down the slope now. "Look well after the cropped head, wilt thou?"

"There is no problem," Agustín said. "Thou hast what thou needest?"

"There are very few shells for this *máquina,* so I will keep it," Robert Jordan said. "Thou canst not get more. For that other and the one of Pablo, yes."

"I cleaned out the barrel," Agustín said. "Where thou plugged it in the dirt with the fall."

"What became of the pack-horse?"

"The gypsy caught it."

Agustín was on the horse now but he did not want to go. He leaned far over toward the tree where Robert Jordan lay.

"Go on, *viejo,*" Robert Jordan said to him. "In war there are many things like this."

"*Qué putá es la guerra,*" Agustín said. "War is a bitchery."

"Yes man, yes. But get on with thee."

"*Salud, Inglés,*" Agustín said, clenching his right fist.

"*Salud,*" Robert Jordan said. "But get along, man."

Augustín wheeled his horse and brought his right fist down as though he cursed again with the motion of it and rode up the draw. All the others had been out of sight long before. He looked back where the draw turned in the timber and waved his fist. Robert Jordan waved and then Agustín, too, was out of sight. . . . Robert Jordan looked down the green slope of the hillside to the road and the bridge. I'm as well this way as any, he thought. It wouldn't be worth risking getting over on my belly yet, not as close as that thing was to the surface, and I can see better this way.

He felt empty and drained and exhausted from all of it and from them going and his mouth tasted of bile. Now, finally and at last, there was no problem. However all of it had been and however all of it would ever be now, for him, no longer was there any problem.

They were all gone now and he was alone with his back against a tree. He looked down across the green slope, seeing the gray horse where Agustín had shot him, and on down the slope to the road with the timber-covered country behind it. Then he looked at the bridge and across the bridge and watched the activity on the bridge and the road. He could see the trucks now, all down the lower road. The gray of the trucks showed through the trees. Then he looked back up the road to where it came down over the hill. They will be coming soon now, he thought.

Pilar will take care of her as well as any one can. You know that. Pablo must have a sound plan or he would not have tried it. You do not have to worry about Pablo. It does no good to think about Maria. Try to believe what you told her. That is the best. And who says it is not true? Not you. You don't say it, any more than you would say the things did not happen that happened. Stay with what you believe now. Don't get cynical. The time is too short and you have just sent her away. Each one does what he can. You can do nothing for yourself but perhaps you can do something for another. Well, we had all our luck in four days. Not four days. It was afternoon when I first got there and it will not be noon today. That makes not quite three days and three nights. Keep it accurate, he said. Quite accurate.

I think you better get down now, he thought. You better get fixed around some way where you will be useful instead of leaning against this tree like a tramp. You have had much luck. There are many worse things than this. Every one has to do this, one day or another. You are not afraid of it once you know you have to do it, are you? No, he said, truly. It was lucky the nerve was crushed, though. I cannot even feel that there is anything below the break. He touched the lower part of his leg and it was as though it were not part of his body.

He looked down the hill slope again and he thought, I hate to leave it, is all. I hate to leave it very much and I hope I have done some good in it. I have tried to with what talent I had. *Have, you mean. All right, have.*

I have fought for what I believed in for a year now. If we win here we will win everywhere. The world is a fine place and worth the fighting for and I hate very much to leave it. And you had a lot of luck, he told himself, to have had such a good life. You've had just as good a life as grandfather's though not as long. You've had as good a life as any one because of these last days. You do not want to complain when you have been so lucky. I wish there was some way to pass on what I've learned, though. Christ, I was learning fast there at the end. . . .

You take it easy, now, he said. Get turned over now while you still have time. . . . Get yourself turned over, Jordan. But he was reluctant to try it.

Then he remembered that he had the small flask in his hip pocket and he thought, I'll take a good spot of the giant killer and then I'll try it. But the flask was not there when he felt for it. Then he felt that much more alone because he knew there was not going to be even that. I guess I'd counted on that, he said.

Do you suppose Pablo took it? Don't be silly. You must have lost it at the bridge. "Come on now, Jordan," he said. "Over you go."

Then he took hold of his left leg with both hands and pulled on it hard, pulling toward the foot while he lay down beside the tree he had been resting his back against. Then lying flat and pulling hard on the leg, so the broken end of the bone would not come up and cut through the thigh, he turned slowly around on his rump until the back of his head was facing downhill. Then with his broken leg, held by both hands, uphill, he put the sole of his right foot against the instep of his left foot and pressed hard while he rolled, sweating, over onto his face and chest. He got onto his elbows, stretched the left leg well behind him with both hands and a far, sweating, push with the right foot and there he was. He felt with his fingers on the left thigh and it was all right. The bone end had not punctured the skin and the broken end was well into the muscle now.

The big nerve must have been truly smashed when that damned horse rolled on it, he thought. It truly doesn't hurt at all. Except now in certain changes of positions. That's when the bone pinches something else. You see? he said. You see what luck is? You didn't need the giant killer at all.

He reached over for the submachine gun, took the clip out that was in the magazine, felt in his pocket for clips, opened the action and looked through the barrel, put the clip back into the groove of the magazine until it clicked, and then looked down the hill slope. Maybe half an hour, he thought. Now take it easy.

Then he looked at the hillside and he looked at the pines and he tried not to think at all.

He looked at the stream and he remembered how it had been under the bridge in the cool of the shadow. I wish they would come, he thought. I do not want to get in any sort of mixed-up state before they come.

Who do you suppose has it easier? Ones with religion or just taking it straight? It comforts them very much but we know there is no thing to fear. It is only missing it that's bad. Dying is only bad when it takes a long time and hurts so much that it humiliates you. That is where you have all the luck, see? You don't have any of that.

It's wonderful they've got away. I don't mind this at all now they are away. It *is* sort of the way I said. It is really very much that way. Look how different it would be if they were all scattered out across that hill where that gray horse is. Or if we were all cooped up here waiting for it. No. They're gone. They're away. Now if the attack were only a success. What do you want? Everything. I want everything and I will take whatever I get. If this attack is no good another one will be. I never noticed when the planes came back. *God, that was lucky I could make her go . . . .*

His leg was hurting very badly now. The pain had started suddenly with the swelling after he had moved and he said, Maybe I'll just do it now. I guess I'm not awfully good at pain. Listen, if I do that now you wouldn't misunderstand, would you? *Who are you talking to?* Nobody, he said. Grandfather, I guess. No. Nobody. Oh bloody it, I wish that they would come.

Listen, I may have to do that because if I pass out or anything like that I am no good at all and if they bring me to they will ask me a lot of questions and do things and all and that is no good. It's much best not to have them do those things. So why wouldn't it be all right to just do it now and then the whole thing would be over with? Because oh, listen, yes, listen, *let them come now.*

You're not so good at this, Jordan, he said. Not so good at this. And who is so good at this? I don't know and I don't really care right now. But you are not. That's right. You're not at all. Oh not at all, at all. I think it would be all right to do it now? Don't you?

No, it isn't. Because there is something you can do yet. As long as you know what it is you have to do it. As long as you remember what it is you have to wait for that. *Come on. Let them come. Let them come. Let them come!*

Think about them being away, he said. Think about them going through the timber. Think about them crossing a creek. Think about them riding through the heather. Think about them going up the slope. Think about them O. K. tonight. Think about them travelling, all night. Think about them hiding up tomorrow. Think about them. God damn it, think about them. *That's just as far as I can think about them,* he said.

Think about Montana. *I can't.* Think about Madrid. *I can't.* Think about a cool drink of water. *All right.* That's what it will be like. Like a cool drink of water. *You're a liar.* It will just be nothing. That's all it will be. Just nothing. Then do it. *Do it.* Do it now. It's all right to do it now. Go on and do it now. *No, you have to wait.* What for? You know all right. *Then wait.*

I can't wait any longer now, he said. If I wait any longer I'll pass out. I know because I've felt it starting to go three times now and I've held it. I held it all right. But I don't know about any more. What I think is you've got an internal hemorrhage there from where that thigh bone's cut around inside. Especially on that turning business. That makes the swelling and that's what weakens you and makes you start to pass. It would be all right to do it now. Really, I'm telling you that it would be all right.

And if you wait and hold them up even a little while or just get the officer that may make all the difference. One thing well done can make—

All right, he said. And he lay very quietly and tried to hold on to himself that he felt slipping away from himself as you feel snow starting to slip sometimes on a mountain slope, and he said, now quietly, then let me last until they come.

Robert Jordan's luck held very good because he saw, just then, the cavalry ride out of the timber and cross the road. He watched them coming riding up the slope. He saw the trooper who stopped by the gray horse and shouted to the officer who rode over to him. He watched them both looking down at the gray horse. They recognized him of course. He and his rider had been missing since the early morning of the day before.

Robert Jordan saw them there on the slope, close to him now, and below he saw the road and the bridge and the long lines of vehicles below it. He was completely integrated now and he took a good long look at everything. Then he looked up at the sky. There were big white clouds in it. He touched the palm of his hand against the pine needles where he lay and he touched the bark of the pine trunk that he lay behind.

Then he rested as easily as he could with his two elbows in the pine needles and the muzzle of the submachine gun resting against the trunk of the pine tree.

As the officer came trotting now on the trail of the horses of the band he would pass twenty yards below where Robert Jordan lay. At that distance there would be no problem. The officer was Lieutenant Berrendo. He had come up from La Granja when they had been ordered up after the first report of the attack on the lower post. They had ridden hard and had then had to swing back, because the bridge had been blown, to cross the gorge high above and come around through the timber. Their horses were wet and blown and they had to be urged into the trot.

Lieutenant Berrendo, watching the trail, came riding up, his thin face serious and grave. His submachine gun lay across his saddle in the crook of his left arm. Robert Jordan lay behind the tree, holding himself very carefully and delicately to keep his hands steady. He was waiting until the officer reached the sunlit place where the first trees of the pine forest joined the green slope of the meadow. He could feel his heart beating against the pine needle floor of the forest.

INVOCATION
HELENE JOHNSON

This work by black poet Helene Johnson expresses one person's attempt to achieve immortality through unity with nature. The dying person requests that her grave and her remains be surrounded by vital, sensuous images and symbols of birth, life, and growth, so that she may live eternally in the "warm, wet breast of Earth." To some this may seem a very unusual quest for immortality, primarily because it is so impersonal. The dying person does not wish to live eternally in her present identity, but rather in several different natural forms, including trees, plants, and flowers. Helene Johnson was born in Boston, Massachusetts, in 1907.

Let me be buried in the rain
In a deep, dripping wood,
Under the warm wet breast of Earth
Where once a gnarled tree stood.
And paint a picture on my tomb
With dirt and a piece of bough
Of a girl and a boy beneath a round, ripe moon
Eating of love with an eager spoon
And vowing an eager vow.
And do not keep my plot mowed smooth
And clean as a spinster's bed,
But let the weed, the flower, the tree,
Riotous, rampant, wild and free,
Grow high above my head.

FOOL'S PARADISE
ISAAC BASHEVIS SINGER

Born in Poland in 1904, Isaac Bashevis Singer worked for the Yiddish Press in Warsaw during the 1920's and later became a staff member of the Jewish Daily Forward. Since 1935 he has been a resident of the United States. His short story, "Fool's Paradise," deals with a lazy young man who strongly desires to die and go to paradise, where he hopes to be free of all labor and enjoy total leisure. His views of what life in paradise must be like reflect one popular notion

*of what happens after death. For many people it is easy to
believe that individuals who lived good lives will be rewarded
with an afterlife that includes none of the bad features of life
on earth. In this story Atzel discovers that even the paradise
he has imagined can become a very tiresome place to spend
eternity.*

Somewhere, sometime, there lived a rich man whose name
was Kadish. He had an only son who was called Atzel. In
the household of Kadish there lived a distant relative, an
orphan girl, called Aksah. Atzel was a tall boy with black
hair and black eyes. Aksah was somewhat shorter than
Atzel, and she had blue eyes and golden hair. Both were
about the same age. As children, they ate together, studied
together, played together. Atzel played the husband;
Aksah, his wife. It was taken for granted that when they
grew up they would really marry.

But when they had grown up, Atzel suddenly became
ill. It was a sickness no one had ever heard of before:
Atzel imagined that he was dead.

How did such an idea come to him? It seems it came
from listening to stories about paradise. He had had an
old nurse who had constantly described the place to him.
She had told him that in paradise it was not necessary to
work or to study or make any effort whatsoever. In paradise one ate the meat of wild oxen and the flesh of
whales; one drank the wine that the Lord reserved for
the just; one slept late into the day; and one had no duties.

Atzel was lazy by nature. He hated to get up early in
the morning and to study languages and science. He
knew that one day he would have to take over his father's
business and he did not want to.

Since his old nurse had told Atzel that the only way to
get to paradise was to die, he had made up his mind to
do just that as quickly as possible. He thought and
brooded about it so much that soon he began to imagine
that he *was* dead.

Of course his parents became terribly worried when
they saw what was happening to Atzel. Aksah cried in
secret. The family did everything possible to try to convince Atzel that he was alive, but he refused to believe
them. He would say, "Why don't you bury me? You see
that I am dead. Because of you I cannot get to paradise."

Many doctors were called in to examine Atzel, and all tried to convince the boy that he was alive. They pointed out that he was talking, eating, and sleeping. But before long Atzel began to eat less and he rarely spoke. His family feared that he would die.

In despair Kadish went to consult a great specialist, celebrated for his knowledge and wisdom. His name was Dr. Yoetz. After listening to a description of Atzel's illness, he said to Kadish, "I promise to cure your son in eight days, on one condition. You must do whatever I tell you to, no matter how strange it may seem."

Kadish agreed, and Dr. Yoetz said he would visit Atzel that same day. Kadish went home to prepare the household. He told his wife, Aksah, and the servants that all were to follow the doctor's orders without question, and they did so.

When Dr. Yoetz arrived, he was taken to Atzel's room. The boy lay on his bed, pale and thin from fasting, his hair disheveled, his nightclothes wrinkled.

The doctor took one look at Atzel and called out, "Why do you keep a dead body in the house? Why don't you make a funeral?"

On hearing these words the parents became terribly frightened, but Atzel's face lit up with a smile and he said, "You see, I was right."

Although Kadish and his wife were bewildered by the doctor's words, they remembered Kadish's promise, and went immediately to make arrangements for the funeral.

Atzel now became so excited by what the doctor had said that he jumped out of bed and began to dance and clap his hands. His joy made him hungry and he asked for food. But Dr. Yoetz replied, "Wait, you will eat in paradise."

The doctor requested that a room be prepared to look like paradise. The walls were hung with white satin, and precious rugs covered the floors. The windows were shuttered, and draperies tightly drawn. Candles and oil lamps burned day and night. The servants were dressed in white with wings on their backs and were to play angels.

Atzel was placed in an open coffin, and a funeral ceremony was held. Atzel was so exhausted with happiness that he slept right through it. When he awoke, he found himself in a room he didn't recognize. "Where am I?" he asked.

KATHE KOLLWITZ / (1867–1945)

Kathe Kollwitz, born in 1867 in Konigsburg, Germany, is one of the most moving artists of our century. For more than sixty years, she used her work to express the ideas that obsessed her: the plight of the oppressed, the causes of peace and social justice, the joys and sorrows of parenthood, and the mystery of death. At 23, she married Karl Kollwitz, a doctor. They had two sons, one of whom was killed in World War I. In her late years she experienced the trauma of Hitler's Germany, where she was forbidden to teach and where her work was labeled "degenerate."

Because she lived through two World Wars and witnessed the death of family and friends, it is understandable that death, which had haunted her life, began to appear more and more as a symbolic figure in her art. One is not surprised that Kollwitz's personal image of death is as moving and as grim as we see it here. She felt that she had to convey these horrors to the public. She said, "This is how it was—this is what we have all borne during these unspeakably bad years." She was convinced that her art had its purpose: ". . . to be effective in this time when people are so helpless and in need of aid."

The *Death* lithographs that follow are strong and gripping. The figures contemplate the coming of death with fear or fascination. The fluid lines of these drawings often make it difficult to distinguish Death from the living; they seem to be merging into one another. In *Death Reaches into a Group of Children*, she seems to foreshadow the death by aerial bombing that was soon to overtake hundreds of thousands in Europe and elsewhere.

Kollwitz loved life and was not one to contemplate or promote suicide herself. Yet, in *Old Man with Noose*, she recognizes that in light of the deprivations and degradations (especially of wartime) that people can be made to endure, it is conceivable that some might consider suicide an option.

Each person's view of death is of a totally personal nature, since it is shaped by the particular experiences of the individual's lifetime. We have seen how Kathe Kollwitz's life influenced her representation of death. Yet this is but a singular view. The artistic expression of death is as variable as the experiences that contribute to it.

KOLLWITZ, Kathe. *Death Seizing a Woman*. (1934). Plate IV from *Death*. Lithograph, 20 x 14⁷⁄₁₆″. Collection, The Museum of Modern Art, New York.

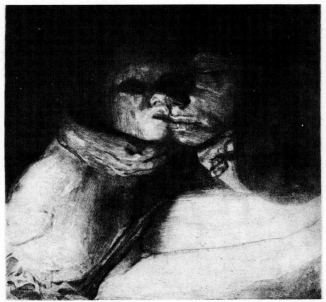

KOLLWITZ, Kathe. *Death, Woman and Child.* (1910). Etching, 16⅛ x 16³⁄₁₆″. Collection, The Museum of Modern Art, New York. Gift of Mrs. Theodore Boettger.

KOLLWITZ, Kathe. *Death Reaching into a Group of Children*. (1934).
Plate III from *Death*. Lithograph, 19$\frac{9}{16}$ x 16$\frac{1}{2}$″. Collection, The Museum
of Modern Art, New York.

KOLLWITZ, Kathe. *Woman Welcoming Death*. (1934). Plate I from *Death*. Lithograph, 18 x 15¹¹/₁₆". Collection, The Museum of Modern Art, New York.

KOLLWITZ, Kathe. *The Call of Death.* (1935 or 1936). Plate VIII from
Death. Lithograph, 14⁷⁄₁₆ x 15¹¹⁄₁₆". Collection, The Museum of Modern
Art, New York.

KOLLWITZ, Kathe. *Girl Held in the Lap of Death.* (1934). Plate II from *Death*. Lithograph, 14⅞ x 16¾". Collection, The Museum of Modern Art, New York.

KOLLWITZ, Kathe. *Old Man with Noose.* (1925). Woodcut, 11⅜ x 5″. Collection, The Museum of Modern Art, New York. Gift of Edward M. N. Warburg.

"In paradise, my lord," a winged servant replied.

"I'm terribly hungry," Atzel said. "I'd like some whale flesh and sacred wine."

"In a moment, my lord."

The chief servant clapped his hands and a door opened through which there came men servants and maids, all with wings on their backs, bearing golden trays laden with meat, fish, pomegranates and persimmons, pineapples and peaches. A tall servant with a long white beard carried a golden goblet full of wine. Atzel was so starved that he ate ravenously. The angels hovered around him, filling his plate and goblet even before he had time to ask for more.

When he had finished eating, Atzel declared he wanted to rest. Two angels undressed and bathed him. Then they brought him a nightdress of fine embroidered linen, placed a nightcap with a tassel on his head, and carried him to a bed with silken sheets and a purple velvet canopy. Atzel immediately fell into a deep and happy sleep.

When he awoke, it was morning but it could just as well have been night. The shutters were closed, and the candles and oil lamps were burning. As soon as the servants saw that Atzel was awake, they brought in exactly the same meal as the day before.

"Why do you give me the same food as yesterday?" Atzel asked. "Don't you have any milk, coffee, fresh rolls, and butter?"

"No, my lord. In paradise one always eats the same food," the servant replied.

"Is it already day, or is it still night?" Atzel asked.

"In paradise there is neither day nor night."

Dr. Yoetz had given careful instructions on how the servants were to talk to Atzel and behave toward him.

Atzel again ate the fish, meat, fruit, and drank the wine, but his appetite was not as good as it had been. When he had finished his meal and washed his hands in a golden finger bowl, he asked, "What time is it?"

"In paradise time does not exist," the servant answered.

"What shall I do now?" Atzel questioned.

"In paradise, my lord, one doesn't do anything."

"Where are the other saints?" Atzel inquired. "I'd like to meet them."

"In paradise the dwellings are too far from each other

for visiting. It would take thousands of years to go from one to the other."

"When will my family come?" Atzel asked.

"Your father still has twenty years to live, your mother thirty. And as long as they live they can't come here."

"What about Aksah?"

"She has more than fifty years to live."

"Do I have to be alone all that time?"

"Yes, my lord."

For a while Atzel shook his head, pondering. Then he asked, "What is Aksah going to do?"

"Right now, she's mourning for you. But you know, my lord, that one cannot mourn forever. Sooner or later she will forget you, meet another young man, and marry. That's how it is with the living."

Atzel got up and began to walk to and fro. His long sleep and the rich food had restored his energy. For the first time in years, lazy Atzel had a desire to do something, but there was nothing to do in his paradise.

For eight days Atzel remained in his false heaven, and from day to day he became sadder and sadder. He missed his father; he longed for his mother; he yearned for Aksah. Idleness did not appeal to him as it had in former times. Now he wished he had something to study; he dreamed of former times. Now he wished to ride his horse, to talk to friends. The food, which had so delighted him the first day, lost its flavor.

The time came when he could no longer conceal his sadness. He remarked to one of the servants, "I see now that it is not as bad to live as I had thought."

"To live, my lord, is difficult. One has to study, work, do business. Here everything is easy," the servant consoled him.

"I would rather chop wood and carry stones than sit here. And how long will this last?"

"Forever."

"Stay here forever?" Atzel began to tear his hair in grief. "I'd rather kill myself."

"A dead man cannot kill himself."

On the eighth day, when it seemed that Atzel had reached the deepest despair, one of the servants, as had been arranged, came to him and said, "My lord, there has been a mistake. You are not dead. You must leave paradise."

"I'm alive?"

"Yes, you are alive, and I will bring you back to earth."

Atzel was beside himself with joy. The servant blind-folded him, and after leading him back and forth through the long corridors of the house, brought him to the room where his family was waiting and uncovered his eyes.

It was a bright day, and the sun shone through the open windows. A breeze from the surrounding fields and orchards freshened the air. In the garden outside, the birds were singing and the bees buzzing as they flew from flower to flower. From the barns and stables Atzel could hear the mooing of cows and the neighing of horses. Joyfully he embraced and kissed his parents and Aksah.

"I didn't know how good it was to be alive," he cried out.

And to Aksah he said, "Haven't you met another young man while I was away? Do you still love me?"

"Yes, I do, Atzel. I could not forget you."

"If that is so, it is time we got married."

It was not long before the wedding took place. Dr. Yoetz was the guest of honor. Musicians played; guests came from faraway cities. Some came on horseback, some drove mules, and some rode camels. All brought fine gifts for the bride and groom, in gold, silver, ivory, and assorted precious stones. The celebration lasted seven days and seven nights. It was one of the gayest weddings that old men had ever remembered. Atzel and Aksah were extremely happy, and both lived to a ripe old age. Atzel stopped being lazy and became the most diligent merchant in the whole region. His trading caravans traveled as far as Baghdad and India.

It was not until after the wedding that Atzel learned how Dr. Yoetz had cured him, and that he had lived in a fool's paradise. In the years to come he often talked with Aksah about his adventures, and later they told the tale of Dr. Yoetz's wonderful cure to their children and grandchildren, always finishing with the words, "But, of course, what paradise is really like, no one can tell."

from SONG OF MYSELF
WALT WHITMAN

*This poem is the final section (52) of "Song of Myself," the
outstanding poetic achievement of Walt Whitman, the nineteenth-century poet credited with having revolutionized American poetry. In this excerpt the narrator bequeaths himself to
the earth in an attempt to achieve unity with immortal nature.
For Whitman, life continues after death because our bodies
revert to the natural universe, from which is fashioned future
life in endless cycle. "Song of Myself" is from Whitman's
famous volume Leaves of Grass. Since grass was one of the
poet's major symbols of immortality, it is not surprising that
he hopes to live forever in "the grass I love."*

I bequeath myself to the dirt to grow from the grass I
love,
If you want me again look for me under your boot-
soles.

You will hardly know who I am or what I mean,
But I shall be good health to you nevertheless,
And filter and fibre your blood.

Failing to fetch me at first keep encouraged,
Missing me one place search another,
I stop somewhere waiting for you.

from THE SEVENTH SEAL
INGMAR BERGMAN

*In his dramatically powerful film, The Seventh Seal, Swedish
director Ingmar Bergman portrays Medieval Europe during
the period of the Black Plague, when death and the fear
of death rampaged across the continent. The movie opens with
death coming to claim the knight. The knight challenges
death to a game of chess, with the terms that as long as he
is winning he may continue to live. Death accepts the challenge.
The knight's bargaining—typical of those who are struggling
to cope with imminent death—stems from a wish to delay
death long enough for one loving or transcendent act. This*

*dialogue reveals how painful it is to face the lack of tangible
evidence of an afterlife for those who are unwilling to accept
faith or dogma as proof.*

The knight is kneeling before a small altar. It is dark and
quiet around him. The air is cool and musty. Pictures of
saints look down on him with stony eyes. Christ's face is
turned upward, His mouth open as if in a cry of anguish.
On the ceiling beam there is a representation of a hideous
devil spying on a miserable human being. The knight hears
a sound from the confession booth and approaches it. The
face of Death appears behind the grill for an instant, but
the knight doesn't see him.

KNIGHT: I want to talk to you as openly as I can, but my
heart is empty.

    Death doesn't answer.

KNIGHT: The emptiness is a mirror turned toward my own
face. I see myself in it, and I am filled with fear and dis-
gust.

    Death doesn't answer.

KNIGHT: Through my indifference to my fellow men, I
have isolated myself from their company. Now I live in a
world of phantoms. I am imprisoned in my dreams and
fantasies.
DEATH: And yet you don't want to die.
KNIGHT: Yes, I do.
DEATH: What are you waiting for?
KNIGHT: I want knowledge.
DEATH: You want guarantees?
KNIGHT: Call it whatever you like. Is it so cruelly incon-
ceivable to grasp God with the senses? Why should He
hide Himself in a mist of half-spoken promises and unseen
miracles?

    Death doesn't answer.

KNIGHT: How can we have faith in those who believe
when we can't have faith in ourselves? What is going to
happen to those of us who want to believe but aren't able

to? And what is to become of those who neither want to
nor are capable of believing?

The knight stops and waits for a reply, but no one
speaks or answers him. There is complete silence.

KNIGHT: Why can't I kill God within me? Why does He
live on in this painful and humiliating way even though I
curse Him and want to tear Him out of my heart? Why,
in spite of everything, is He a baffling reality that I can't
shake off? Do you hear me?

DEATH: Yes, I hear you.

KNIGHT: I want knowledge, not faith, not suppositions,
but knowledge. I want God to stretch out His hand toward
me, reveal Himself and speak to me.

DEATH: But He remains silent.

KNIGHT: I call out to Him in the dark but no one seems to
be there.

DEATH: Perhaps no one is there.

KNIGHT: Then life is an outrageous horror. No one can
live in the face of death, knowing that all is nothingness.

DEATH: Most people never reflect about either death or
the futility of life.

KNIGHT: But one day they will have to stand at that last
moment of life and look toward the darkness.

DEATH: When *that* day comes . . .

KNIGHT: In our fear, we make an image, and that image
we call God.

DEATH: You are worrying . . .

KNIGHT: Death visited me this morning. We are playing
chess together. This reprieve gives me the chance to ar-
range an urgent matter.

DEATH: What matter is that?

KNIGHT: My life has been a futile pursuit, a wandering, a
great deal of talk without meaning. I feel no bitterness or
self-reproach because the lives of most people are very
much like this. But I will use my reprieve for one meaningful deed.

DEATH: Is that why you are playing chess with Death?

KNIGHT: He is a clever opponent, but up to now I haven't
lost a single man.

DEATH: How will you outwit Death in your game?

KNIGHT: I use a combination of the bishop and the knight

which he hasn't yet discovered. In the next move I'll shatter one of his flanks.
DEATH: I'll remember that.

Death shows his face at the grill of the confession booth for a moment but disappears instantly.

KNIGHT: You've tricked and cheated me! But we'll meet again, and I'll find a way.
DEATH (*invisible*): We'll meet at the inn, and there we'll continue playing.

The knight raises his hand and looks at it in the sunlight which comes through the tiny window.

KNIGHT: This is my hand. I can move it, feel the blood pulsing through it. The sun is still high in the sky and I, Antonius Block, am playing chess with Death.

He makes a fist of his hand and lifts it to his temple.

IV

"PERFORMING THE RITES":

Customs for Coping with Death

Rituals and ceremonies are one way that groups of people mark important occasions. For example, most societies have some special way of acknowledging that a couple has chosen to start living together and raising a family. The wedding is the group's way of giving public recognition to the couple's new status and of providing support and encouragement as they undertake new roles.

Similarly, rituals and ceremonies have been developed by virtually all societies around the globe for coping with the impact of death. Just as weddings are quite different from society to society, so too are death rituals. Each society has evolved its own unique type of ceremony in keeping with their particular beliefs about the nature of death and the afterlife. Yet despite the differences, the purposes of all death rituals are much the same: to pay tribute to the dead person, to ease the survivors into the mourning process, and to provide a sense of companionship for the survivors at a time when they feel abandoned and bereft. And since rituals are almost by definition procedures that have not changed through the years, they are a way of reminding both the survivors and the community as a whole that despite the death of a person they love, things will continue to go on much as before. By virtue of their conservative, seemingly timeless nature, these rituals are like a wise old doctor in a time of confusion who says, "Don't be afraid; I have handled many of these cases before." Because tradition is so reassuring at such times, a society's death rituals rarely change.

The most familiar type of death ritual in our society is, of course, the funeral service. In addition, a "wake" is sometimes held during which friends and relatives of the deceased sit with the body prior to burial, or "calling hours" are observed during which friends can visit the family of the deceased and express their sympathy. If the body is to be buried, another brief ceremony is often held at the graveside before the body is placed in the ground. Besides these more formal rituals, our society has others for coping with death, such as showing support for the survivors by writing condolence letters or taking food to the home.

It is easy, especially for a young person, to look upon these customs as outdated, unnecessary, and perhaps unpleasant or even morbid. But each of our funeral customs developed as a way of meeting the needs of the deceased, friends of the deceased, or the family of the deceased. Only by understanding what purposes the funeral rituals are intended to serve can we decide if a particular practice is useful or not.

For the person who has died (or is in the process of dying) traditional funeral practices provide a means through which other people can express honor by going to extra effort to attend the ceremony, send flowers, or make donations to a charitable cause in memory of the deceased. For the person who is dying, anticipating one's funeral can give a positive focus to one's final days. The chance to give by choosing a charity, the expectation of having many friends attend the ceremony (an expectation the dying person will never see refuted)—all can add to the self-esteem of the patient during those difficult final days. For members of some religious groups, the expectation of a final official blessing and forgiveness is consoling.

For the friends and acquaintances of the deceased, mourning is facilitated by most traditional funeral practices. The person is seen for the last time in a situation that allows remembrance of the whole person, as "John Jones, the person," not "John Jones, the cancer patient." Equally important, funeral customs provide the opportunity for friends to talk about the life of the deceased and acknowledge its worth. Seeing the social group together is also beneficial, for it reinforces the idea that despite the death of this individual, the society will endure. A funeral is also a last chance to "do something," however symbolic, for the dead friend, a last opportunity to demonstrate affection, to forgive, and to be forgiven.

The funeral enables the surviving family members to share their grief with friends. In many cultures, it is almost demanded of the family that they express their grief openly. The funeral customs of a group may prescribe a particular length of time during which the needs of the family are taken care of by friends so that the family does not need to focus their attention on anything but their loss. It's almost as though the group is saying, "Your friends not only know you feel empty, they expect you to for this period of time, and they will help you with the everyday details of living so that you can." The Jewish custom of "sitting shiva" and the Irish wake both allow the bereaved family to forget everyday responsibilities to a certain extent for a prescribed length of time while friends provide food and emotional support. A similar custom among Moslems is the basis for the short story, "Feast of the Dead," which appears in this section.

Because they evolved to meet the emotional needs of the people involved, funeral practices are usually helpful. However, it is sometimes the case that a particular tradition may not be appropriate for a certain individual's grief. Viewing the restored body of the deceased is often a healthy experience for the grieving survivors, for example, but if this practice encourages a person to deny that the deceased is really dead, then it is not appropriate. Judgment about the value of a particular death ritual is possible only in terms of what it contributes to helping the survivors—acquaintances as well as close friends and family—come to terms with the loss they have suffered.

Finally, the details of a society's death rituals shed light on its value system, its beliefs about death, the extent of its preoccupation with death, and its attitudes toward emotional expression. The ancient Egyptians, for example, were so preoccupied with death that preparations for it could occupy a lifetime. Their elaborate mummification procedures indicated their belief that the physical body itself made the trip to the hereafter; and pictures depicting their entire way of daily life and values were often carved into the walls of the tomb. The Egyptians paid a price for their secure and prosperous eternity: they were so obsessed with death that their culture stagnated for three thousand years. By contrast, the United States is very life-oriented, and preparations for burial are made almost hastily. We act most of the time as though death doesn't exist, and so when it does occur we are left bewildered. Perhaps through understanding, we can learn to shun all extremes and serve the needs of both life and death with dignity and harmony.

from TRYING HARD
TO HEAR YOU
SANDRA SCOPPETTONE

The author of the novel from which this selection is excerpted is known chiefly as a playwright. She presently lives in Southhold, New York. In Trying Hard to Hear You she explores the problems young people have in accepting those who are different. The passage below appears near the end of the novel, after two of the narrator's friends have been killed in an automobile accident. The friends' funerals are dramatically different in both what takes place at the service and their effects on the young people who attend.

There was no cast party that night, and two days later we went to the funerals. Phil's was eleven in the morning and Penny's was at one that afternoon. Everyone but Eben and Bruce came to Phil's funeral.

I had never been to a funeral before but I'd seen them in movies and on television so I knew pretty much what to expect. Mother was there but she said she didn't expect Rachel or me to sit with her. All the kids sat together in our various groups. None of us had been asked to be pallbearers because the Chrysties really didn't know any of us. I'd asked Jeff if he wanted me to sit with him but he said he'd rather sit alone. He looked awful. I don't think he'd slept since it happened and he was thinner than I'd ever seen him.

The casket was, of course, at the front of the church. And it was open. I was surprised about that because I had heard all kinds of rumors that both of them had been terribly disfigured.

Mr. and Mrs. Chrystie and Phil's brother sat in front on the right-hand side. There were two much older people next to them and I assumed they were Phil's grandparents. They were both crying a lot but not as much as Mrs. Chrystie. Or at least not as loud. Mr. Chrystie didn't seem to be crying at all. I remembered what Phil had told me about his father not liking him too much and I wondered if he wasn't crying because he didn't care or because he was doing the old male thing of being a stoic. I decided it was the second.

Then the hymns stopped and the eulogy began. I have to confess I really didn't hear a word of it. Oh, maybe a word here and there, but I wasn't actually listening. My mind was on the casket. It wasn't that I was afraid . . . I don't think. I mean what's to be afraid of? When people are dead they're dead. They can't hurt you. And yet it *was* fear I was feeling. There was no mistaking that crawly dampness on the back of my neck or the heavy pounding my heart was doing. It may have been my first experience with death but it certainly wasn't my first with fear. I couldn't figure out what was making me feel that way until I noticed that people were getting up and going to the casket. Then I knew. It was simply the thought of looking at Phil. Here I was, sixteen years old, and I had never seen a dead person. What if I fainted? Or threw up or something? But that was silly—why should that happen? What was it about looking at dead people that might make you do that? They were just lying there like they were sleeping, weren't they?

"Camilla?"

I felt a tug at my arm. It was Janet who was sitting next to me.

"C'mon . . . we have to go look at Phil."

"Why?" I asked.

"Because we have to," Mary El said, leaning across Janet. "Move."

I was on the aisle. "Why do we *have* to?"

"Oh, don't start," Janet said. "If you're not going to look, at least move so we can go up."

So that's what I did. I stood up and stepped out into the aisle and let them go past.

"Gross," Mary El whispered as she passed me.

Was it? Or was it gross to go and stare at him? I really didn't know. I stood in the aisle a few seconds, watching the people file past the casket, and then I decided that to make a decision about it I had to go up. There would be lots more funerals in my lifetime and if I was going to have a point of view about them, I should experience at least one the way everybody else did.

Slowly I walked down the aisle. When I got to the casket I stopped, took two more steps, and looked in. As I had expected, his eyes were closed and his hands were

folded across his chest. I had seen enough movies to
know that would be his position. But movies are one
thing, and real life . . . real death is another. There was
rouge on his cheeks and his lips were colored and he
looked like he was made of wax. It was awful. That body
lying there in the blue-lined coffin was no more Phil
than I was. I turned away quickly and started back up the
aisle. Before I had even gotten to my seat I had made my
decision. Never, never again would I look at a dead person if I had a choice. There was no point. It certainly did
nothing for the person who was dead and served no purpose for the person who was looking, as far as I could
figure. It was just some terrible old custom that people
followed without thinking about it. I made up my mind
right there and then to leave instructions that I was to
have a closed casket. *I was to have a closed casket.* The
words bounced around my head like a tennis ball gone
wild. Someday I was going to die. It was the first time I
had ever *really* thought about my own death.

Not that up until this point I had thought I was immortal or anything. It was just that I hadn't thought about
it at all. But now, sitting in this church with Phil lying in
his casket, there was no way I couldn't think about it. If
it could happen to him and Penny so suddenly, it could
happen to me. It was a terrible thought and one I wanted
to push aside. I guess that's called not facing reality. And
the reality was that even if I didn't die suddenly or die
young, someday I *was* going to die. I began to feel like I
couldn't breathe. I knew from listening to my mother talk
about patients with other analysts that I was having an
anxiety attack. I guess knowing that helped a bit because
soon my breathing was okay.

Okay, I said to myself, so someday I was going to die.
I was no different from anyone else in that regard. There
was no reason to dwell on it, make myself sick about it.
It was a fact and there was nothing I could do about it.
The important thing was to live . . . and to live the best
way I knew how. I couldn't do anything about my death
but I could do something about my life, and that's what
I would concentrate on: getting the most out of life that
I possibly could without hurting anyone else's life. I felt
better.

Everyone was rising. The pallbearers were picking up

the casket and leaving the church. Phil's family followed the casket out and then we all left.

The service at the cemetery was short. The minister said a prayer and then the casket was lowered into the grave. Everybody cried a lot, including me, and then it was over. We all got back into our cars and headed for the church where Penny's funeral was being held.

Hers was altogether different from Phil's. While his was what you might call traditional, Penny's was kind of off-beat. For instance, at Phil's they played hymns and at Penny's they had a friend of the Lademans' playing the score from *Jesus Christ Superstar,* which was some of Penny's favorite music. A lot of older people were commenting on it, saying it was shocking and dreadful and stuff like that, but I thought it was neat. I mean, what did hymns have to do with Penny? The second thing that was different was that Penny's casket was closed. I thought it was because the rumors I had heard were true but later I learned that the Lademans didn't believe in open caskets. The third thing that was different was the service. Byron Krausse, the minister, was very different from any other minister on the North Fork. He was very young and he had a full reddish beard. He started the service by saying that he didn't know Penny too well and rather than say a lot of ordinary things about her it was his wish, as well as her family's, to have anyone who wanted to, come up and say something about Penny. There was a lot of buzzing and clucking of tongues from some of the older people, and then I saw Sam walking up to the front. He cleared his throat and pushed his hair out of his eyes.

"Once when Penny and I were walking on the beach we found a sea gull with a broken leg. Penny took the sea gull home and put a splint on his leg and took care of him for a whole month. When he was better she let him go. She cried for a whole day because she'd grown to love that bird, whom she called Joshua. I probably would have kept him but Penny thought more about the bird's feelings than her own. That's the way she was."

Then Sam went back to his seat. Janet went up next.

Her voice cracked slightly as she began to talk. "Whenever I was depressed Penny could make me laugh. She always had a funny story to tell and, if she knew you were upset, even when she was herself, she concentrated on making *you* laugh."

One by one the kids went up. I was really surprised when Maura walked to the front.

"I didn't know Penny too well but, well, she very much wanted the part of Reno Sweeney that I got this summer. For a long time I thought she hated me, and maybe she did, but about two weeks ago she came up to me after a rehearsal and said: 'Maura, I gotta tell ya . . . you're really good. I'm not sure I could've done it.' That meant more to me than if the biggest producer on Broadway had said I was good. And all I could think was that if things had been reversed I don't know if I would have had the guts to say it to her. I think she was a super person."

By now everyone was crying. None of us had known that Penny had said that to Maura and it showed us a side of her we hadn't known.

Finally, I went up. "After listening to everything that everyone else has said I'm really sorry I didn't know Penny a lot better. What I knew I liked but it makes me realize that there's a whole lot more to people than we know. Penny made me laugh too and sometimes she made me mad and sometimes I just didn't know what to make of her, but basically I think she was a good person and made the most of her life and that's what's most important. I'll miss her a lot."

There were three or four people after me and then Byron Krausse said a short prayer. When that was over the pallbearers, who consisted of Sam, Walt, Eben, Penny's brother, and two men, led the procession out of the church.

After the service at the cemetery we all went to the Sweet Shop. All except Jeff, who went home I guess. We all agreed that when we died we wanted to have a funeral like Penny's. Sam said he wanted to be cremated and Walt said he wanted to be frozen. Mary El said she couldn't stand to think about it and couldn't we talk about something else.

"You can talk all you want about something else," Janet said, "but it's going to happen to you too someday. This we know."

"Well, it's gross to go on and on about it."

"No it isn't. It's dumb not to face it," I said.

"You face it if you want to, Camilla. I'm going to put it out of my mind."

"Are you going to put Phil and Penny out of your mind, too?"

"Well, no, but I'm not going to dwell on them either," Mary El said.

"I, for one," Janet said, "will never forget them."

"I didn't mean I'd forget them. I just mean I don't want to dwell on them forever. I don't see what good it'll do anybody to keep thinking . . ."

I interrupted. "You don't want to face that they're dead. Well, the fact is that they are. We're never going to see either of them again and we can't run away from that."

Nobody said anything then and one by one we made excuses and left for our various destinations. I went home and stayed in my room for the rest of the afternoon, listening to music and thinking about Penny and Phil and the pleasure each of them had given me. I guess you could say it was my own memorial. That night I went off to do the show.

FOREST LAWN
TOM PAXTON

Tom Paxton, singer and songwriter, was born in 1937. His essence as a songwriter is in his involvement, his integrity, and his humor. He makes appropriate and moving songs out of today's complexities, and is said to have added the dimension of depth to the folk revival. These satirical song lyrics poke fun at elaborate, tasteless funerals such as those frequently conducted at Forest Lawn cemetery in Los Angeles, which sometimes resemble a dramatic spectacle or a circus sideshow.

Oh, lay me down in Forest Lawn in a silver casket,
Put golden flowers over my head in a silver basket.
Let the Drum and Bugle corps blow Taps while cannons roar,
Let sixteen liveried employees pass out souvenirs from the funeral store.

I want to go simply when I go,
They'll give me a simple fun'ral there I know.

With a casket lined in fleece and fireworks spelling out "Rest in Peace."

Oh, take me when I'm gone to Forest Lawn.

Oh, lay me down in Forest Lawn they understand there,
They have a heavenly choir and a military band there.
Just put me in their care, I'll find my comfort there,
With sixteen planes in a last salute dropping a cross in
   a parachute.

I want to go simply when I go,
They'll give me a simple fun'ral there I know.

With a hundred strolling strings and topless dancers in
   golden wings,
Oh, take me when I'm gone to Forest Lawn.

Oh, come, come, come, come, come to the church in
   the wildwood,
Kindly leave a contribution in the pail.
Be as simple and as trusting as a child would,
And we'll sell you the church in the Dale.

To find a simple resting place is my desire,
To lay me down with a smiling face comes a little bit
   higher.
My likeness done in brass will stand in plastic grass,
And weights and hidden springs will tip its hat to the
   mourners filing past.

I want to go simply when I go,
They'll give me a simple fun'ral there I know.

I'll sleep beneath the sand, with piped in music of Billy
   Graham.
Oh, take me when I'm gone to Forest Lawn.

Rock of Ages cleft for me, for a slightly higher fee,
Oh, take me when I'm gone to Forest Lawn.

THE UNDERTAKER'S CHAT
MARK TWAIN

Although one purpose of a funeral is to honor the deceased person, the primary function is to meet the needs of the mourners. But sometimes in attempting to meet these needs, the funeral becomes something very different from what the deceased would have wanted, a point made emphatically in this humorous sketch written by Mark Twain in 1870.

"Now that corpse," said the undertaker, patting the folded hands of deceased approvingly, "was a brick—every way you took him he was a brick. He was so real accommodating, and so modest-like and simple in his last moments. Friends wanted metallic burial-case—nothing else would do. *I* couldn't get it. There warn't going to be time—anybody could see that.

"Corpse said never mind, shake him up some kind of a box he could stretch out in comfortable, *he* warn't particular 'bout the general style of it. Said he went more on room than style, anyway in a last final container.

"Friends wanted a silver door-plate on the coffin, signifying who he was and wher' he was from. Now *you* know a fellow couldn't roust out such a gaily thing as that in a little country-town like this. What did corpse say?

"Corpse said, whitewash his old canoe and dob his address and general destination onto it with a blacking-brush and a stencil-plate, 'long with a verse from some likely hymn or other, and p'int him for the tomb, and mark him C. O. D., and just let him flicker. *He* warn't distressed any more than you be—on the contrary, just as ca'm and collected as a hearse-horse; said he judged that wher' he was going to a body would find it considerable better to attract attention by a picturesque moral character than a natty burial-case with a swell door-plate on it.

"Splendid man, he was. I'd druther do for a corpse like that 'n any I've tackled in seven year. There's some satisfaction in buryin' a man like that. You feel that what you're doing is appreciated. Lord bless you, so's he got planted before he sp'iled, he was perfectly satisfied; said his relations meant well, *per*fectly well, but all them prep-

arations was bound to delay the thing more or less, and
he didn't wish to be kept layin' around. You never see
such a clear head as what he had—and so ca'm and so
cool. Jist a hunk of brains—that is what *he* was. Perfectly
awful. It was a ripping distance from one end of that
man's head to t'other. Often and over again he's had
brain-fever a-raging in one place, and the rest of the pile
didn't know anything about it—didn't affect it any more
than an Injun insurrection in Arizona affects the Atlantic
States.

"Well, the relations they wanted a big funeral, but
corpse said he was down on flummery—didn't want any
procession—fill the hearse full of mourners, and get out
a stern line and tow *him* behind. He *was* the most down
on style of any remains I ever struck. A beautiful, simple-
minded creature—it was what he was, you can depend
on that. He was just set on having things the way he
wanted them, and he took a solid comfort in laying his
little plans. He had me measure him and take a whole raft
of directions; then he had the minister stand up behind
a long box with a table-cloth over it, to represent the
coffin, and read his funeral sermon, saying 'Angcore,
angcore!' at the good places, and making him scratch out
every bit of brag about him, and all the hifalutin; and
then he made them trot out the choir, so's he could help
them pick out the tunes for the occasion, and he got them
to sing 'Pop Goes the Weasel,' because he'd always liked
that tune when he was downhearted, and solemn music
made him sad; and when they sung that with tears in their
eyes (because they all loved him), and his relations grieving around, he just laid there as happy as a bug, and
trying to beat time and showing all over how much he
enjoyed it; and presently he got worked up and excited,
and tried to join in, for, mind you, he was pretty proud of
his abilities in the singing line; but the first time he opened
his mouth and was just going to spread himsel' his breath
took a walk.

"I never see a man snuffed out so sudden. Ah, it was a
great loss—a powerful loss to this poor little one-horse
town. Well, well, well, I hain't got time to be palavering
along here—got to nail on the lid and mosey along with
him; and if you'll just give me a lift we'll skeet him into
the hearse and meander along. Relations bound to have
it so—don't pay no attention to dying injunctions, minute

a corpse's gone; but, if I had *my* way, if I didn't respect his last wishes and tow him behind the hearse *I'll* be cuss'd. I consider that whatever a corpse wants done for his comfort is little enough matter, and a man hain't got no right to deceive him or take advantage of him; and whatever a corpse trusts me to do I'm a-going to *do*, you know, even if it's to stuff him and paint him yaller and keep him for a keepsake—you hear *me!*"

He cracked his whip and went lumbering away with his ancient ruin of a hearse, and I continued my walk with a valuable lesson learned—that a healthy and wholesome cheerfulness is not necessarily impossible to *any* occupation. The lesson is likely to be lasting, for it will take many months to obliterate the memory of the remarks and circumstances that impressed it.

from THE GRAPES OF WRATH
JOHN STEINBECK

During the Great Depression of the 1930's, thousands of farming families from the midwestern United States were forced off their lands. They made their way west to California in search of work, penniless but determined. John Steinbeck dramatically focused the world's attention on these families with his novel The Grapes of Wrath. *In the excerpt below, the Joad family has been limping west in a dilapidated truck, and the grandfather dies of a stroke en route. His is the simplest of funerals, stripped by harsh necessity of all but homemade preparation of the body, with a heartfelt attempt to bury him with respect and dignity. What is most striking about this account is the comfort and familiarity this rural family feels in the face of death, despite their acute sadness.*

A long gasping sigh came from the open mouth, and then a crying release of air.

"Give us this day—our daily bread—and forgive us—" The breathing had stopped. Casy looked down into Grampa's eyes and they were clear and deep and penetrating, and there was a knowing serene look in them.

"Hallelujah!" said Granma. "Go on."

"Amen," said Casy.

Granma was still then. And outside the tent all the noise had stopped. A car whished by on the highway.

Casy still knelt on the floor beside the mattress. The people outside were listening, standing quietly intent on the sounds of dying. Sairy took Granma by the arm and led her outside, and Granma moved with dignity and held her head high. She walked for the family and held her head straight for the family. Sairy took her to a mattress lying on the ground and sat her down on it. And Granma looked straight ahead, proudly, for she was on show now. The tent was still, and at last Casy spread the tent flaps with his hands and stepped out.

Pa asked softly, "What was it?"

"Stroke," said Casy. "A good quick stroke."

Life began to move again. The sun touched the horizon and flattened over it. And along the highway there came a long line of huge freight trucks with red sides. They rumbled along, putting a little earthquake in the ground, and the standing exhaust pipes sputtered blue smoke from the Diesel oil. One man drove each truck, and his relief man slept in a bunk high up against the ceiling. But the trucks never stopped; they thundered day and night and the ground shook under their heavy march.

The family became a unit. Pa squatted down on the ground, and Uncle John beside him. Pa was the head of the family now. Ma stood behind him. Noah and Tom and Al squatted, and the preacher sat down, and then reclined on his elbow. Connie and Rose of Sharon walked at a distance. Now Ruthie and Winfield, clattering up with a bucket of water held between them, felt the change, and they slowed up and set down the bucket and moved quietly to stand with Ma.

Granma sat proudly, coldly, until the group was formed, until no one looked at her, and then she lay down and covered her face with her arm. The red sun set and left a shining twilight on the land, so that faces were bright in the evening and eyes shone in reflection of the sky. The evening picked up light where it could.

Pa said, "It was in Mr. Wilson's tent."

Uncle John nodded. "He loaned his tent."

"Fine friendly folks," Pa said softly.

Wilson stood by his broken car, and Sairy had gone to the mattress to sit beside Granma, but Sairy was careful not to touch her.

Pa called, "Mr. Wilson!" The man scuffed near and

squatted down, and Sairy came and stood beside him. Pa said, "We're thankful to you folks."

"We're proud to help," said Wilson.

"We're beholden to you," said Pa.

"There's no beholden in a time of dying," said Wilson, and Sairy echoed him, "Never no beholden."

Al said, "I'll fix your car—me an' Tom will." And Al looked proud that he could return the family's obligation.

"We could use some help." Wilson admitted the retiring of the obligation.

Pa said, "We got to figger what to do. They's laws. You got to report a death, an' when you do that, they either take forty dollars for the undertaker or they take him for a pauper."

Uncle John broke in, "We never did have no paupers."

Tom said, "Maybe we got to learn. We never got booted off no land before, neither."

"We done it clean," said Pa. "There can't no blame be laid on us. We never took nothin' we couldn' pay; we never suffered no man's charity. When Tom here got in trouble we could hold up our heads. He only done what any man would a done."

"Then what'll we do?" Uncle John asked.

"We go in like the laws says an' they'll come out for him. We on'y got a hundred an' fifty dollars. They take forty to bury Grampa an' we won't get to California— or else they'll bury him a pauper." The men stirred restively, and they studied the darkening ground in front of their knees.

Pa said softly, "Grampa buried his pa with his own hand, done it in dignity, an' shaped the grave nice with his own shovel. That was a time when a man had the right to be buried by his own son an' a son had the right to bury his own father."

"The law says different now," said Uncle John.

"Sometimes the law can't be foller'd no way," said Pa. "Not in decency, anyways. They's lots a times you can't. When Floyd was loose an' goin' wild, law said we got to give him up—an' nobody give him up. Sometimes a fella got to sift the law. I'm sayin' now I got the right to bury my own pa. Anybody got somepin to say?"

The preacher rose high on his elbow. "Law changes," he said, "but 'got to's' go on. You got the right to do what you got to do."

Pa turned to Uncle John. "It's your right too, John. You got any word against?"

"No word against," said Uncle John. "On'y it's like hidin' him in the night. Grampa's way was t'come out a-shootin'."

Pa said ashamedly, "We can't do like Grampa done. We got to get to California 'fore our money gives out."

Tom broke in, "Sometimes fellas workin' dig up a man an' then they raise hell an' figger he been killed. The gov'ment's got more interest in a dead man than a live one. They'll go hell-scrapin' tryin' to fin' out who he was and how he died. I offer we put a note of writin' in a bottle an' lay it with Grampa, tellin' who he is an' how he died, an' why he's buried here."

Pa nodded agreement. "Tha's good. Wrote out in a nice han'. Be not so lonesome too, knowin' his name is there with 'im, not jus' a old fella lonesome underground. Any more stuff to say?" The circle was silent.

Pa turned his head to Ma. "You'll lay 'im out?"

"I'll lay 'im out," said Ma. "But who's to get supper?"

Sairy Wilson said, "I'll get supper. You go right ahead. Me an' that big girl of yourn."

"We sure thank you," said Ma. "Noah, you get into them kegs an' bring out some nice pork. Salt won't be deep in it yet, but it'll be right nice eatin'."

"We got a half sack a potatoes," said Sairy.

Ma said, "Gimme two half-dollars." Pa dug in his pocket and gave her the silver. She found the basin, filled it full of water, and went into the tent. It was nearly dark in there. Sairy came in and lighted a candle and stuck it upright on a box and then she went out. For a moment Ma looked down at the dead old man. And then in pity she tore a strip from her own apron and tied up his jaw. She straightened his limbs, folded his hands over his chest. She held his eyelids down and laid a silver piece on each one. She buttoned his shirt and washed his face.

Sairy looked in, saying, "Can I give you any help?"

Ma looked slowly up. "Come in," she said. "I like to talk to ya."

"That's a good big girl you got," said Sairy. "She's right in peelin' potatoes. What can I do to help?"

"I was gonna wash Grampa all over," said Ma, "but he got no other clo'es to put on. An' 'course your quilt's spoilt. Can't never get the smell a death from a quilt. I seen a dog growl an' shake at a mattress my ma died on, an' that was two years later. We'll wrop 'im in your quilt. We'll make it up to you. We got a quilt for you."

Sairy said, "You shouldn' talk like that. We're proud to help. I ain't felt so—safe in a long time. People needs —to help."

Ma nodded. "They do," she said. She looked long into the old whiskery face, with its bound jaw and silver eyes shining in the candlelight. "He ain't gonna look natural. We'll wrop him up."

"The ol' lady took it good."

"Why, she's so old," said Ma, "maybe she don't even rightly know what happened. Maybe she won't really know for quite a while. Besides, us folks takes a pride holdin' in. My pa used to say, 'Anybody can break down. It takes a man not to.' We always try to hold in." She folded the quilt neatly about Grampa's legs and around his shoulders. She brought the corner of the quilt over his head like a cowl and pulled it down over his face. Sairy handed her half-a-dozen big safety pins, and she pinned the quilt neatly and tightly about the long package. And at last she stood up. "It won't be a bad burying," she said. "We got a preacher to see him in, an' his folks is all aroun'." Suddenly she swayed a little, and Sairy went to her and steadied her. "It's sleep—" Ma said in a shamed tone. "No, I'm awright. We been so busy gettin' ready, you see."

"Come out in the air," Sairy said.

"Yeah, I'm all done here." Sairy blew out the candle and the two went out.

A bright fire burned in the bottom of the little gulch. And Tom, with sticks and wire, had made supports from which two kettles hung and bubbled furiously, and good steam poured out under the lids. Rose of Sharon knelt on the ground out of range of the burning heat, and she had a long spoon in her hand. She saw Ma come out of the tent, and she stood up and went to her.

"Ma," she said. "I got to ask."

"Scared again?" Ma asked. "Why, you can't get through nine months without sorrow."

"But will it—hurt the baby?"

Ma said, "They used to be a sayin', 'A chile born outa sorrow'll be a happy chile.' Isn't that so, Mis' Wilson?"

"I heard it like that," said Sairy. "An' I heard the other: 'Born outa too much joy'll be a doleful boy.' "

"I'm all jumpy inside," said Rose of Sharon.

"Well, we ain't none of us jumpin' for fun," said Ma. "You jes' keep watchin' the pots."

On the edge of the ring of firelight the men had gathered. For tools they had a shovel and a mattock. Pa marked out the ground—eight feet long and three feet wide. The work went on in relays. Pa chopped the earth with the mattock and then Uncle John shoveled it out. Al chopped and Tom shoveled, Noah chopped and Connie shoveled. And the hole drove down, for the work never diminished in speed. The shovels of dirt flew out of the hole in quick spurts. When Tom was shoulder deep in the rectangular pit, he said, "How deep, Pa?"

"Good an' deep. A couple feet more. You get out now, Tom, and get that paper wrote."

Tom boosted himself out of the hole and Noah took his place. Tom went to Ma, where she tended the fire. "We got any paper an' pen, Ma?"

Ma shook her head slowly, "No-o. That's one thing we didn' bring." She looked toward Sairy. And the little woman walked quickly to her tent. She brought back a Bible and a half pencil. "Here," she said. "They's a clear page in front. Use that an' tear it out." She handed book and pencil to Tom.

Tom sat down in the firelight. He squinted his eyes in concentration, and at last wrote slowly and carefully on the end paper in big clear letters: "This here is William James Joad, dyed of a stroke, old old man. His fokes bured him becaws they got no money to pay for funerls. Nobody kilt him. Jus a stroke an he dyed." He stopped. "Ma, listen to this here." He read it slowly to her.

"Why, that soun's nice," she said. "Can't you stick on somepin from Scripture so it'll be religious? Open up an' git a-sayin' somepin outa Scripture."

"Got to be short," said Tom. "I ain't got much room lef' on the page."

Sairy said, "How 'bout 'God have mercy on his soul'?"

"No," said Tom. "Sounds too much like he was hung. I'll copy somepin." He turned the pages and read, mumbling his lips, saying the words under his breath. "Here's a good short one," he said. " 'An' Lot said unto them, Oh, not so, my Lord.' "

"Don't mean nothin'," said Ma. "Long's you're gonna put one down, it might's well mean somepin."

Sairy said, "Turn to Psalms, over further. You kin always get somepin outa Psalms."

Tom flipped the pages and looked down the verses. "Now here *is* one," he said. "This here's a nice one, just blowed full a religion: 'Blessed is he whose transgression is forgiven, whose sin is covered.' How's that?"

"That's real nice," said Ma. "Put that one in."

Tom wrote it carefully. Ma rinsed and wiped a fruit jar and Tom screwed the lid down tight on it. "Maybe the preacher ought to wrote it," he said.

Ma said, "No, the preacher wan't no kin." She took the jar from him and went into the dark tent. She unpinned the covering and slipped the fruit jar in under the thin cold hands and pinned the comforter tight again. And then she went back to the fire.

The men came from the grave, their faces shining with perspiration. "Awright," said Pa. He and John and Noah and Al went into the tent, and they came out carrying the long, pinned bundle between them. They carried it to the grave. Pa leaped into the hole and received the bundle in his arms and laid it gently down. Uncle John put out a hand and helped Pa out of the hole. Pa asked, "How about Granma?"

"I'll see," Ma said. She walked to the mattress and looked down at the old woman for a moment. Then she went back to the grave. "Sleepin'," she said. "Maybe she'd hold it against me, but I ain't a-gonna wake her up. She's tar'd."

Pa said, "Where at's the preacher? We oughta have a prayer."

Tom said, "I seen him walkin' down the road. He don't like to pray no more."

"Don't like to pray?"

"No," said Tom. "He ain't a preacher no more. He figgers it ain't right to fool people actin' like a preacher when he ain't a preacher. I bet he went away so nobody wouldn' ast him."

Casy had come quietly near, and he heard Tom speaking. "I didn' run away," he said. "I'll he'p you folks, but I won't fool ya."

Pa said, "Won't you say a few words? Ain't none of our folks ever been buried without a few words."

"I'll say 'em," said the preacher.

Connie led Rose of Sharon to the graveside, she reluctant. "You got to," Connie said. "It ain't decent not to. It'll jus' be a little."

The firelight fell on the grouped people, showing their faces and their eyes, dwindling on their dark clothes. All the hats were off now. The light danced, jerking over the people.

Casy said, "It'll be a short one." He bowed his head, and the others followed his lead. Casy said solemnly, "This here ol' man jus' lived a life an' jus' died out of it. I don' know whether he was good or bad, but that don't matter much. He was alive, an' that's what matters. An' now he's dead, an' that don't matter. Heard a fella tell a poem one time, an' he says 'All that lives is holy.' Got to thinkin', an' purty soon it means more than the words says. An' I wouldn' pray for a ol' fella that's dead. He's awright. He got a job to do, but it's all laid out for 'im an' there's on'y one way to do it. But us, we got a job to do, an' they's a thousan' ways, an' we don' know which one to take. An' if I was to pray, it'd be for the folks that don' know which way to turn. Grandpa here, he got the easy straight. An' now cover 'im up and let 'im get to his work." He raised his head.

Pa said, "Amen," and the others muttered, "A-men." Then Pa took the shovel, half filled it with dirt, and spread it gently into the black hole. He handed the shovel to Uncle John, and John dropped in a shovelful. Then the shovel went from hand to hand until every man had his turn. When all had taken their duty and right, Pa attacked the mound of loose dirt and hurriedly filled the hole. The women moved back to the fire to see to supper. Ruthie and Winfield watched, absorbed.

Ruthie said solemnly, "Grampa's down under there." And Winfield looked at her with horrified eyes. And then he ran away to the fire and sat on the ground and sobbed to himself.

from ERIC
DORIS LUND

The book Eric *is the true story of a teen-ager dying of
leukemia, as told by his mother, a free-lance writer and car-
toonist who lives in Rowayton, Connecticut. In the excerpt
below, Eric is in the final stages of his illness, after a heroic
fight to experience life to the fullest for as long as possible.
Throughout the long illness Eric's family has gone through
the process of saying "good-bye," as innumerable medical
crises brought him close to death. Thus, it is somewhat easier
for them to say their final farewell when the end comes at
last. Although in the past Eric's family has been active in
helping him fight for life, they now offer him permission and
support toward letting go of life. When Eric finally dies, the
family can deal very matter-of-factly with the question of how
to dispose of his body, refusing to spend a large amount of
money on a funeral that for them would be "phony," "useless,"
and "wasteful."*

I went in to see him alone. There was a hush in the room.
A nurse and an intern were quietly checking dials, needles,
charts. But I saw only the figure on the bed. I had been
frightened at the thought of watching Eric die. The actual
moment when he would cease to exist. Wouldn't it be
more than I could bear? Wouldn't my heart stop, too?
Yet here, close to the end, there was no fear.

In the hour of his death, I searched Eric's face with
wonder and awe, much as I'd searched it the day he was
born. A son! From darkness he had come, the mystery of
who he was still hidden behind the small brow, the closed
eyes. Into darkness he was going (not fighting off the
oxygen mask any longer . . . going . . . accepting),
eyes closed once again, taking with him still too much of
the mystery of who he was, yet leaving me unbelievably
rich.

Pain waited for me when this hour was over. I had no
time for it now. All the life force in my body was focused
on knowing what little there was left to know. No tears,
for I wanted to see. No faintness, for I wanted to be *there*
in case he came back once more from the blackness. Only
sixteen or so hours ago—was it afternoon, was it morning?

—he'd opened his eyes for a moment, after hours of unconsciousness, and struggled to speak through broken lips.

"Come closer. Mom? Come closer—

"Have to get to Westport," he gasped. "Can't find the way. Please, Mom—help me? Westport?"

"You'll get there," I whispered back, not knowing what he meant, thinking he was delirious but wanting to comfort him. "You'll find the way, Eric. I know you will."

He hadn't roused again. And it was half an hour since Dr. Dowling had said he was dying. I took his hand. The cool, translucent fingers lay very still in mine, not responding, not curling in the fierce life grip of the baby. Strange, strange, I never thought you'd grow old before I did, Eric, that you'd die while I held your hand—

MaryLou darted in at that moment and came up to me. Urgently she whispered, "Talk to him! I just remembered, hearing is the last sense to go. Say something to him quickly." She left us.

Now! Now it must happen. I put my hand on his shoulder and bent close to the pale curved ear, the delicate microphone waiting for its last message. What could I tell him for the journey?

"I love you," I said. "I'm here with you, Eric, and you're almost there."

Suddenly I thought I understood. Westport! Scene of hard-won victories on the playing field, where he and his soccer companions became county champions long ago. There was one more game to be played, and he wanted to play it well. Death is an act to be well performed. It seemed to me he was out on the field again, lone player running through the darkness, trying to head off the enemy, trying to score just one more time before he went down forever.

"You're beautiful, Eric. You were beautiful all the way. You did it just right. You're almost there. I love you!"

He died in MaryLou's arms a few minutes later. Her head was on the pillow next to his. It was a good and gentle death, the death she'd promised him with peace and dignity. Her last great gift.

Most of us had spoken to him by then, given him our messages for the journey. The words were not remarkable in any way.

"I told him, 'You're a good brother,'" said Mark.

"I told him, 'Eric, it's good to be with you. I love you,'" said his father.

Love is the only message, after all.

We stood together in the doorway just outside his room to stop them if they tried to have a Code Alert.

A nurse came out and started to run.

"No Code," we said.

She stopped, surprised. No paddles for the heart, no holes or tubes for the throat, no machinery for the lungs?

"But—" she said.

Sidney looked at her hard. "No Code," he said again.

Afterward. I'd forgotten there would be an "afterward." We stood in the hallway, crying, hugging, once in a while laughing. We had suddenly lost our balance. The center of our world, on which we'd all been focused for so long, had suddenly been taken away. We were swaying dizzily around the edges, holding on to each other, feeling tears on each other's cheeks, not knowing yet how to let go.

I held MaryLou and said, "You've lost your lover and your best friend. But you haven't lost us as a family. We'll be yours as long as you need us and want us."

Then I remembered Mrs. Hardy. Let her not hear it from anyone but me. I walked quickly down the hall to her ward. She was sitting by her bed, little frail bird of a woman with sandpiper legs, a foolish ruffled shower cap covering her bald head, reading *McCall's* magazine. I saw the headline: Fashions for Spring.

She looked up as I came nearer, and her eyes were frightened.

"I'm sorry I have to tell you this. Eric lost his fight."

She cried, then, and I was afraid she might drown because she didn't have a whole face left to cry with. I put my arms around her and kissed her cheek; it was burning. She pulled away, signaling me to wait while she found her pad and began to write feverishly. Her handwriting was getting harder and harder to read. But I made out, "God bless you and give you peace. You were a wonderful mother."

We hugged once more. "I'll try to come and see you," I said. "I really will."

There were others to tell, others to comfort. I remem-

bered what Eric had told me about the night Abby died.
"Her husband tried to comfort *us*—he didn't want us to
give up or be afraid because Abby died."

I remembered, and now I understood. I tried to think
of what to say to the ones I knew.

There was the autopsy form. "Sign here, please." There
was the Eye Bank form. "Sign here—below." Eric had
already signed it himself. And there were two brown shopping bags with the possessions of Eric Lund. The nurse
who handed them to us said, "We're sorry it turned out
this way." Then she turned to me. "Do you want a
tranquilizer?"

"No, thank you." I know all the stops from Librium to
Miltown, from the hills of Dexamil to the Valium of tran-
quillity, and there isn't a pill in the world that can put
things right now. I'll take my pain straight, undulled, and
with it the glory of knowing how much he was, the sense
of his strength shoring up my life. Even though all seems
to be lost, much will be found again. I want it all—as
Eric wanted it all. I can wait. And trust. Life will begin
again.

"Let's go home," I said.

Lisa had lived out the hours in the home of one of
our oldest friends. It was a beautiful house. From nearly
every window you can look out on a great pond, willows
bending down, swans sailing grandly beyond the yellow
marsh grass. Lisa told me later she walked from room to
room that day looking at the calm, gray winter world
outside, the serene, rich world inside—paintings, water-
colors, etchings, jade figures, porcelain, crystal. Why is
nothing shattering? Why am I not crying?

Around three in the afternoon she began to write. "Oh,
I am shaking. Today is the day Eric dies. . . ." She
wrote a sort of poem as she sat there in the peaceful library looking at the pond, a fourteen-year-old girl struggling with mortality. She wrote, ". . . yet I will endure."

It was ten o'clock that night before she heard our car
in the driveway. We hadn't called. I'd wanted to be there
when she learned about it. Nothing had to be said. She
saw us. She ran to my arms in a burst of tears.

It was close to midnight when she found herself in her
own room again after a vigil of thirty-three hours. She

went to her desk and sat down. She unfolded the paper on which she'd written her poem. At the bottom of the page she wrote in very small letters, "He is dead."

In our room, lying in the dark, Sidney kept saying, "I never thought Eric would die. I never thought Eric would die."

Dr. Dowling called me the next morning. "What are you going to do about disposing of Eric's body?"

"Can we give him to a medical school—or something like that?"

"It's not easy," said Dr. Dowling thoughtfully. "*We* can't take him because we'd be accused of body-snatching. I think maybe I can help you, though. Let me give you the name of a doctor across the street at Cornell. Tell him I said to call."

"First, tell me how *you* feel about it," I said, knowing how much Dr. Dowling had cared about Eric.

His answer was quick. "The bodies you get in medical school are pretty bad. I'd have been honored to work on a beautiful body like Eric's."

All right. Let's go. Sidney had been listening. He agreed.

The next morning I sat up in bed next to the telephone and tried to give away my son's body. I looked first for signs of revulsion or horror in myself. There were none. He had given himself to science long ago, that part of him that was becoming less and less important. As his athlete's body finally failed, Eric—the essential Eric—had re-treated to his skull. His eyes held all his life those last few days. His face had a purity and stark beauty that con-stantly reminded me of someone else. But who?

Later, when I went to Spain and saw Goya's etchings, and the face of El Greco's Christ on the cross, I saw the Eric of those last days. Still later, among photographs of the survivors of the Andes air crash who had cannibalized to survive, I saw—in the face of a young, near-starved youth—again, Eric. When we are reduced to the last essence of what is valuable in man, do we become more and more alike, as the newborn are alike? In the hos-pital where Eric was born, a nurse had brought out a tiny infant to demonstrate "The Bath" to a class of new mothers. "Whose baby is this?" she asked, before unwrapping it and putting it in the soapy little tub. There were about eleven of us sitting around in our wrappers or flannel bathrobes. Six hands went up! Mine almost did. I am ashamed and amused about that moment to this day. The baby was a girl! Now I think that the very old or the dying may be like the very new—less personalized, less stylish and defined. They are vessels that hold the deeply common experience.

It is not easy to give away a body. I called the number Dr. Dowling had given me. Four times. The doctor's secretary seemed embarrassed. Finally I was put through to the doctor himself. He was cautiously grateful. But the problems seemed to be legion. Forms. Red tape. And we would have to hire a hearse to take the body over to Cornell.

"But it's just across the street!"

I have since heard of other instances where people were successful in donating a body to scientific research in some hospitals in New York. But at that time and that place there seemed to be no legal way to transport a body several hundred yards across York Avenue between 68th and 69th streets. I was too tired to go into all the reasons why, but I did protest. "I thought all you medical schools needed bodies." (I'd just read an article in the *New York Times* the week before entitled "The Grave Shortage of Bodies.")

"That's true," said the doctor seriously. "But of course we can't look too interested. In any case, you'd have to claim the body again after we'd used it and have a funeral home furnish a casket and—"

"Casket!" Ye gods! What for? For what would be left of Eric then? Odds and ends. What was left of Eric now but the beauty of his spirit, the memory of his laugh, his wicked humor, his open-eyed honesty? You can't tell me I have to put up with this. I thanked the man for talking to me and said we'd have to think of something else.

I decided to talk to Susan, who usually knows about things. "You know," I said, "we've shot our savings these past few years. Mark's going to have to drop out of Yale next year to earn money, and he already owes them three thousand dollars for loans. And Lisa needs a new piano. She's been trying to play Bach and Chopin on that barroom upright in the basement that has half the keys sticking. Now they tell me we've got to have a casket and the works for Eric. Even with cremation. What's it going to cost?"

"No way you can get out for less than a thousand dollars, Doris," Susan said.

So for a thousand dollars I could buy a casket to get Eric taken to the crematorium; then eventually Eric's ashes would be delivered to my doorstep in a small wooden box with "Eric Lund" on the cover. "Sign here, please," the messenger would say. What if I wasn't home? What if Lisa answered the door?

I called Dr. Dowling. "I'm not getting very far." I explained the difficulties. "So it looks like no matter what we do, we've got to buy Eric a revolting, candy-box casket. Eric would absolutely hate that. It's phony, it's useless, it's wasteful!"

"You can let the city claim the body."

"Then what?"

"He goes to potter's field."

Suddenly it sounded beautiful. Potter's field! Where the poor, lost, bottom-of-the-ladder people go. Eric belonged with them. He would have cared for them if he had lived. He was no rich kid from the suburbs. He belonged to the city where he'd loved MaryLou, where they'd ridden their bicycles, walked the avenues holding hands—where he'd loved so many other people, too.

When we were all together I asked each member of the family what they thought of letting the city claim Eric's body, of sending him to potter's field, with love?

MaryLou said, "As long as I can go, too, what do I care?"

Susan thought Eric would have loved the joke of outwitting the system.

Sidney, struggling with tears, laughed and said, "Well, the human body is about ninety-seven percent water and twenty cents' worth of other ingredients—even with inflation. So why not?"

Meredith and Jim thought it was a good, practical idea.

Mark said, "I'll go along. I'll go to potter's field, too—only I'm not ready just yet."

"But how do you feel, Mommy?" Lisa asked.

"Oh, I guess the only thing I really would have wanted is a funeral pyre with beautiful flames soaring seventy-five feet in the air. And maybe a parade with lots of

music and flags and everybody in town, especially the little boys he played with—and maybe *Aida*'s elephants and
all the animals from Noah's Ark, too—marching down
the main street right by Eric's bonfire."

"Pollution, Mommy!" said Lisa, my child of the seven-
ties. "Bonfires make too much smoke. No. This is better. Give Eric back to the earth. We should send him to
potter's field. Then he'll be recycled."

So it was settled. Eric went to potter's field. We're all
going to potter's field, if we can manage it. It's the family
plot. And now when somebody asks me where Eric is
buried, I just say, "In the family plot."

There was a memorial service in the church by the
river. It's the same church where Eric had started out to
be head counselor in the boys' camp the summer before
he died. Each of us wrote something for Eric, and the
minister, who was Eric's friend, read our words. The
pews were nearly full, and there were many small boys
among the soccer teammates, college boys and girls, old
family friends and relatives.

Afterward a great many people came back to the house.
Then it was over. Hard to believe, but it was really over.

from I HEARD THE OWL
CALL MY NAME
MARGARET CRAVEN

*In the culture of the Kwakiutl Indians of the Canadian west
coast, legend has it that when someone "hears the owl call his
name," it is a sign that he or she is about to die. Mark, the
young priest in this story, has been sent to work among the
Indians in this remote and beautiful part of the world. Through
a number of clues, including hearing the owl call his name,
Mark gradually learns that he has a terminal illness. The loving
support given to Mark by the villagers allows him to make
peace with his fate and live out what remains of his life
productively and peacefully. Having lived in intimate contact
with nature, the Kwakiutl Indians were fully aware of the
natural end of a dead body: it became food for scavengers. Their
customs clearly reflect their wish to control and prevent this end
through the use of magic and ritual.*

On the second night of Mark's return from his holiday, Marta asked him to dinner, and she did not ask Jim also, which was unusual.

"After the dinner the old will come," she told him. "They have something to request."

"You don't suppose they are still grieving about the drinking, or the boys going out to school," Mark asked Jim. "You don't suppose they are going to leave the village again?"

Jim did not think so.

"If this were it, I am sure I would be told. It is something which concerns only the old."

At dinner Marta did not mention what it was the elders wished. She asked of the holiday in Vancouver and she asked of Gordon and the boys.

"The younger ones will adjust more easily," Mark told her. "For Gordon it will be harder. He is much older than the boys he will meet at school. But he will endure, Marta, and he will win his battle."

After dinner there was a knock at the door and the elders entered: Mrs. Hudson, T. P., Peter the carver, and several others whom Mark did not know well, who still thought in Kwákwala, dreamed in Kwákwala, and spoke little English.

When they were seated there was a long silence, as the old watched Mark intently and soberly. It was not the drinking that had brought them here. It was not even the loss of the young. It was something that led back into the deepest beliefs of the tribe, and Mark sensed it and waited.

T. P. spoke for them.

"We have come about the ancient burial ground," he said. "Except for the weesa-bedó, it has not been used for many years."

"And you want the body of the weesa-bedó moved to the new graveyard. Is that it, T. P.?"

"No—he is well where he is. In the early days we buried our dead in a square box and we placed the box about a third of the way up a large tree, and we cut off the limbs below the box so the animals could not reach it, and later, other boxes were hauled up by ropes and each family had its own burial tree."

"I have seen them."

"Later we cut down a large tree ten feet from the ground and on its stump we built a house, and in the house we placed ten boxes and sometimes more."

"I have seen them also."

"But now many boxes have fallen from the trees and other trees have fallen on the grave houses built on the stumps. The bones of our ancestors lie scattered on the ground, and the old totems and the carvings are broken and beyond repair."

"If this disturbs you," Mark said, choosing his words carefully, "we can build a large communal grave and in it we can place all the boxes and the broken carvings. And if you wish in the morning I will go with you and the older men to start the clearing."

The old people rose.

"It is well," T. P. said. "I will stop by for you in the morning."

The next day the fine weather holding, Mark went with the elder men of the tribe, and what had seemed so reasonable a project became suddenly huge and macabre.

The little path that led to the ancient burial ground was overgrown. When they had cut their way through it, they saw that the year's windfall had been severe and that the old grave houses and the boxes that had fallen from the trees were covered with brush and branches.

For five days the men of the tribe worked at the clearing, and when this was done, Jim and other younger men went up the huge spruce trees with ropes to lower the grave boxes that were still intact. Where any box had fallen and touched the ground, only bones were left, but where the boxes had remained in the air, the bodies were partially mummified, the wrists still holding the copper bracelets, green now and paper-thin; and beside the heads were ancient water vessels placed there in case the soul of the dead thirsted on his journey.

When the huge grave was dug and ready, forty boxes were placed in it, and all the broken bones and bits of ancient grave posts and carvings. The men who had done the work buried also the clothes they had worn. Then on a sunny, clear morning, Mark held a brief service and the grave was covered. When it was over, he saw relief in the eyes of the old, and again T. P. spoke for them.

"At last a man has come to us who has seen to it that our dead can rest in peace."

from GRATEFUL TO
LIFE AND DEATH
R. K. NARAYAN

A contemporary Indian novelist, R. K. Narayan describes a
burial custom very different from what most Americans are
used to. The form of cremation used in India, as depicted in
this excerpt from Grateful to Life and Death, *involves the*
close participation of the family in a way that would be
distressing in our culture. We are more often sheltered from
direct involvement in the care of the dying.

I looked at the patient. She had grown a shade whiter,
and breathed noisily. There were drops of perspiration on
her forehead. I touched it, and found it very cold. "Doctor, the temperature is coming down."

"Yes, yes, I knew it would . . ." he said, biting his
nails. Nothing seemed to be right anywhere. "Doctor
. . . tell me. . . ."

"For heaven's sake, don't ask questions," he said. He
felt the pulse; drew aside the blanket and ran his fingers
over her abdomen which appeared slightly distended. He
tapped it gently, and said: "Run to the car and fetch the
other bag please, which you will find in the back
seat. . . ."

The doctor opened it. "Hot water, hot water, please."
He poured turpentine into the boiling water, and applied
fomentations to her abdomen. He took out a hypodermic
syringe, heated the needle, and pushed it into her arm:
at the pressure of the needle she winced. "Perhaps it
hurts her," I muttered. The doctor looked at me without
an answer. He continued the fomentation.

An hour later, he drew up the blanket and packed
his bag. I stood and watched in silence. All through this,
he wouldn't speak a word to me. I stood like a statue. The
only movement the patient showed was the heaving of her
bosom. The whole house was silent. The doctor held his
bag in one hand, patted my back and pursed his lips. My
throat had gone dry and smarted. I croaked through this
dryness: "Don't you have to remain, doctor?" He shook
his head: "What can we do? We have done our best. . . ."
He stood looking at the floor for a few moments, heaved

a sigh, patted my back once again, and whispered: "You may expect a change in about two and a half hours." He turned and walked off, I stood stock still, listening to his shoe creaks going away, the starting of his car; after the car had gone, a stony silence closed in on the house, punctuated by the stentorian breathing, which appeared to me the creaking of the hinges of a prison gate, opening at the command of a soul going into freedom.

Here is an extract from my diary: The child has been cajoled to sleep in the next house. The cook has been sent there to keep her company. Two hours past midnight. We have all exhausted ourselves, so a deep quiet has descended on us (moreover a great restraint is being observed by all of us for the sake of the child in the next house, whom we don't wish to scare). Susila lies there under the window, laid out on the floor. For there is the law that the body, even if it is an Emperor's, must rest only on the floor, on Mother Earth.

We squat on the bare floor around her, her father mother and I. We mutter, talk among ourselves, and wail between convulsions of grief; but our bodies are worn out with fatigue. An unearthly chill makes our teeth chatter as we gaze on the inert form and talk about it. Gradually, unknown to ourselves, we recline against the wall and sink into sleep. The dawn finds us all huddled on the cold floor.

The first thing we do is to send for the priest and the bearers. . . . And then the child's voice is heard in the next house. She is persuaded to have her milk there, dress, and go out with a boy in the house, who promises to keep her engaged and out of our way for at least four hours. She is surprised at the extraordinary enthusiasm with which people are sending her out today. I catch a glimpse of her as she passes on the road in front of our house, wearing her green velvet coat, bright and sparkling.

Neighbours, relations and friends arrive, tears and lamentations, more tears and lamentations, and more and more of it. The priest roams over the house, asking for one thing or other for performing the rites. . . . The corpse-bearers, grim and sub-human, have arrived with their equipment—bamboo and coir ropes. Near the front step they raise a small fire with cinders and faggots

—this is the fire which is to follow us to the cremation ground.

A bamboo stretcher is ready on the ground in front of the house. Some friends are hanging about with red eyes. I am blind, dumb, and dazed.

The parting moment has come. The bearers, after brief and curt preliminaries, walk in, lift her casually without fuss, as if she were an empty sack or a box, lay her on the stretcher, and tie her up with ropes. Her face looks at the sky, bright with the saffron touched on her face, and the vermilion on the forehead, ans a string of jasmine somewhere about her head.

The downward curve of her lips gives her face a repressed smile. . . . Everyone gathers a handful of rice and puts it between her lips—our last offering.

They shoulder the stretcher. I'm given a pot containing the fire and we march out, down our street, Ellamman Street. Passers-by stand and look for a while. But every face looks blurred to me. The heat of the sun is intense. We cut across the sands, ford the river at Nallappa's Grove, and on to the other bank of the river, and enter the cremation ground by a small door on its southern wall.

The sun is beating down mercilessly, but I don't feel it. I feel nothing, and see nothing. All sensations are blurred and vague.

They find it necessary to put down the stretcher a couple of times on the roadside. Half a dozen flies are dotting her face. Passers-by stand and look on sadly at the smiling face. A madman living in Ellamman Street comes by, looks at her face and breaks down, and follows us on, muttering vile and obscure curses on fate and its ways.

Stretcher on the ground. A deep grove of tamarind trees and mangoes, full of shade and quiet—an extremely tranquil place. Two or three smouldering pyres are ranged about, and bamboos and coirs lie scattered, and another funeral group is at the other end of this grove. "This is a sort of cloakroom, a place where you leave your body behind," I reflect as we sit down and wait. Somebody appears carrying a large notebook, and writes down name, age, and disease; collects a fee, issues a receipt, and goes away.

The half a dozen flies are still having their ride. After weeks, I see her face in daylight, in the open, and note the devastation of the weeks of fever—this shrivelling heat has baked her face into a peculiar tinge of pale yellow. The purple cotton saree which I bought her on another day is wound round her and going to burn with her.

The priest and the carriers are ceaselessly shouting for someone or other. Basket after basket of dry cow-dung fuel is brought and dumped. . . . Lively discussion over prices and quality goes on. The trappings of trade do not leave us even here. Some hairy man sits under a tree and asks for alms. I am unable to do anything, but quietly watch in numbness. . . . I'm an imbecile, incapable of doing anything except what our priest orders me to do. Presently I go over, plunge in the river, return, and perform a great many rites and mutter a lot of things which the priest asks me to repeat.

They build up a pyre, place her on it, cover her up with layers of fuel. . . . Leaving only the face and a part of her chest out, four layers deep down. I pour ghee on and drop the fire.

We are on our homeward march, a silent and benumbed gang. As we cross Nallappa's Grove once again, I cannot resist the impulse to turn and look back. Flames appear over the wall. . . . It leaves a curiously dull pain at heart. There are no more surprises and shocks in life, so that I watch the flame without agitation. For me the greatest reality is this and nothing else. . . . Nothing else will worry or interest me in life hereafter.

FEAST OF THE DEAD
Cevdet Kudret

Cevdet Kudret, born in Istanbul in 1907, is a well-known Turkish writer of poetry and plays as well as prose fiction. In this short story he describes a social custom designed to alleviate grief and ease the suffering of the bereaved. When the father in a poor family dies, his wife and children are aided by kind neighbors who send them baskets of food. This practice is similar to the way people in other cultural groups, including Americans, show their concern for grieving survivors.

January changed the color of the air. Under the ash-color sky, the world seemed grimmer. People went out only for work. The streets, especially the back streets, often stretched bare and empty. There was nobody under the oak trees, in the courtyards of the mosques, at the fountains—the spots of coolness and gathering places for the children of the street in the summer. The fountains were never completely deserted. Almost every day there would be someone to go there to fetch the day's water.

A boy who had been to the fountain for water that noon ran back to his street panting, and told the first man he saw:

"Dursun Agha is dead"

Dursun Agha was a familiar figure of the street. He was about fifty; a sturdy man with a round black beard. He was the water carrier, who barely made both ends meet, with a wife and two children in his small, two-story house. His entire capital consisted of two water cans and a pole, with a chain dangling from either end. Mounting the pole on his shoulder every morning, hooking the cans by their handles to the chains, he set out with his first call, in his own street:

"Water. Anybody need water?"

His low, resonant voice could carry as far as the last house in the street. Those who needed water would call back, "Dursun Agha, one trip," or "Two trips," or "Three trips." "One trip" meant two cans of water. Then Dursun Agha woud climb up to the fountain on the hill, fill up his cans, and thus go to and fro, between the fountain and the houses, all day long. He got three *kurush* for each trip; this way of earning the day's bread was like digging a well with a needle, earning it drop by drop. If they had had to rely only on his earnings, it would have been impossible to feed four mouths; but thank God, his wife Gulnaz was called upon, three or four times a week, as a charwoman. Within the limited opportunities of her work, she tried to help her husband earn just a little bit more, cheating in small ways that were pathetic, harmless, and even innocent—using up a little extra water, just a can or two, so that her husband could earn a few more three *kurush*.

Now all this had ended suddenly. The cause of Dursun Agha's death was soon discovered. After he had hooked the brimful cans to the pole, he had slipped while trying to stand up on the ice that had hardened during the night before, ice polished slippery as glass with water continuously dripping over it. He could not get his balance again because of the load of full water cans, and he had hit his

head on the stone bowl under the tap. Who could ever
have expected him to die so suddenly? Looking at Dursun
Agha, one could sooner imagine a stone being fragile and
getting hurt. But *he?* Who would have thought that he
could smash his skull? However, even if a man looked
tough and durable, he could die, just like that, all of a
sudden.

When Gulnaz heard the news, she froze. Could this be
the punishment for her little tricks, for her cheating? No,
oh no, God could not be that cruel. This could not be
anything but an accident. There were witnesses: he
slipped, fell down, and died. Anybody could fall this way
and die.

Perhaps they could, but at least they would have left
something behind them to support their family. All the
estate that Dursun Agha had left was his two cans and
a pole.

What was Gulnaz going to do now? She thought and
thought but could make no decision. It was not easy to be
left all alone with two children, one nine years old, the
other six. How could she feed these two mouths by wash-
ing clothes only twice or three times a week? She remembered all the water she had used up so freely. She might
just as well not think of the water any more. In an instant all had changed. Now there was no difference between using much water or using little. If she could only
find a way out and give up being a charwoman altogether.
The water she had loved so long had suddenly become a
thing to hate—there was treachery in its glitter, enmity
in its flow. She no more wanted to see or hear it.

When death occurs in a house, no one thinks of cook-
ing. The first thing the household forgets is food. This
goes on for thirty-six, or maybe forty-eight hours at
the most, but as soon as a gnawing is felt in the stomach,
or a listlessness in the limbs, someone in the house says
"Come, we must have food," and thus, with eating, starts
the return to the usual course of living.

It is a Moslem tradition for the neighbors to send food,
for a day or two, to the bereaved household. The first
meal came to Gulnaz and her children from the white
house at the corner. Raif Efendi, the businessman, lived
there. One could see from a mile off that this was the
home of a wealthy man. At noon on the day after Dursun
Agha died, the maid from the white house appeared with

a large tray in her hands at Gulnaz' house and rang the bell. On the tray were dishes of noodles cooked in chicken broth, some meat with a good, rich sauce, cheese rolls, and sweets.

To tell the truth, no one had thought of eating that day; but as soon as the cover was lifted from the tray there was a giving in, a relaxation of feelings. Silently they all gathered around the table. Maybe it was because they had never had such good food before, or maybe because pain had sharpened their senses, but they all found the food exceptionally delicious. Having eaten once, they found it natural to sit around the table at suppertime and satisfy their hunger with the leftovers of their lunch.

Another neighbor took care of the food for the next day. This went on for three or four days. Of course, none of the later meals was as tasty or as generous as the trayful from the white house, but they were all a great deal better than any that was ever cooked in Gulnaz' pot. If this had only continued, Gulnaz and her children could easily have borne their sorrow to the end of their lives, but when the trays stopped coming in and the coal which they were buying, pound by pound, from the store on the main street could not be bought any more, they began to realize that their sorrow was unbearable.

The first day food stopped coming in, they kept their hopes up till noontime, running to the door with the sound of each footstep in the street outside, hoping to see a big tray with a white cloth cover over it. But instead they saw people simply going about their daily lives, merely passing by, their empty hands hanging at the ends of their arms. At suppertime, they realized that no one was going to bring food, so they had to cook at home as they had done before. They had got used to quite another type of food during the past few days and found it difficult to readjust to the meager dish of potatoes Gulnaz had cooked with hardly a trace of butter. They had no choice but to get used to it again. They were not really hungry for about three or four days, until their staples were all used up. But then they ran out of butter, flour, and potatoes. For the next few days they ate whatever they found here and there in the house: two onions, one clove of garlic, a handful of dry lima beans found in the corner of the cupboard. Finally, there came a day when all the pots, baskets, bottles, and boxes in the house were empty. That day, for the first time, they went to bed on empty stomachs.

The next day was the same. In the late afternoon, the little boy started crying, "Mother, it hurts inside!" His mother said, "Be patient, children, be patient just a little! Something must happen" They all felt that their stomachs had shrunk to the size of a baby's fist. They all felt dizzy when standing up—it was best to lie flat on the back; then you felt as if you were dreaming. They all saw green-and-red forms fluttering in front of their eyes; there was also a hollow, echoing sound in their ears. They noticed their voices were gradually getting softer.

The day after, Gulnaz had a dream: maybe there was someone in the street who needed a charwoman. You could never tell. Maybe she would receive a message one morning: "Tell Gulnaz to come for laundry today." Yes, Gulnaz, who had vowed never to look at a pail of water again, now was longing for this call. But the people of the street thought it would be inconsiderate to call her for work. "Poor woman," they all said, "sorrow must be gnawing at her heart now. She is in no shape to do laundry, poor thing."

That morning no one in the household thought of getting up. They all had visions of food. The little boy talked occasionally. "I can see bread. Look, look, Mother (putting out his hand as if to grab it), bread—how fluffy it is —so soft—so nicely baked. . . ."

The older boy saw sweets instead. How stupid he had been, how very stupid not to have savored them when they came on the trays—how stupid to have eaten all his share at once, when they were given to him. If only he had them once more he knew what he would do: he would eat them very slowly, savoring each mouthful, one by one.

Gulnaz lay in her bed, listening to the murmurs of her children, biting her lips in order not to cry out, tears flowing down her temples from under her closed lids. Life outside went on as before. She could follow all that happened by just listening—all of the life of this street where she had lived for many years.

A door closed. The little boy next door, Cevat, is going to school; he always banged the door. If it had been the older boy, Suleyman, he would close the door gently; the

two brothers are so different in nature. Now a rheumatic
old lady shuffling her feet slowly. That is the mother of
Salih, who works on a ship as cabin boy. She is going out
for shopping. More footsteps. This time it is Tahsin Efendi,
the barber, who lives in the red house at the end of the
street. He always walks by at this time of the morning to
open up his shop on the main street. The next one is
Hasan Bey, the grandson of Idris Agha, the jobber; he is a
clerk in the electric company. He will move away from
this street as soon as he finds an educated girl and marries
her. This one is the schoolteacher, Nuriye Hanim. Then
there is Feyzullah Efendi, who makes slippers. Then
Cemil Bey, the tax collector. And there is the bread man,
who always stops at Rifky Bey's house. He comes every
day, at exactly this same hour. The big baskets tied to
both sides of the horse are full of bread. The creaking of
the baskets can be heard from far away.

It was the older boy who first heard the creaking of the
baskets and looked toward his brother. The younger boy
heard it next. He, too, turned his head to his brother;
their eyes met. The younger one murmured, "Bread!"

The sound was coming closer. Gulnaz got up slowly in
the chill room and put a wrap around her to go out. She
had decided to ask for two loaves of bread on credit. She
could pay when she got money from laundering. Her hand
on the latch; she paused inside the door. Her whole attention was concentrated on listening. The approaching
sound of hoofs crushed her courage—crushed and
crushed; finally, when the sounds were only a few steps
away, they forced her to throw open the door. Gulnaz,
with eyes growing larger, stared at this food, this grace,
passing by. The square baskets on the white horse were
so wide that they covered the entire side of the animal,
and so deep that they almost touched the ground. Both
baskets were full to the brim. The bread was made of
pure white flour. The loaves all seemed so fresh and
spongy; it must be such a joy to touch them; why, one's
fingers would simply sink into their soft texture. A beautiful smell went up through one's nose, down the throat.
Gulnaz swallowed. Just as she was about to open her
mouth and say something to the bread man, he shouted
in a high-pitched voice, "Giddy-yap." She lost all her
courage, could not say a word, just stood there frozen,
staring at the baskets brushing against the woodwork of

the house. The food, the grace of God, was passing by her house, but she could not stretch out her hand and take it. The horse walked slowly on, waving his long white tail like a handkerchief. "Good-by, Gulnaz! Good-by! Good-by!"

Banging the door, she returned to the room, She dared not look into the fevered eyes of the boys, who had been waiting hopefully. She could not find a place to hide her empty hands. Suddenly it was as if she were ashamed of having hands at all. Not a word was said in the room; the boys simply turned the other way; the older boy closed his eyes in order not to see the emptiness of his mother's hands; his brother did the same. Gulnaz went to a cushion on the floor and dropped herself onto it with the softness and lightness of a shadow, her feet under her skirts, her arms covered by the shabby wrap on her shoulders; she hid in her corner as if she wanted to dissolve into nothingness. She looked like a bundle of old rags. The atmosphere in the room became tenser; silence increased. No one made the slightest movement for half an hour or more. Finally, it was again the younger boy who broke the silence. He called out from his bed:

"Mother! Mother!"

"Yes, son?"

"I can't stand it any more. Something is happening in my insides."

"Oh, my sweet boy, my little boy."

"Here, in my tummy. Something is moving."

"It's from hunger. I feel it, too. Don't worry, it's nothing. Your intestines are moving."

"I'm dying. I'm dying."

The older boy opened his eyes and looked at his brother. Gulnaz looked at both of them. The little boy was silent. His eyes looked darker; his lips dry, parched, and white; his cheeks hollow; his bloodless skin faded and sallow. Finally, Gulnaz beckoned to the older boy. He got up and both left the room. In the hallway between the two rooms, she whispered as if afraid of being overheard, "We must go to Bodos, the grocer. We must! Ask for some rice, flour, and potatoes. Tell him we'll pay him in a few days."

The boy's shabby coat was not heavy enough to keep out the cold of the street. He had no strength in his legs. He had to steady himself against the walls as he walked.

Finally, he reached the store on the hill to Cerrahpasha and went through the door into the warmth of the store, heated by a large fire pot. He let others take his turn, hoping to be able to talk to the grocer in privacy and to enjoy the warmth a little longer. After everyone had gone, he left his place by the fireside, ordered a pound of rice, a pound of flour, and a pound of potatoes, put his hand in his pocket as if reaching for his money, and then pretending to have left it at home, looking annoyed, he said, "Oh, I left the money home. How do you like that! I'd hate to have to go all the way home in this cold and come back again. Write it down, won't you, and I'll bring it when I come tomorrow."

Bodos knew the tricks of the game only too well. Looking over his glasses, he said, "You've become so thin. Someone who has money at home doesn't get so thin."

He put the boy's order to one side. "First bring the money and then you take this," he said. "All right," the boy said, embarrassed to see his lie found out. "I'll bring it." He hurried out.

After the boy had left, Bodos Agha turned to his wife, who helped him in the store. "Poor souls," he said. "I feel so sorry for them. What on earth will they live on from now on, I wonder?"

His wife nodded. "Yes. I feel sorry for them, too. Poor souls."

The boy was finding the iciness of the street more unbearable than he had before he entered the store. At the corner smoke was coming out of the chimney of the white house. How happy were the people who lived in it! It did not even occur to him to be jealous; he had only admiration for these people who had fed him the best meal of his life.

The boy walked toward his own house as quickly as he could, his teeth chattering. Entering the room, he said nothing to his mother and brother. His empty hands spoke for him.

Before their questioning eyes, he took off his clothes and went to his bed, which had not yet lost all its warmth; but when he spoke, he said, "I am cold. I am cold." The blanket rose and fell on his trembling body.

Gulnaz piled on him whatever she could find and looked with fearful eyes at the bundle rising and falling on the boy's trembling body. The trembling lasted for an hour and a half or more. Then came the fever and exhaustion. The boy lay flat on his back, stretched out, motionless, his eyes staring vacantly. Gulnaz lifted the covers and tried to cool his burning head with her cold hands.

The woman paced through the house till evening, desperate. She did not know what to do. She couldn't think. She kept on going into the room and out again, looking with empty, glazed eyes at the walls, the ceilings, the furniture. Suddenly, she noticed that she was no longer hungry. It was like the numbness from excessive heat or cold. The edges and tips of the nerves must be blunted by hunger.

The sun had just gone down. The covers, taken off the fevered boy's bed and piled on the floor, were a bundle of darkness. Looking at the small pile, she had a sudden rational thought: wouldn't there be anybody to give some money for all that? She remembered the neighbors' having talked of a junk store in the Grand Bazaar where they bought used things—but it must be closed. Now she had to wait till the morning.

With the peace of mind she had from having found a solution, she gave up her walking from room to room and sat by the bedside of her son.

The boy's fever went up. The woman sat motionless, staring. The younger boy could not sleep, from hunger. He too, was watching, his eyes open. The sick boy moaned slowly, tossed and turned in his fever, finding no comfort. His cheeks were burning. He talked in delirium, his eyes fixed on a spot on the ceiling—looking, looking, not seeing. Large, fixed, glassy eyes. The younger boy was watching him closely from his bed. When the sick boy started talking again with the fever, the younger boy sat up in his bed and said, in a low, soft voice audible only to his mother, "Mother, will my brother die?"

The woman shivered as if touched by a cold wind on her skin. She looked at her son with frightened eyes. "Why do you ask that?"

The boy paused for a minute under his mother's gaze; then he leaned close to her ear and said softly, trying hard to hide his voice from his brother:

"Because, then food will come from the white house."

(Translated by Filiz Ofluoglu)

V

"ON A JOURNEY WITHOUT ME":

Grief and Mourning

Grief and mourning are frequently used to describe a person's reaction to the death of someone close. Grief can be thought of as the pain of the loss. Mourning is the process that the survivor goes through to diminish that pain. Grief is an emotion that we have all either experienced or seen in others. Mourning, however, is a word that describes a very specific process that may be less well understood.

Mourning involves remembering repetitively and over a long period of time experiences that were shared with the dead person, until the devastating potency of the loss in its entirety is neutralized. The brain is very wise in this regard and protects us by breaking up the experience into many small component parts, and these small memories are played through over and over again individually until the pain of grief is diminished. It's a form of "divide and conquer." The entire picture of the loss is too overwhelming to be faced all together and at once, but the smaller, partial memories are not. For example, if your favorite aunt has died, there may be a song that reminds you of her. There will be a memory of a day at the beach together, and many more elements—each a small component part of your total experience of your aunt. In the mourning process, each of these is brought up separately and repeatedly played through conscious awareness until the pangs of remembering are diminished. For example, hearing the song may initially bring out a deeply sad memory, but after you hear it and remember your aunt fifteen times, the song may only evoke a wistful nostalgia.

One cannot rush through the mourning process. For at least the first year, as each birthday, anniversary, holiday, and special occasion comes around, the loss is likely to be keenly felt. With a major loss, mourning will last roughly six months to a year and a half, although residual sadness may last a lifetime. To expect a grieving person to "snap out of it" before the end of the first year is to misunderstand the nature of satisfactory mourning.

The expression "satisfactory mourning" may strike some people as strange. Since mourning is both involuntary and uncomfortable, they may feel that one should try to end it as soon as possible. In reality, mourning is a healing process—a very necessary, very helpful way of diminishing the grief one feels as a result of a loss. Mourning is, therefore, not something to be avoided or interfered with, since only through mourning can someone's grief be satisfactorily resolved.

People who do not understand the importance of confronting grief directly or are too overwhelmed by a loss try to push it out of their minds, perhaps by "bearing up bravely," and then find themselves fifteen years later with the pain and the need for forgetting every bit as sharp as on the day of the death. They have become locked into a pattern of lifelong mourning which is never concluded because the grief feelings have never been allowed to gain expression. This is called "pathological mourning" (or "unresolved grief") and is far more common than most people suspect. Through professional help to encourage them to face the grief, the mourning can proceed in its natural course to a natural conclusion, even if the loss happened thirty years previously.

What are some of the emotional reactions of the survivors at the time they learn of their loss and in the weeks and months following it? Interestingly, the process of satisfactory mourning is very similar to the process of dying which we examined in Part II, except that for the dying person *every* pleasant memory must be mourned, whereas only the ones related to the deceased must be mourned by the grieving survivor.

The first reaction at a time of loss is often numbness. The news of the loss, even if one has been prepared for it, is so overwhelming that the person goes numb, much as does one's thumb when struck by a hammer. The numbness is a temporary protection against pain, making it possible for the survivor to cope with the countless details of arranging the funeral and adjusting to new circumstances.

In some cases, the death has been anticipated for so long by the family that they have to a certain extent completed the process of mourning before the actual death of the person. This is known as "anticipatory grief," and occurs when, for example, a cancer patient lingers on and on longer than the doctors predicted. The family, having lived so long with the expectation that the patient would soon be dead, has hastened the process of mourning. Consequently, when the death actually occurs, they may react calmly—or even with relief. This phenomenon is well illustrated in the excerpt from *Eric* in Part IV.

Perhaps the most common feelings a person has after the death of a loved one are extreme sadness or depression. He or she feels empty, lonely, and worthless and experiences a general lack of joy in life. A typical response is to withdraw from most human affairs for a while. Other symptoms of depression are a poor appetite, insomnia, general lack of energy, and an inability to concentrate. The bereaved person often feels desperately alone and is often plagued with memories of episodes in childhood when he or she felt alone and abandoned. Feelings of depression may continue for many months after the death of the loved one, even though the person thinks he should be "getting over it."

Frequently, anger is one of the many kinds of feelings experienced by the grieving person. This anger is sometimes directed at other people (a doctor who didn't diagnose the disease early enough to prevent the death of the loved one, for example) or at God or Fate for acting so cruelly. The anger may even be directed at the dead person himself. It may seem ironic that a grieving survivor would be angry at the dead person, but it is not an unusual occurrence. For the survivor feels abandoned, and thus the dead person is responsible for the pain and unhappiness that the survivor is experiencing. Such feelings are, of course, not rational; but feelings rarely are.

Anxiety is another emotional reaction that is frequently present when a person loses a loved one. For one thing, the survivor may be fearful that "that could have been me," since the death of someone close almost always reminds us of our own mortality. Or the anxiety may spring from feelings of helplessness: "How am I going to manage without this person who has been so important to me?" Unless the bereaved person has been through the process of mourning previously, he or she may feel anxiety about the painful emotions that the loss has produced and may wonder, "Will the pain ever go away?" or "Is it normal to react this way or am I losing my mind?"

Still another characteristic response is guilt feelings. Guilt is a frequent emotional reaction to the death of a loved one, since the survivors often feel somehow responsible for not preventing the death: "If only I had bought my father an air conditioner for his home, he would not have had a heart attack on that hot day," or "I should have insisted that Raymond have a physical examination regularly. If I had, he might still be alive today." Grieving persons remember countless things they wish they had done for the deceased or they remember things they did to hurt the deceased and never apologized for. No matter how well a person has treated the loved one during his or her life, there are always things to regret, and at the time of death the feelings of regret frequently turn to guilt since there is no longer any opportunity to do things differently.

Considering the kind of feelings that the grieving person is experiencing as part of the mourning process, what can friends and family do to be most helpful? First of all, they should not stay away from the grieving person just because of their own feelings of discomfort. Sending flowers or a preprinted sympathy card is no substitute for being present to offer the support that only a caring friend can give. Don't worry if you don't know what to say; your mere presence is a clear message in itself.

Secondly, help the grieving person express his or her feelings, even though the process may be painful. There is a frequent misconception that it is cruel to remind the grieving person of his/her loss. As in the case of the terminally ill patient who wishes to talk, it facilitates the mourning process to talk freely about the person who has died. Grief is eased by its sharing. Therefore, we may not always be helpful when we try to distract grieving persons by "being cheerful" and avoiding any mention of the deceased. Instead, we should give them opportunities to reminisce about the person who has died and to talk about the experiences they shared. By being willing to listen, we can help the grieving person work through the painful but essential process of mourning.

HEARTACHE
ANTON CHEKHOV

At a time of grief, many people feel the need to talk about their loss. Usually a friend or family member will listen sympathetically. But if friends or family are not available,

*even a stranger will do. The old man in this short story
written in 1886 by the great Russian writer, Anton Chekhov,
tries to find someone to whom he can pour out his grief.
The indifference he encounters and the loneliness he feels are
no less common today than they were in nineteenth-century
Russia.*

*"To whom shall I tell my sorrow?"**

Evening twilight. Large flakes of wet snow are circling
lazily about the street lamps which have just been lighted,
settling in a thin soft layer on roofs, horses' backs, peoples'
shoulders, caps. Iona Potapov, the cabby, is all white
like a ghost. As hunched as a living body can be, he
sits on the box without stirring. If a whole snowdrift were
to fall on him, even then, perhaps he would not find it
necessary to shake it off. His nag, too, is white and motionless. Her immobility, the angularity of her shape, and
the sticklike straightness of her legs make her look like a
penny gingerbread horse. She is probably lost in thought.
Anyone who has been torn away from the plow, from the
familiar gray scenes, and cast into this whirlpool full of
monstrous lights, of ceaseless uproar and hurrying people, cannot help thinking.

Iona and his nag have not budged for a long time.
They have driven out of the yard before dinnertime and
haven't had a single fare yet. But now evening dusk is
descending upon the city. The pale light of the street
lamps changes to a vivid color and the bustle of the street
grows louder.

"Sleigh to the Vyborg District!" Iona hears. "Sleigh!"

Iona starts, and through his snow-plastered eyelashes
sees an officer in a military overcoat with a hood.

"To the Vyborg District!" repeats the officer. "Are you
asleep, eh? To the Vyborg District!"

As a sign of assent Iona gives a tug at the reins, which
sends layers of snow flying from the horse's back and
from his own shoulders. The officer gets into the sleigh.
The driver clucks to the horse, cranes his neck like a swan,
rises in his seat and, more from habit than necessity,
flourishes his whip. The nag, too, stretches her neck,
crooks her sticklike legs and irresolutely sets off.

"Where are you barging in, damn you?" Iona is

* From an old Russian song comparable to a Negro Spiritual.

promptly assailed by shouts from the massive dark wavering to and fro before him. "Where the devil are you going? Keep to the right!"

"Don't you know how to drive? Keep to the right," says the officer with vexation.

A coachman driving a private carriage swears at him; a pedestrian who was crossing the street and brushed against the nag's nose with his shoulder, looks at him angrily and shakes the snow off his sleeve. Iona fidgets on the box as if sitting on needles and pins, thrusts out his elbows and rolls his eyes like a madman, as though he did not know where he was or why he was there.

"What rascals they all are," the officer jokes. "They are doing their best to knock into you or be trampled by the horse. It's a conspiracy."

Iona looks at his fare and moves his lips. He wants to say something, but the only sound that comes out is a wheeze.

"What is it?" asks the officer.

Iona twists his mouth into a smile, strains his throat and croaks hoarsely: "My son, sir . . . er, my son died this week."

"H'm, what did he die of?"

Iona turns his whole body around to his fare and says, "Who can tell? It must have been a fever. He lay in the hospital only three days and then he died. . . . It is God's will."

"Get over, you devil!" comes out of the dark. "Have you gone blind, you old dog? Keep your eyes peeled!"

"Go on, go on," says the officer. "We shan't get there until tomorrow at this rate. Give her the whip!"

The driver cranes his neck again, rises in his seat, and with heavy grace swings his whip. Then he looks around at the officer several times, but the latter keeps his eyes closed and is apparently indisposed to listen. Letting his fare off in the Vyborg District, Iona stops by a teahouse and again sits motionless and hunched on the box. Again the wet snow paints him and his nag white. One hour passes, another. . . .

Three young men, two tall and lanky, one short and hunchbacked, come along swearing at each other and loudly pound the pavement with their galoshes.

"Cabby, to the Police Bridge!" the hunchback shouts

in a cracked voice. "The three of us . . . twenty kopecks!"

Iona tugs at the reins and clucks to his horse. Twenty
kopecks is not fair, but his mind is not on that. Whether
it is a ruble or five kopecks, it is all one to him now, so
long as he has a fare. . . . The three young men, jostling
each other and using foul language, go up to the sleigh
and all three try to sit down at once. They start arguing
about which two are to sit and who shall be the one to
stand. After a long ill-tempered and abusive altercation,
they decide that the hunchback must stand up because he
is the shortest.

"Well, get going," says the hunchback in his cracked
voice, taking up his station and breathing down Iona's
neck. "On your way. What a cap you've got, brother! You
won't find a worse one in all Petersburg—"

"Hee, hee . . . hee, hee . . ." Iona giggles, "as you
say—"

"Well, then, 'as you say,' drive on. Are you going to
crawl like this all the way, eh? D'you want to get it in
the neck?"

"My head is splitting," says one of the tall ones. "At
the Dukmasovs' yesterday, Vaska and I killed four bottles of cognac between us."

"I don't get it, why lie?" says the other tall one angrily.
"He is lying like a trouper."

"Strike me dead, it's the truth!"

"It is about as true as that a louse sneezes."

"Hee, hee," giggles Iona. "The gentleman are feeling
good!"

"Faugh, the devil take you!" cries the hunchback in-
dignantly. "Will you get a move on, you old pest, or won't
you? Is that the way to drive? Give her a crack of the
whip! Giddap, devil! Giddap! Let her feel it!"

Iona feels the hunchback's wriggling body and quivering voice behind his back. He hears abuse addressed to
him, sees people, and the feeling of loneliness begins little
by little to lift from his heart. The hunchback swears till
he chokes on an elaborate three-decker oath and is overcome by cough. The tall youths begin discussing a certain
Nadezhda Petrovna. Iona looks round at them. When at
last there is a lull in the conversation for which he has
been waiting, he turns around and says: "This week . . .
er . . . my son died."

"We shall all die," says the hunchback, with a sigh wiping his lips after his coughing fit. "Come, drive on, drive on. Gentlemen, I simply cannot stand this pace! When will he get us there?"

"Well, you give him a little encouragement. Biff him in the neck!"

"Do you hear, you old pest? I'll give it to you in the neck. If one stands on ceremony with fellows like you, one may as well walk. Do you hear, you old serpent? Or don't you give a damn what we say?"

And Iona hears rather than feels the thud of a blow on his neck.

"Hee, hee," he laughs. "The gentlemen are feeling good. God give you health!"

"Cabby, are you married?" asks one of the tall ones.

"Me? Hee, hee! The gentlemen are feeling good. The only wife for me now is the damp earth. . . . Hee, haw, haw! The grave, that is! . . . Here my son is dead and me alive. . . . It is a queer thing, death comes in at the wrong door. . . . It don't come for me, it comes for my son. . . ."

And Iona turns round to tell them how his son died, but at that point the hunchback gives a sigh of relief and announces that, thank God, they have arrived at last. Having received his twenty kopecks, for a long while Iona stares after the revelers, who disappear into a dark entrance. Again he is alone and once more silence envelops him. The grief which has been allayed for a brief space comes back again and wrenches his heart more cruelly than ever. There is a look of anxiety and torment in Iona's eyes as they wander restlessly over the crowds moving to and fro on both sides of the street. Isn't there someone among those thousands who will listen to him? But the crowds hurry past, heedless of him and his grief. His grief is immense, boundless. If his heart were to burst and his grief to pour out, it seems that it would flood the whole world, and yet no one sees it. It has found a place for itself in such an insignificant shell that no one can see it in broad daylight.

Iona notices a doorkeeper with a bag and makes up his mind to speak to him.

"What time will it be, friend?" he asks.

"Past nine. What have you stopped here for? On your way!"

Iona drives a few steps away, hunches up and surrenders himself to his grief. He feels it is useless to turn to people. But before five minutes are over, he draws himself up, shakes his head as though stabbed by a sharp pain and tugs at the reins. . . . He can bear it no longer.

"Back to the yard!" he thinks. "To the yard!"

And his nag, as though she knew his thoughts, starts out at a trot. An hour and a half later, Iona is sitting beside a large dirty stove. On the stove, on the floor, on benches are men snoring. The air is stuffy and foul. Iona looks at the sleeping figures, scratches himself and regrets that he has come home so early.

"I haven't earned enough to pay for the oats," he reflects. "That's what's wrong with me. A man that knows his job . . . who has enough to eat and has enough for his horse don't need to fret."

In one of the corners a young driver gets up, hawks sleepily and reaches for the water bucket.

"Thirsty?" Iona asks him.

"Guess so."

"H'm, may it do you good, but my son is dead, brother . . . did you hear? This week in the hospital. . . . What a business!"

Iona looks to see the effect of his words, but he notices none. The young man has drawn his cover over his head and is already asleep. The old man sighs and scratches himself. Just as the young man was thirsty for water so he thirsts for talk. It will soon be a week since his son died and he hasn't talked to anybody about him properly. He ought to be able to talk about it, taking his time, sensibly. He ought to tell how his son was taken ill, how he suffered, what he said before he died, how he died. . . . He ought to describe the funeral, and how he went to the hospital to fetch his son's clothes. His daughter Anisya is still in the country. . . . And he would like to talk about her, too. Yes, he has plenty to talk about now. And his listener should gasp and moan and keen. . . . It would be even better to talk to women. Though they are foolish, two words will make them blubber.

"I must go out and have a look at the horse," Iona thinks. "There will be time enough for sleep. You will have enough sleep, no fear. . . ."

He gets dressed and goes into the stable where his horse is standing. He thinks about oats, hay, the weather.

When he is alone, he dares not think of his son. It is possible to talk about him with someone, but to think of him when one is alone, to evoke his image is unbearably painful.

"You chewing?" Iona asks his mare seeing her shining eyes. "There, chew away, chew away. . . . If we haven't earned enough for oats, we'll eat hay. . . . Yes. . . . I've grown too old to drive. My son had ought to be driving, not me. . . . He was a real cabby. . . . He had ought to have lived. . . ."

Iona is silent for a space and then goes on: "That's how it is, old girl. . . . Kuzma Ionych is gone. . . . Departed this life. . . . He went and died to no purpose. . . . Now let's say you had a little colt, and you were that little colt's own mother. And suddenly, let's say, that same little colt departed this life. . . . You'd be sorry, wouldn't you?"

The nag chews, listens, and breathes on her master's hands. Iona is carried away and tells her everything.

(Translated by Avrahm Yarmolinsky)

SONNET 71
WILLIAM SHAKESPEARE

In Sonnet 71 William Shakespeare (1564–1616), speaking of his own death, advises his beloved friend not to mourn or grieve when the separation of death finally occurs. He would rather his friend forget and be happy and strong, than grieve and suffer. It is interesting to note that during the sixteenth and seventeenth centuries the therapeutic value of mourning was not understood. Shakespeare often spoke of grieving and weeping as weak and "womanish."

No longer mourn for me when I am dead
Than you shall hear the surly sullen bell
Give warning to the world that I am fled
From this vile world, with vilest worms to dwell.
Nay, if you read this line, remember not
The hand that writ it, for I love you so
That I in your sweet thoughts would be forgot,
If thinking on me then should make you woe.
Oh, if, I say, you look upon this verse

When I, perhaps, compounded am with clay,
Do not so much as my poor name rehearse,
But let your love even with my life decay,
    Lest the wise world should look into your moan
    And mock you with me after I am gone.

from MADAME BOVARY
GUSTAVE FLAUBERT

*This excerpt from a classic nineteenth-century French novel
describes the reaction of Charles, her husband, to Madame
Bovary's death by suicide. (Her death itself is described in
another excerpt which appears in Part VI.) His grief is typical
of the reaction many people have to the loss of someone they
love. At first he seems unaware that she has really died, telling
the pharmacist that there won't be a funeral ceremony because
he "wants to keep her." He is numb, responding "like a
machine" when Homais tries to engage him in conversation.
But as he gradually starts to realize the enormity of his loss,
the numbness and denial turn to anger.*

There is always after the death of anyone a kind of
stupefaction; so difficult is it to grasp this advent of nothingness and to resign ourselves to believe in it. But still,
when he saw that she did not move, Charles threw himself
upon her, crying—

"Farewell! farewell!"

Homais and Canivet dragged him from the room.

"Restrain yourself!"

"Yes," said he, struggling, "I'll be quiet. I'll not do
anything. But leave me alone. I want to see her. She is
my wife!"

And he wept.

"Cry," said the chemist; "let nature take her course;
that will solace you."

Weaker than a child, Charles let himself be led downstairs into the sitting-room, and Monsieur Homais soon
went home. On the Place he was accosted by the blind
man, who, having dragged himself as far as Yonville, in
the hope of getting the antiphlogistic pomade, was asking
every passer-by where the druggist lived.

"There now! as if I hadn't got other fish to fry. Well, so
much the worse; you must come later on."

And he entered the shop hurriedly.

He had to write two letters, to prepare a soothing potion for Bovary, to invent some lie that would conceal the poisoning, and work it up into an article for the "Fanal," without counting the people who were waiting to get the news from him; and when the Yonvillers had all heard his story of the arsenic that she had mistaken for sugar in making a vanilla cream, Homais once more returned to Bovary's.

He found him alone (Monsieur Canivet had left), sitting in an arm-chair near the window, staring with an idiotic look at the flags of the floor.

"Now," said the chemist, "you ought yourself to fix the hour for the ceremony."

"Why? What ceremony?" Then, in a stammering, frightened voice, "Oh, no! not that. No! I want to see her here."

Homais, to keep himself in countenance, took up a water-bottle on the whatnot to water the geraniums.

"Ah! thanks," said Charles; "you are good."

But he did not finish, choking beneath the crowd of memories that this action of the druggist recalled to him.

Then to distract him, Homais thought fit to talk a little horticulture: plants wanted humidity. Charles bowed his head in sign of approbation.

"Besides, the fine days will soon be here again."

"Ah!" said Bovary.

The druggist, at his wit's end, began softly to draw aside the small window-curtain.

"Hallo! there's Monsieur Tuvache passing."

Charles repeated like a machine—

"Monsieur Tuvache passing!"

Homais did not dare to speak to him again about the funeral arrangements; it was the priest who succeeded in reconciling him to them.

He shut himself up in his consulting-room, took a pen, and after sobbing for some time, wrote—

"I wish her to be buried in her wedding-dress, with white shoes, and a wreath. Her hair is to be spread out over her shoulders. Three coffins, one of oak, one of mahogany, one of lead. Let no one say anything to me. I shall have strength. Over all there is to be placed a large piece of green velvet. This is my wish; see that it is done."

The two men were much surprised at Bovary's romantic ideas. The chemist at once went to him and said—

"This velvet seems to me a superfetation. Besides, the expense—"

"What's that to you?" cried Charles. "Leave me! You did not love her. Go!"

The priest took him by the arm for a turn in the garden. He discoursed on the vanity of earthly things. God was very great, was very good: one must submit to his decrees without a murmur; nay, must even thank him.

Charles burst out into blasphemies: "I hate your God!"

"The spirit of rebellion is still upon you," sighed the ecclesiastic.

Bovary was far away. He was walking with great strides along by the wall, near the espalier, and he ground his teeth; he raised to heaven looks of malediction, but not so much as a leaf stirred.

(Translated by Eleanor Marx-Aveling)

I REMEMBER THE RIVER
AT WU SUNG
Mei Yao Ch'en

Sometimes the most poignant triggers of grief come unexpectedly. An aroma, melody, building, season, holiday, color, or some other unpredictable stimulus can elicit sharp pangs of remembrance. Although this poem, written by the founder of the poetic style of the Chinese Sung Dynasty (1002 to 1060 A.D.), is remote from us in time and setting, the sentiments it expresses are universal in their application.

I remember once, on a journey to the west,
An evening at the mouth of the river, at Wu Sung.
Along the banks a fresh breeze blew against the current.
The pale moon rose between two willow trees.
A single night bird flew far away.
Fishing boats wandered on the river.
And who was with me then?
I weep and think of my dead wife.

(Translated by Kenneth Rexroth)

from A GRIEF OBSERVED

C. S. LEWIS

In this excerpt from the diary he kept as a chronicle of his grief over the death of his wife, C. S. Lewis (1898–1963) attempts to describe as specifically as possible the feelings associated with grief and the way he is treated by people he encounters during the time when he is mourning his loss.

No one ever told me that grief felt so like fear. I am not afraid, but the sensation is like being afraid. The same fluttering in the stomach, the same restlessness, the yawning. I keep on swallowing.

At other times it feels like being mildly drunk, or concussed. There is a sort of invisible blanket between the world and me. I find it hard to take in what anyone says. Or perhaps, hard to want to take it in. It is so uninteresting. Yet I want the others to be about me. I dread the moments when the house is empty. If only they would talk to one another and not to me.

There are moments, most unexpectedly, when something inside me tries to assure me that I don't really mind so much, not so very much, after all. Love is not the whole of a man's life. I was happy before I ever met H. I've plenty of what are called "resources." People get over these things. Come, I shan't do so badly. One is ashamed to listen to this voice but it seems for a little to be making out a good case. Then comes a sudden jab of red-hot memory and all this "commonsense" vanishes like an ant in the mouth of a furnace.

On the rebound one passes into tears and pathos. Maudlin tears. I almost prefer the moments of agony. These are at least clean and honest. But the bath of self-pity, the wallow, the loathsome sticky-sweet pleasure of indulging it—that disgusts me. And even while I'm doing it I know it leads me to misrepresent H. herself. Give that mood its head and in a few minutes I shall have substituted for the real woman a mere doll to be blubbered over. Thank God the memory of her is still too strong (will it always be too strong?) to let me get away with it.

For H. wasn't like that at all. Her mind was lithe and

184

quick and muscular as a leopard. Passion, tenderness and pain were all equally unable to disarm it. It scented the first whiff of cant or slush; then sprang, and knocked you over before you knew what was happening. How many bubbles of mine she pricked! I soon learned not to talk rot to her unless I did it for the sheer pleasure—and there's another red-hot jab—of being exposed and laughed at. I was never less silly than as H's lover.

And no one ever told me about the laziness of grief. Except at my job—where the machine seems to run on much as usual—I loathe the slightest effort. Not only writing but even reading a letter is too much. Even shaving. What does it matter now whether my cheek is rough or smooth? They say an unhappy man wants distractions—something to take him out of himself. Only as a dog-tired man wants an extra blanket on a cold night; he'd rather lie there shivering than get up and find one. It's easy to see why the lonely become untidy; finally, dirty and disgusting.

. . . An odd by-product of my loss is that I'm aware of being an embarrassment to everyone I meet. At work, at the club, in the street, I see people, as they approach me, trying to make up their minds whether they'll "say something about it" or not. I hate it if they do, and if they don't. Some funk it altogether. R. has been avoiding me for a week. I like best the well brought-up young men, almost boys, who walk up to me as if I were a dentist, turn very red, get it over, and then edge away to the bar as quickly as they decently can. Perhaps the bereaved ought to be isolated in special settlements like lepers.

THE MOTHER
PADRAIC PEARSE

As commander-in-chief of Irish forces during the 1916 Easter Rebellion, Padraic Pearse supported the struggle of the Irish to prevent England from extending home rule to Ireland. He was executed in 1919 after surrendering his troops. His personal experiences with war may have produced the attitudes expressed in this poem. The mother has ambivalent feelings about the deaths of her two soldier sons. She is proud because they died in the service of their country; yet she is also deeply saddened by the loss of the sons she loves so much.

I do not grudge them: Lord, I do not grudge
My two strong sons that I have seen go out
To break their strength and die, they and a few,
In bloody protest for a glorious thing,
They shall be spoken of among their people,
The generations shall remember them,
And call them blessed;
But I will speak their names to my own heart
In the long nights;
The little names that were familiar once
Round my dead hearth.
Lord, thou art hard on mothers:
We suffer in their coming and their going;
And tho' I grudge them not, I weary, weary
Of the long sorrow—And yet I have my joy:
My sons were faithful, and they fought.

WAR
LUIGI PIRANDELLO

A recipient, in 1934, of the Nobel Prize for Literature, Pirandello was born in 1867 in Sicily and died in 1936. In his short story "War" he describes a man who, although he lost his son in war, advises other parents not to worry about their sons because war is a part of life, and death in war is an honor. When this seemingly strong, fearless man is later forced to talk specifically about his own son's death, his reaction is a powerful mixture of terror, grief, and self-discovery. We realize that he has never completely acknowledged the loss of his son, using denial to protect himself from the painful truth. "War" is an excellent example of how grief which is not properly faced and dealt with can resurface in a violent and unexpected manner.

The passengers who had left Rome by the night express had to stop until dawn at the small station of Fabriano in order to continue their journey by the small old-fashioned "local" joining the main line with Sulmona.

At dawn, in a stuffy and smoky second-class carriage

in which five people had already spent the night, a bulky
woman in deep mourning was hoisted in—almost like a
shapeless bundle. Behind her—puffing and moaning—
followed her husband, a tiny man, thin and weakly, his
face death-white, his eyes small and bright and looking
shy and uneasy.

Having at last taken a seat, he politely thanked the
passengers who had helped his wife and who had made
room for her. Then he turned round to the woman trying
to pull down the collar of her coat and politely inquired:
"Are you all right, dear?"

The wife, instead of answering, pulled up her collar
again to her eyes, so as to hide her face.

"Nasty world," muttered the husband with a sad smile.

And he felt it was his duty to explain to his traveling
companions that the poor woman was to be pitied, for the
war was taking away from her her only son. He was a
boy of twenty to whom both had devoted their entire
life, even breaking up their home at Sulmona to follow
him to Rome, where he had to go as a student. Then they
had allowed him to volunteer for war, with an assurance,
however, that at least for six months he would not be
sent to the front. And now, all of a sudden, they had received a wire that he was due to leave in three days'
time and asking them to go and see him off.

The woman under the big coat was twisting and wriggling, at times growling like a wild animal, feeling certain
that all those explanations would not have aroused even
a shadow of sympathy from those people who—most
likely—were in the same plight as herself. One of them,
who had been listening with particular attention, said:

"You should thank God that your son is only leaving
now for the front. Mine has been sent there the first day
of the war. He has already come back twice wounded and
been sent back again to the front."

"What about me? I have two sons and three nephews
at the front," said another passenger.

"Maybe, but in our case it is our *only* son," ventured
the husband.

"What difference can it make? You may spoil your
only son with excessive attentions, but you cannot love
him more than you would all your other children if you
had any. Paternal love is not like bread that can be broken
into pieces and split among the children in equal shares.

A father gives *all* his love to each one of his children without discrimination, whether it be one or ten, and if I am suffering now for my two sons, I am not suffering half for each of them but double. . . ."

"True . . . true . . ." sighed the embarrassed husband, "but suppose (of course, we all hope it will never be your case) a father has two sons at the front and he loses one of them, there is still one left to console him . . . while . . ."

"Yes," answered the other, getting cross, "a son left to console him but also a son left for whom he must survive, while in the case of the father of an only son, if the son dies, the father can die, too, and put an end to his distress. Which of the two positions is worse? Don't you see how my case would be worse than yours?"

"Nonsense," interrupted another traveler, a fat, red-faced man with bloodshot eyes of the palest gray.

He was panting. From his bulging eyes seemed to spurt inner violence of an uncontrolled vitality which his weakened body could hardly contain.

"Nonsense," he repeated, trying to cover his mouth with his hand so as to hide the two missing front teeth. "Nonsense. Do we give life to our children for our own benefit?"

The other travelers stared at him in distress. The one who had had his son at the front since the first day of the war sighed: "You are right. Our children do not belong to us, they belong to the Country. . . ."

"Bosh," retorted the fat traveler. "Do we think of the Country when we give life to our children? Our sons are born because . . . well, because they must be born and when they come to life they take our own life with them. This is the truth. We belong to them but they never belong to us. And when they reach twenty, they are exactly what we were at their age. We, too, had a father and mother, but there were so many other things as well —girls, cigarettes, illusions, new ties—and the Country, of course, whose call we would have answered, when we were twenty, even if father and mother had said no. Now, at our age, the love of our Country is still great, of course, but stronger than it is the love for our children. Is there any one of us here who wouldn't gladly take his son's place at the front if he could?"

There was a silence all round, everybody nodding as to approve.

"Why, then," continued the fat man, "shouldn't we consider the feelings of our children when they are twenty? Isn't it natural that at their age they should consider the love for their Country (I am speaking of decent boys, of course) even greater than the love for us? Isn't it natural that it should be so, as after all they must look upon us as upon old boys who cannot move any more and must stay at home? If Country exists, if Country is a natural necessity like bread, of which each of us must eat in order not to die of hunger, somebody must go to defend it. And our sons go, when they are twenty, and they don't want tears, because if they die, they die inflamed and happy (I am speaking, of course, of decent boys). Now, if one dies young and happy, without having the ugly sides of life, the boredom of it, the pettiness, the bitterness of disillusion . . . what more can we ask for him? Everyone should stop crying: everyone should laugh, as I do . . . or at least thank God—as I do—because my son, before dying, sent me a message saying that he was dying satisfied at having ended his life in the best way he could have wished. That is why, as you see, I do not even wear mourning. . . ."

He shook his light fawn coat as to show it. His livid lip over his missing teeth was trembling, his eyes were watery and motionless and soon after, he ended with a shrill laugh which might well have been a sob.

"Quite so . . . quite so . . ." agreed the others.

The woman who, bundled in a corner under her coat, had been sitting and listening had—for the last three months—tried to find in the words of her husband and her friends something to console her in her deep sorrow, something that might show her how a mother should resign herself to send her son not even to death but to a probable danger of life. Yet not a word had she found among the many which had been said . . . and her grief had been greater in seeing that nobody—as she thought—could share her feelings.

But now the words of the traveler amazed and almost stunned her. She suddenly realized that it wasn't the others who were wrong and could not understand her but herself who could not rise up to the same height of those fathers and mothers willing to resign themselves, without crying, not only to the departure of their sons but even to their death.

She lifted her head, she bent over from her corner trying to listen with great attention to the details which the fat man was giving to his companions about the way his son had fallen as a hero, for his King and his Country, happy and without regrets. It seemed to her that she had stumbled into a world she had never dreamt of, a world so far unknown to her, and she was so pleased to hear everyone joining in congratulating that brave father who could so stoically speak of his child's death.

Then suddenly, just as if she had heard nothing of what had been said and almost as if waking up from a dream, she turned to the old man, asking him:

"Then . . . is your son really dead?"

Everybody stared at her. The old man, too, turned to look at her, fixing his great, bulging, horribly watery light gray eyes, deep in her face. For some little time he tried to answer, but words failed him. He looked and looked at her, almost as if only then—at that silly, incongruous question—he had suddenly realized at last that his son was really dead . . . gone for ever . . . for ever. His face contracted, became horribly distorted, then he snatched in haste a handkerchief from his pocket and, to the amazement of everyone, broke into harrowing, heart-rending, uncontrollable sobs.

(Translated by Michael Pettinati)

TO W. P., II
RUDYARD KIPLING

This sonnet by the well-known British author Rudyard Kipling expresses the mixed feelings typically experienced by grieving persons. Emotions of sorrow, loss, and loneliness exist alongside the happy memories of constant love and lasting enrichment. The object of love is taken away, and this causes sadness and pain; but the love itself remains, and this continues to be a source of comfort and joy. Kipling was born in 1865 and died in 1936. He was the recipient of the Nobel Prize for Literature in 1907.

With you a part of me hath passed away;
For in the peopled forest of my mind

A tree made leafless by this wintry wind
Shall never don again its green array.
Chapel and fireside, country road and bay,
Have something of their friendliness resigned;
Another, if I would, I could not find,
And I am grown much older in a day.
But yet I treasure in my memory
Your gift of charity, and young heart's ease,
And the dear honour of your amity;
For these once mine, my life is rich with these.
And I scarce know which part may greater be,
What I keep of you, or you rob from me.

from BLOOD OF THE LAMB
PETER DeVRIES

This excerpt from a novel by a contemporary American writer deals with a father's inconsolable pain and grief as a result of the death of his little daughter, Carol. The first section relates an incident in the final days of her illness, in which the father, who narrates the story, attempts to bargain with God for just one more year with his daughter. The events in the second section take place after Carol's death, when the father is struggling to come to terms with his loss.

I walked out past St. Catherine's to the bar and grill and back again so often through so many hospitalizations that I cannot remember which time it was that I stopped in the church on the way back to sit down and rest. I was dead-drunk and stone-sober and bone-tired, my head split and numbed by the plague of voices in eternal disputation. I knew why I was delaying my return to the hospital. The report on the morning's aspiration would be phoned up to the ward from the laboratory any minute, and what I died to learn I dreaded to hear.

I got up and walked to the center aisle, where I stood looking out to the high altar and the soaring windows. I turned around and went to the rear corner, where stood the little shrine to St. Jude, Patron of Lost Causes and Hopeless Cases. Half the candles were burning. I took a taper and lit another. I was alone in the church. The gentle flames wavered and shattered in a mist of tears spilling from my eyes as I sank to the floor.

"I do not ask that she be spared to me, but that her life be spared to her. Or give us a year. We will spend it as we have the last, missing nothing. We will mark the dance of every hour between the snowdrop and the snow: crocus to tulip to violet to iris to rose. We will note not only the azalea's crimson flowers but the red halo that encircles a while the azalea's root when her petals are shed, also the white halo that rings for a week the foot of the old catalpa tree. Later we will prize the chrysanthemums which last so long, almost as long as paper flowers, perhaps because they know in blooming not to bloom. We will seek out the leaves turning in the little-praised bushes and the unadvertised trees. Everyone loves the sweet, neat blossom of the hawthorn in spring, but who lingers over the olive drab of her leaf in autumn? We will. We will note the lost yellows in the tangles of that bush that spills over the Howards' stone wall, the meek hues among which it seems to hesitate before committing itself to red, and next year learn its name. We will seek out these modest subtleties so lost in the blare of oaks and maples, like flutes and woodwinds drowned in brasses and drums. When winter comes, we will let no snow fall ignored. We will again watch the first blizzard from her window like figures locked snug in a glass paperweight. 'Pick one out and follow it to the ground!' she will say again. We will feed the plain birds that stay to cheer us through the winter, and when spring returns we shall be the first out, to catch the snowdrop's first white whisper in the wood. All this we ask, with the remission of our sins, in Christ's name. Amen."

Summer passed into autumn, and when in November a few white flakes sifted down out of the sky, Mrs. Brodhag decided to make the journey to her sister in Seattle of which she had for so long restively spoken. Perhaps she would make "other connections" there, in view of my having the house on the market. If I sold it—a result little foreshadowed by the processions marching through it behind an ever-changing leadership of brokers— and did move into a city apartment, I would hardly be needing her help. The trip to the airport was the first down the Parkway since the days when we had made so many. "—In both our prayers—" she raged in my ear against the roar of jets. I pressed into her hand a St.

Christopher medal, extricated with difficulty from the chain of the crucifix with which it had become entangled in my pocket. We smiled as she nodded thanks. Then she was a bird in the sky, then a bee, then nothing.

It was as many months again before I could bring myself to explore at any length the bright front bedroom, then only because the sudden sale of the house required its cleaning out. Dresses and toys and bureau articles were put into boxes and carried into the garage for the charity truck to haul away. Among the books and papers in the large desk drawer was a class letter from the sixth grade, a monumental scroll on which each individual note was pasted, wound upon two sticks like an ancient document. I read a few before stowing it into a carton of things to be kept for a still further future. One was a note from a boy reputed to have lost his heart to her, commanding her early return and with a P.S. reading, "You and I up in a tree, K-I-S-S-I-N-G." Into the carton were also tucked the home movies still sealed in their original tins. At last I found the courage to turn on the tape recorder.

I carried it down into the living room, of which the windows were open, the year being now once again well advanced into spring. It was twilight, and I turned on all the lamps.

After a whir of scratches and laughing whispers began some absurd dialogue Carol had picked up between Mrs. Brodhag and me, without our knowing it, about leaking eaves and how they should be got at. "You might as well be married the way she nags you," Carol said into the machine she had herself initiated with this prank. Then followed some of her piano pieces, including the Chopin *Nocturne* I had managed to get on the tape the night of the unfortunate television program. I stood at the window with a heavy drink as each molten note dropped out of nowhere onto my heart. There was a long silence after the music, and I was about to end the entertainment as a poor idea when my hand was arrested at the switch by the sound of her voice. This time she read a selection to which she had a few words of preface:

"I want you to know that everything is all right, Daddy. I mean you mustn't worry, really. You've helped me a lot—more than you can imagine. I was digging around in the cabinet part at the bottom of the bookshelves for

something to read that you would like. I mean, not
something from your favorite books of poetry and all, but
something of your own. What did I come across but that
issue of the magazine put out by your alma mater, with
the piece in it about your philosophy of life. Do you remember it? I might as well say that I know what's going
on. What you wrote gives me courage to face whatever
there is that's coming, so what could be more appropriate
than to read it for you now? Remember when you explained it to me? Obviously, I don't understand it all, but
I think I get the drift:

"I believe that man must learn to live without those
consolations called religions, which his own intelligence
must by now have told him belong to the childhood of
the race. Philosophy can really give us nothing perma-
nent to believe either; it is too rich in answers, each can-
celing out the rest. The quest for Meaning is foredoomed.
Human life 'means' nothing. But that is not to say that it
is not worth living. What does a Debussy *Arabesque*
'mean,' or a rainbow or a rose? A man delights in all of
these, knowing himself to be no more—a wisp of music
and a haze of dreams dissolving against the sun. Man has
only his own two feet to stand on, his own human trinity
to see him through: Reason, Courage, and Grace. And
the first plus the second equals the third."

I reached the couch at last, on which I lay for some
hours as though I had been clubbed, not quite to death. I
wished that pound of gristle in my breast would stop its
beating, as once in the course of that night I think it
nearly did. The time between the last evening songs of the
birds and their first cries at daybreak was a span of night
without contents, blackness as stark as the lights left burning among the parlor furniture. Sometime towards its close
I went to my bedroom, where from a bureau drawer I
drew a small cruciform trinket on a chain. I went outside,
walking down the slope of back lawn to the privet hedge,
over which I hurled it as far as I could into the trees beyond. They were the sacred wood where we had so often
walked, looking for the first snowdrops, listening for
peepers, and in the clearings of which we had freed from
drifts of dead leaves the tender heads of early violets.

I looked up through the cold air. All the stars were
out. That pit of jewels, heaven, gave no answer. Among
them would always be a wraith saying, "Can't I stay up a

little longer?" I hear that voice in the city streets or on country roads, with my nose in a mug of cocoa, walking in the rain or standing in falling snow. "Pick one out and follow it to the ground."

How I hate this world. I would like to tear it apart with my own two hands if I could. I would like to dismantle the universe star by star, like a treeful of rotten fruit. Nor do I believe in progress. A vermin-eaten saint scratching his filth in the hope of heaven is better off than you damned in clean linen. Progress doubles our tenure in a vale of tears. Man is a mistake, to be corrected only by his abolition, which he gives promise of seeing to himself. Oh, let him pass, and leave the earth to the flowers that carpet the earth, wherever he explodes his triumphs. Man is inconsolable, thanks to that eternal "Why?" when there is no Why, that question mark twisted like a fishhook in the human heart. "Let there be light," we cry, and only the dawn breaks.

What are these thoughts? They are the shadow, no doubt, reaching out to declare me my father's son. But before that I shall be my daughter's father. Not to say my brother's brother. Now through the meadows of my mind wander hand in hand Louie and Carol and at last little Rachel, saying, "My grace is sufficient for thee." For we are indeed saved by grace in the end—but to give, not take. This, it seems then, is my Book of the Dead. All I know I have learned from them—my long-suffering mother and my crazy father, too, and from Greta, gone frowning somewhere, her secret still upon her brow. All I am worth I got from them. And Rena too, and Dr. Simpson's little boy, whom I never saw. What was his name? Stevie. "A dolphin boy," the doctor had said. in trying to describe him to me. I sometimes see him when I'm out walking on my lunch hour in New York, wading through the pigeons beside the defunct fountain in Bryant Park, behind the library. "Can't I stay up a little longer?"

I could not decline the burden of resumption. The Western Gate is closed. That exit is barred. One angel guards it, whose sword is a gold head smiling into the sun in a hundred snapshots. The child on the brink of whose grave I tried to recover the faith lost on the edge of my brother's is the goalkeeper past whom I can now never get. In the smile are sealed my orders for the day. One has heard of people being punished for their sins, hardly for their piety. But so it is. As to that other One, whose voice I thought I heard, I seem to be barred from everything it speaks in comfort, only the remonstrance remaining: "Verily, I say unto thee, Thou shalt by no means come out thence, till thou hast paid the uttermost farthing."

I went inside and brewed some coffee. It seemed feat enough not to reach for another beverage, even at that early hour. The stars had paled and day was breaking. As I sat waiting for the pot to boil, I thought that later in the morning I would telephone the Steins in Trenton and ask about Rachel. I hoped the 6-MP would take her a long way, till school started again, at least. That was always the most important milestone among us parents. Going Back to School. More than making another Christmas, somehow. It didn't take a wise man to understand why. That's the one thing we never stop doing: Going Back to School.

As I sat in the kitchen drinking the coffee, I set my mind to the problem of taking Rachel something of Carol's without letting on anything. Down in the garden amid the lilacs' wasted scent the bees hummed and the hummingbirds shot. It would be a clear morning. The sun had poured its first light through the trees below the garden, gilding the papered wall. The glance directed by the new owners at its ranks of yellow stripes and clumps of bruised fruit gave assurance that this paper would soon be coming down. Truth to tell, we had never liked it much ourselves. There were distant sounds of neighbors stirring, starting the day. An early riser called to someone in the farm below the trees. A wood thrush sang in the merciless summer boughs.

Sometime later, there was a footstep on the path and a knock on the door. It was Omar Howard, come to say good morning and to ask if I had found the Egyptian scarab ring of Carol's, which I had promised him. I had indeed, and, pressing it into his hand, received in return a volume I might find of interest—*Zen: The Answer?*

I sat paging through it for a few minutes after he had gone, sampling what would be perused at more leisure later. ". . . detached attachment . . . roll with nature . . . embrace her facts so as not to be crushed by them . . . swim with the . . ." And of course the Chinese original of that invisible wall-motto in the hospital corridor: "No fuss." On the jacket was a picture of the author, seen trimming a gardenia bush, his hobby. I boarded a train to California, in one or another of whose hanging gardens the wise man dwelt, and, bearding him there, asked whether there were any order of wisdom by which the sight of flowers being demolished could be readily borne. "Watch," I said, and tore from a branch the most perfect of his blossoms and mangled it into the dirt with my heel. Then I tore another, then another, watching studiously his expression as I ground the white blooms underfoot. . . .

These thoughts were cut short with the reminder that I must write a letter of recommendation for Omar to a prep school he was trying to get into, for which I had also promised to kick in a little tuition money, if memory served.

Time heals nothing—which should make us the better able to minister. There may be griefs beyond the reach of solace, but none worthy of the name that does not set free the springs of sympathy. Blessed are they that comfort, for they too have mourned, may be more likely the human truth. "You had a dozen years of perfection. That's a dozen more than most people get," a man had rather sharply told me one morning on the train. He was the father of one of Carol's classmates, a lumpish girl of no wiles and ways, whose Boston mother had long since begun to embalm her dreams in alcohol. I asked him to join me sometime in a few beers and a game or two at the bowling alleys, where one often saw him hanging about alone. He agreed. Once I ran into Carol's teacher, Miss Halsey. "Some poems are long, some are short. She was a short one," Miss Halsey had summed up, smiling, with the late-Gothic horse face which guarantees that she will never read any poems, long or short, to any children of her own. Again the throb of compassion rather than the breath of consolation: the recognition of how long, how long is the mourners' bench upon which we sit, arms linked in undeluded friendship, all of us, brief links, ourselves, in the eternal pity.

from THE ARLESIAN GIRL
ALPHONSE DAUDET

*This selection is part of a story by Alphonse Daudet, a French
novelist who was born in 1840 and died in 1897. There are
two "deaths" in this tale—the death of Jan's love for the
Arlesian girl and the resulting death of Jan himself—and
both provoke dramatic grief reactions. When Jan's relationship
with the Arlesian girl ends he suffers a loss as great as if the
girl had died. His grief goes unexpressed, however, and
ultimately leads him to suicide. His death, in turn, brings grief
to his mother, who in her hysteria tears off her clothes and
stands "naked in the courtyard near the stone table covered
with dew and blood."*

In order to reach the village by way of my mill, I must
pass a farmhouse built close to the road, in back of a
large courtyard planted with nettle trees. It is a typical
Provencal farmhouse with red tiles, a large brown facade
with irregular openings, and then, over a tall weathervane
on the hayloft, a pulley for raising the bales of hay and
some wisps of brown hay which have dropped out.

Why did this house attract me? Why did this closed
gate move me? I could not say, and yet the place somehow gave me the chills. There was an unearthly silence
about this home; when I was passing the dogs never
barked, the hens fled without a sound. Inside the house, not
a murmur! Nothing, not even the tinkling of a mule's bell.
Without the white curtains in the windows and the smoke
which rose above the roof, one would think the place un-
inhabited.

Yesterday at noon I was returning from the village,
and to keep out of the sun I passed beside the walls of
the farm in the shade of the nettle trees. On the road in
front of the house silent farmhands were loading a cart
with hay. The gate was ajar. While passing I glanced in
and I saw at the back of the courtyard, leaning his elbows on a large stone table, his head in his hands, a large
white-haired man wearing a short jacket and tattered
pants. I stopped. One of the men said to me quietly:

"*Chut!* That is the master. He has been like this since
the misfortune with his son."

At that moment a woman and a small boy dressed in black passed next to us with gilt-edged prayerbooks and entered the farmyard.

The man added: "The mistress and her little boy are returning from Mass. They have gone there every day since the boy was killed. Oh, sir, such sorrow! The father continues to wear the dead boy's clothes. No one can make him take them off. *Dia! hue!* Get along, girl!"

The cart started to leave. Wanting to learn more of the story, I asked one of the hands if I could ride beside him, and it was there, high up in the hay, I learned all of the tragic story.

He was called Jan. He was an admirable peasant of twenty years, quiet as a girl, solid and with an open face. Because he was very handsome, the girls all admired him, but he had only one on his mind—a little Arlesian girl—dressed all in velvet and lace, whom he had met only once at Lice d'Arles. At the house no one viewed this affair with pleasure at first. The girl was thought to be a coquette and her parents were not natives of the country. But Jan wanted his Arlesian girl in the face of all opposition. He said: "I will die if you do not give her to me."

They had no choice. They decided to let them marry after the harvest.

Then, one Sunday evening, in the courtyard of the house, the family was finishing its dinner. It was almost a wedding feast. The fiancée was not there, but everyone drank to her health all evening. Then, a man appeared at the door and asked in a trembling voice to speak to Mr. Esteve alone. Esteve rose and went out to the road.

"Sir," the man said to him. "You are going to allow your son to marry a hussy who has been my mistress for two years. What I am saying can be proved—here are letters! Her parents know everything and have promised her to me, but since your son has been pursuing her neither they nor the girl would have anything more to do with me. I would have believed, however, that after what has happened she would not become the wife of anyone else."

"So!" said Mr. Esteve, when he had looked at the letters. "Come in and have a glass of muscat."

The man replied, "Thank you, but I am too troubled to drink," and so he left.

The father went back into the house, his face expressionless; he took his seat again and the dinner ended gaily.

That evening Mr. Esteve and his son went out to the fields together. They remained outside for a long time. When they returned, the mother was waiting for them.

"Wife," said the husband, leading their son to her, "kiss him, he is unhappy."

Jan never spoke again of the Arlesian girl. He always loved her, however, and now more than ever since they had shown her to him in the arms of another. But he was too proud to say anything, and that's what killed the poor boy. Sometimes he spent whole days alone in a corner, without moving. During other days he threw himself on the land in a rage, and almost killed himself doing the work of ten men. When night fell, he would take the road to Arles and walk straight ahead until he saw the sun rising, framed by the slender steeples of that town. Then he would return. He never traveled the full distance.

To see him thus, always sad and alone, made his family feel helpless. They dreaded a calamity. One time at the table, his mother, watching him with eyes filled with tears, said to him, "All right, listen, Jan, if you want her still, we will give her to you."

The father, red with embarrassment, bowed his head.

Jan shook his head and went out.

From that day he changed his ways and seemed always to be gay in order to reassure his parents. People saw him at dances, at cabarets, and at the *ferrades*. At Fonteville it was he who led the *farandole*.

The father said, "He is cured." The mother, however, was still afraid and watched her son more than ever. Jan slept with his younger brother, and the poor old woman made herself a bed outside their door.

Then came the festival of St. Eloi, the patron saint of householders.

There was great happiness in the household. There was *chateauneuf* for everyone, and wine flowed like rain. Then there were firecrackers, fires on the threshing floor, lanterns of all colors in the trees. Vive St. Eloi! They danced the *farandole* to exhaustion. The little boy scorched his new shirt. Jan seemed to be happy; he wanted to dance with his mother; the poor woman was crying with joy.

At midnight they went to bed. Everyone needed sleep. Jan remained awake. His little brother later told them that he had sobbed all night. Ah, I tell you he was really bitten, that one.

The next day, at dawn, the mother heard someone running through her room. She had something like a premonition.

"Jan, is that you?"

Jan did not answer; he was already on the stairs.

Very quickly the mother got up.

He was climbing to the hayloft; she climbed after him.

"My son, in the name of heaven!"

He closed the door and drew the bolt.

"Jan, my little Jan, answer me! What are you doing?"

Groping, with trembling hands, she searched for the lock. Then a window opened. There was the sound of a body breaking on the tiles of the courtyard, and that was all.

He must have said to himself, the poor child: "I love her too much, I am going away." Oh, miserable souls that we are; it is strange, after all, that scorn cannot kill love.

That morning, the village people had asked each other who was crying down there at the Esteve house.

It was the mother, standing naked in the courtyard near the stone table covered with dew and blood, sobbing, with her dead son in her arms.

(Translated by Janet E. Levy)

FOR YOU
BRUCE SPRINGSTEEN

In these song lyrics by rock composer-performer Bruce Springsteen, the main character is overcome by grief which he expresses as pervasive anger at his girl friend who has committed suicide. Such an expression of remorse, frustration, and anger by a person who has lost a friend through suicide is a characteristic grief reaction. He has received more critical acclaim from the nation's rock-music critics than any other performer in recent memory.

Princess cards she sends me
    with her regards
barroom eyes shine vacancy, to

see her you gotta look hard
Wounded deep in battle, I
stand stuffed like some soldier
undaunted
To her Cheshire smile. I'll stand on
file, she's all I ever wanted.
But you let your blue walls get
in the way of these facts
honey, get your carpetbaggers
off my back
you wouldn't even give me time
to cover my tracks,
You said, "Here's your mirror
and your ball and jacks." But
they're not what I came for,
and I'm sure you see that too
I came for you, for you, I came
for you, but you did not need
my urgency
I came for you, for you, I came
for you, but your life was one
long emergency
and your cloud line urges me,
and my electric surges free.
Crawl into my ambulance, your
pulse is getting weak,
reveal yourself all now to me
girl while you've got the
strength to speak
Cause they're waiting for you at
Bellevue with their oxygen
masks
But I could give it all to you now if
only you could ask
And don't call for your surgeon
even he says it's too late
It's not your lungs this time, it's
your heart that holds your fate.
Don't give me back my money, honey,
I don't want it back
you and your pony face and
your union jack
well take your local joker and
teach him how to act

I swear I was never that way even
   when I really cracked
Didn't you think I knew that you
   were born with the power of
   a locomotive
able to leap tall buildings in a
   single bound?
And your Chelsea suicide with
   no apparent motive
you could laugh and cry in a
   single sound.
And your strength is devastating
   in the face of all these odds
Remember how I kept you
   waiting when it was my turn to
   be the god?
You were not quite half so
   proud when I found you
   broken on the beach
Remember how I poured salt
   on your tongue and hung just
   out of reach
And the band they played the
   homecoming theme as I
   caressed your cheek
That ragged, jagged melody she
   still clings to me like a leech.
But that medal you wore on your
   chest always got in the way
like a little girl with a trophy so
   soft to buy her way.
We were both hitchhikers but you
   had your ear tuned to the roar
of some metal tempered engine
   on an alien, distant shore
So you left to find a better
   reason than the one we were
   living for
and it's not that nursery mouth
   I came back for,
It's not the way you're stretched
   out on the floor
cause I've broken all your
   windows and I've jammed

through all your doors
And who am I to ask you to
    lick my sores?
And you should know
    that's true . . .
I came for you, for you, I came
    for you, but you did not need
    my urgency
I came for you, for you, I came
    for you, but your life was one
    long emergency
and your cloud line urges me,
    and my electric surges free.

ACCEPTING DEATH

BARBARA STANFORD WITH GENE STANFORD

One of the reassuring aspects of death and grief is that suffering continues only for those left behind. Some grieving people, such as the scholar in this Taoist parable retold by Barbara and Gene Stanford in Myths *and* Modern Man, *find solace in the realization that by taking on the burden of survivorship they have spared a loved one that unhappiness.*

There is a story of an old Taoist scholar who lost his dearly beloved wife. His friends and relatives came to mourn with him, but they found him sitting on the floor and beating a drum and singing.

"How can you do this?" his friends demanded. "After all of the years you spent with her, how can you be cheerful at her death?"

"I do love my wife," replied the Taoist. "And when she died I despaired because she was gone. But then I began to think and realized that this is what life is. After all, if I had died first, she would have had to remarry, perhaps someone she did not love, and our children would have been hungry and abused.

"Tears will not change the way life is. My wife is now at peace. If I were to make a lot of noise weeping and wailing, I would disturb her rest. It would show that I know nothing of the ways of life and death."

VI

"UNSPEAKABLE DARKNESS"

Suicide

We all feel depressed at points in our lives, often as the direct result of some loss or sad occurrence, and for most of us time is the medicine that heals and revitalizes our spirits. Some people, for a variety of reasons, are not so fortunate. Their depression deepens, becomes chronic and hopess. Often these people consider or even commit suicide. Successful suicide is most frequently committed by older isolated men. Although women are more likely to attempt suicide, they are far less often successful. Adolescence is another period of high risk, because it is a time of disruption and rapid change. People who attempt suicide usually have told someone else about their despair, either directly or symbolically. They are usually ambivalent about their desire to die; they both wish to live and wish to die at the same time. This is one of the reasons why many suicide attempts are not successful.

Nevertheless, all suicide attempts should be taken very seriously. Even halfhearted attempts at suicide are evidence of emotional problems, and people who make such attempts should be encouraged to seek professional counseling. A common misconception is that people who talk about suicide do not commit suicide. They most certainly can, and in fact the great majority of people who successfully commit suicide have talked about it with someone.

What are some of the things that motivate people to commit suicide? Deep depression, occasionally of an organic or physical nature, is certainly one motivation. Invariably a sense of helplessness fills the person with a feeling of being cornered and without resources to overcome problems and bad feelings. Quite frequently, the loss of a vital human link or relationship proves to be the trigger for suicide. Rage, usually at someone close to them, can also be the cause for a suicide attempt. In such cases the person feels a desire to "get even" and to "show them." Rage, while sometimes a major factor in suicidal behavior, is rarely the only factor. Some people feel suicide may be the only way to show the world how badly they are feeling and to get a response. Fantasies about the experience of being dead may also play a role. Someone convinced of eternal tranquility and freedom from care "on the farther shore" is more likely to choose suicide as an alternative to a frustrating life. States of psychosis or of confusion can sometimes lead to inadvertent suicide or can loosen the person's control over suicidal impulses that were previously held in check. The altered state induced by too much alcohol or other drugs quite commonly brings out suicidal behavior.

It is essential to note that suicidal wishes almost always go away if they are not acted upon successfully. Despite what suicidal persons say about the hopelessness of their futures, they are almost invariably pleased—when they have gained a better perspective on things—that they have been prevented from ending their lives.

"Suicide" does not need to be an external act. It can also be an internal decision, conscious or unconscious, to let some aspect of oneself die. Even the body itself will die when the mind gives up totally. This phenomenon occurred frequently in the concentration camps in World War II; it can happen in children and even in animals. It usually involves a deep sense of loss of faith, a sense of severed connections with other people in society, and a loss of will. In such cases, death can occur from no apparent physical cause at all. The persons simply "turn their face to the wall" and die.

In some other cultures suicide is regarded differently than in our own. In societies in which families are frequently close to starvation, older people will sometimes commit suicide so there will be enough food for the rest. Eskimos who become too old to be of use will sometimes voluntarily go out on an ice floe and "wait for the polar bear." Old people in Persia practice a similar withdrawal. Each year, at the time of the "crossing of the great river," they voluntarily stay behind on the other shore to die and allow the tribe to continue its wanderings to better pasture without being burdened by their helplessness. Among people who live closer to nature and feel that death is a natural part of life, a decision to die may not seem as radical as it does in our culture. A number of stories of the deaths of old American Indians show them recognizing that death was approaching and apparently choosing the time and place to die.

In some cultures, suicide is seen as the appropriate response to certain situations. In Japanese culture, suicide was considered a rational choice to be made when confronted by disgrace or any kind of intolerable situation. Suicide in support of one's country or beliefs is also endorsed in some cultures. During World War II, Japanese Kamikaze pilots flew suicide missions, and during the Vietnam war, Buddhists burned themselves to death to draw attention to their cause.

Yet most Americans do not consider suicide to be a rational choice. While people do sometimes find themselves in an emotional Alamo, it is important to remember that time will almost always bring some better alternative, that suicide is more tragic than glorious, and that, rather than solving the problem, suicide forever prevents a solution from being found.

RICHARD CORY
Edwin Arlington Robinson

This poem, written by Edwin Arlington Robinson (1896– 1935), one of America's best-known poets, makes clear that the pain a person experiences within is not always apparent from the face he or she prepares for the world. Suicide occurs, among people of all social, ethnic, political, and economic groups. Regarded as almost perfect, Richard Cory, with the ideal life, envied by all, is not immune to loneliness, depression, despair, or suicide.

Whenever Richard Cory went down town
    We people on the pavement looked at him:
He was a gentleman from sole to crown,
    Clean favored, and imperially slim.

And he was always quietly arrayed,
    And he was always human when he talked;
But still he fluttered pulses when he said,
    "Good-morning," and he glittered when he walked.

And he was rich—yes, richer than a king—
    And admirably schooled in every grace:

In fine, we thought that he was everything
    To make us wish that we were in his place.

So on we worked, and waited for the light,
    And went without the meat, and cursed the bread;
And Richard Cory, one calm summer night,
    Went home and put a bullet through his head.

from MADAME BOVARY
GUSTAVE FLAUBERT

*Perhaps the most graphic death scene in all of literature is
to be found in this excerpt from the famous nineteenth-century
French novel* Madame Bovary. *Emma (Madame Bovary)
poisons herself with arsenic and lies down quietly to die. At
first it seems that death will come peacefully, but soon the
poison causes agony and convulsions, which make the death
—witnessed by her husband, Charles, her child, and several
other persons—a horrible one indeed. (In Part V appears
another excerpt from this novel, which portrays Charles's grief
over Emma's death.) As in the case of Emma Bovary, suicide
is often attempted with the expectation of being quickly soothed
into a blissful and endless sleep. The realities, however, are more
often ugly, painful, nightmarish, and frightening for the
family, and the worst part, as Emma Bovary here discovers
to her horror, is that you may not be able to change your
mind and turn back.*

"The key! the one for upstairs where he keeps the—"
    "What?"
    And he looked at her, astonished at the pallor of her
face, that stood out white against the black background
of the night. She seemed to him extraordinarily beautiful and majestic as a phantom. Without understanding
what she wanted, he had the presentiment of something
terrible.
    But she went on quickly in a low voice, in a sweet,
melting voice, "I want it; give it to me."
    As the partition wall was thin, they could hear the clat-
ter of the forks on the plates in the dining-room.
    She pretended that she wanted to kill the rats that kept
her from sleeping.
    "I must tell master."

"No, stay!" Then with an indifferent air, "Oh, it's not worth while; I'll tell him presently. Come, light me up-stairs."

She entered the corridor into which the laboratory door opened. Against the wall was a key labelled *Caphar-naüm*.

"Justin!" called the druggist impatiently.

"Let us go up."

And he followed her. The key turned in the lock, and she went straight to the third shelf, so well did her mem-ory guide her, seized the blue jar, tore out the cork, plunged in her hand, and withdrawing it full of a white powder, she began eating it.

"Stop!" he cried, rushing at her.

"Hush! someone will come."

He was in despair, was calling out.

"Say nothing, or all the blame will fall on your master."

Then she went home, suddenly calmed, and with something of the serenity of one that had performed a duty.

When Charles, distracted by the news of the distraint, returned home, Emma had just gone out. He cried aloud, wept, fainted, but she did not return. Where could she be? He sent Félicité to Homais, to Monsieur Tuvache, to Lheureux, to the "Lion d'Or," everywhere, and in the intervals of his agony he saw his reputation destroyed, their fortune lost, Berthe's future ruined. By what?—Not a word! He waited till six in the evening. At last, unable to bear it any longer, and fancying she had gone to Rouen, he set out along the highroad, walked a mile, met no one, again waited, and returned home. She had come back.

"What was the matter? Why? Explain to me."

She sat down at her writing-table and wrote a letter, which she sealed slowly, adding the date and the hour. Then she said in a solemn tone:

"You are to read it to-morrow; till then, I pray you, do not ask me a single question. No, not one!"

"But—"

"Oh, leave me!"

She lay down full length on her bed. A bitter taste that she felt in her mouth awakened her. She saw Charles, and again closed her eyes.

She was studying herself curiously, to see if she were

not suffering. But no! nothing as yet. She heard the ticking of the clock, the crackling of the fire, and Charles breathing as he stood upright by her bed.

"Ah! it is but a little thing, death!" she thought. "I shall fall asleep and all will be over."

She drank a mouthful of water and turned to the wall. The frightful taste of ink continued.

"I am thirsty; oh! so thirsty," she sighed.

"What is it?" said Charles, who was handing her a glass.

"It is nothing! Open the window; I am choking."

She was seized with a sickness so sudden that she had hardly time to draw out her handkerchief from under the pillow.

"Take it away," she said quickly; "throw it away."

He spoke to her; she did not answer. She lay motionless, afraid that the slightest movement might make her vomit. But she felt an icy cold creeping from her feet to her heart.

"Ah! it is beginning," she murmured.

"What did you say?"

She turned her head from side to side with a gentle movement full of agony, while constantly opening her mouth as if something very heavy were weighing upon her tongue. At eight o'clock the vomiting began again.

Charles noticed that at the bottom of the basin there was a sort of white sediment sticking to the sides of the porcelain.

"This is extraordinary—very singular," he repeated.

But she said in a firm voice, "No, you are mistaken."

Then gently, and almost as caressing her, he passed his hand over her stomach. She uttered a sharp cry. He fell back terror-stricken.

Then she began to groan, faintly at first. Her shoulders were shaken by a strong shuddering, and she was growing paler than the sheets in which her clenched fingers buried themselves. Her unequal pulse was now almost imperceptible.

Drops of sweat oozed from her bluish face, that seemed as if rigid in the exhalations of a metallic vapour. Her teeth chattered, her dilated eyes looked vaguely about her, and to all questions she replied only with a shake of the head; she even smiled once or twice. Gradually, her moaning grew louder; a hollow shriek burst from her; she pretended she was better and that she would get up presently. But she was seized with convulsions and cried out—

"Ah! my God! It is horrible!"

He threw himself on his knees by her bed.

"Tell me! what have you eaten? Answer, for heaven's sake!"

And he looked at her with a tenderness in his eyes such as she had never seen.

"Well, there—there!" she said in a faint voice. He flew to the writing-table, tore open the seal, and read aloud: "Accuse no one." He stopped, passed his hands across his eyes, and read it over again.

"What! help—help!"

He could only keep repeating the word: "Poisoned! poisoned!" Félicité ran to Homais, who proclaimed it in the market-place; Madame Lefrançois heard it at the "Lion d'Or"; some got up to go and tell their neighbours, and all night the village was on the alert.

Distraught, faltering, reeling, Charles wandered about the room. He knocked against the furniture, tore his hair, and the chemist had never believed that there could be so terrible a sight.

He went home to write to Monsieur Canivet and to Doctor Larivière. He lost his head, and made more than fifteen rough copies. Hippolyte went to Neufchâtel, and Justin so spurred Bovary's horse that he left it foundered and three parts dead by the hill at Bois-Guillaume.

Charles tried to look up his medical dictionary, but could not read it; the lines were dancing.

"Be calm," said the druggist; "we have only to administer a powerful antidote. What is the poison?"

Charles showed him the letter. It was arsenic.

"Very well," said Homais, "we must make an analysis."

For he knew that in cases of poisoning an analysis must be made; and the other, who did not understand, answered—

"Oh, do anything! save her!"

Then going back to her, he sank upon the carpet, and lay there with his head leaning against the edge of her bed, sobbing.

"Don't cry," she said to him. "Soon I shall not trouble you any more."

"Why was it? Who drove you to it?"

She replied. "It had to be, my dear!"

"Weren't you happy? Is it my fault? I did all I could!"

"Yes, that is true—you are good—you."

And she passed her hand slowly over his hair. The sweetness of this sensation deepened his sadness; he felt his whole being dissolving in despair at the thought that he must lose her, just when she was confessing more love for him than ever. And he could think of nothing; he did not know, he did not dare; the urgent need for some immediate resolution gave the finishing stroke to the turmoil of his mind.

So she had done, she thought, with all the treachery, and meanness, and numberless desires that had tortured her. She hated no one now; a twilight dimness was settling upon her thoughts, and, of all earthly noises, Emma heard none but the intermittent lamentations of this poor heart, sweet and indistinct like the echo of a symphony dying away.

"Bring me the child," she said, raising herself on her elbow.

"You are not worse, are you?" asked Charles.

"No, no!"

The child, serious, and still half-asleep, was carried in on the servant's arm in her long white nightgown, from which her bare feet peeped out. She looked wonderingly at the disordered room, and half-closed her eyes, dazzled by the candles burning on the table. They reminded her, no doubt, of the morning of New Year's day and Mid-Lent, when thus awakened early by candle-light she came to her mother's bed to fetch her presents, for she began saying—

"But where is it, mamma?" And as everybody was silent, "But I can't see my little stocking."

Félicité held her over the bed while she still kept looking towards the mantelpiece.

"Has nurse taken it?" she asked.

And at this name, that carried her back to the memory of her adulteries and her calamities, Madame Bovary turned away her head, as at the loathing of another bitter poison that rose to her mouth. But Berthe remained perched on the bed.

"Oh, how big your eyes are, mamma! How pale you are! how hot you are!"

Her mother looked at her. "I am frightened!" cried the child, recoiling.

Emma took her hand to kiss it; the child struggled.

"That will do. Take her away," cried Charles, who was sobbing in the alcove.

Then the symptoms ceased for a moment; she seemed less agitated; and at every insignificant word, at every respiration a little more easy, he regained hope. At last, when Canivet came in, he threw himself into his arms.

"Ah! it is you. Thanks! You are good! But she is better. See! look at her."

His colleague was by no means of this opinion, and, as he said of himself, "never beating about the bush," he prescribed an emetic in order to empty the stomach completely.

She soon began vomiting blood. Her lips became drawn. Her limbs were convulsed, her whole body covered with brown spots, and her pulse slipped beneath the fingers like a stretched thread, like a harp-string nearly breaking.

After this she began to scream horribly. She cursed the poison, railed at it, and implored it to be quick, and thrust away with her stiffened arms everything that Charles, in more agony than herself, tried to make her drink. He stood up, his handkerchief to his lips, with a rattling sound in his throat, weeping, and choked by sobs that shook his whole body. Félicité was running hither and thither in the room. Homais, motionless, uttered great sighs; and Monsieur Canivet, always retaining his self-command, nevertheless began to feel uneasy.

"The devil! yet she has been purged, and from the moment that the cause ceases—"

"The effect must cease," said Homais, "that is evident."

"Oh, save her!" cried Bovary.

And, without listening to the chemist, who was still venturing the hypothesis, "It is perhaps a salutary paroxysm," Canivet was about to administer some theriac, when they heard the cracking of a whip; all the windows rattled, and a post-chaise drawn by three horses abreast, up to their ears in mud, drove at a gallop round the corner of the market. It was Doctor Larivière.

The apparition of a god would not have caused more commotion. Bovary raised his hands; Canivet stopped short; and Homais pulled off his skull-cap long before the doctor had come in.

He belonged to that great school of surgery begotten of Bichat, to that generation, now extinct, of philosophical practitioners, who, loving their art with a fanatical love, exercised it with enthusiasm and wisdom. Everyone in his hospital trembled when he was angry; and his students so revered him that they tried, as soon as they were themselves in practice, to imitate him as much as possible. So that in all the towns about they were found wearing his long wadded merino overcoat and black frock-coat, whose buttoned cuffs slightly covered his brawny hands—very beautiful hands, and that never knew gloves, as though to be more ready to plunge into suffering. Disdainful of honours, of titles, and of academies, like one of the old Knight-Hospitallers, generous, fatherly to the poor, and practising virtue without believing in it, he would almost have passed for a saint if the keenness of his intellect had not caused him to be feared as a demon. His glance, more penetrating than his bistouries, looked straight into your soul, and dissected every lie athwart all assertions and all reticences. And thus he went along, full of that debonair majesty that is given by the consciousness of great talent, of fortune, and of forty years of a labourious and irreproachable life.

He frowned as soon as he had passed the door when he saw the cadaverous face of Emma stretched out on her back with her mouth open. Then, while apparently listening to Canivet, he rubbed his fingers up and down beneath his nostrils, and repeated—

"Good! good!"

But he made a slow gesture with his shoulders. Bovary watched him; they looked at one another; and this man, accustomed as he was to the sight of pain, could not keep back a tear that fell on his shirt-frill.

He tried to take Canivet into the next room. Charles followed him.

"She is very ill, isn't she? If we put on sinapisms? Anything! Oh, think of something, you who have saved so many!"

Charles caught him in both his arms, and gazed at him wildly, imploringly, half-fainting against his breast.

"Come, my poor fellow, courage! There is nothing more to be done."

And Doctor Larivière turned away.

"You are going?"

"I will come back."

He went out only to give an order to the coachman,

with Monsieur Canivet, who did not care either to have Emma die under his hands.

The chemist rejoined them on the Place. He could not by temperament keep away from celebrities, so he begged Monsieur Larivière to do him the signal honour of accepting some breakfast.

He sent quickly to the "Lion d'Or" for some pigeons; to the butcher's for all the cutlets that were to be had; to Tuvache for cream; and to Lestiboudois for eggs; and the druggist himself aided in the preparation, while Madame Homais was saying as she pulled together the strings of her jacket—

"You must excuse us, sir, for in this poor place, when one hasn't been told the night before—"

"Wine glasses!" whispered Homais.

"If only we were in town, we could fall back upon stuffed trotters."

"Be quiet! Sit down, doctor!"

He thought fit, after the first few mouthfuls, to give some details as to the catastrophe.

"We first had a feeling of siccity in the pharynx, then intolerable pains at the epigastrium, super-purgation, coma."

"But how did she poison herself?"

"I don't know, doctor, and I don't even know where she can have procured the arsenious acid."

Justin, who was just bringing in a pile of plates, began to tremble.

"What's the matter?" said the chemist.

At this question the young man dropped the whole lot on the ground with a crash.

"Imbecile!" cried Homais, "awkward lout! block-head! confounded ass!"

But suddenly controlling himself—

"I wished, doctor, to make an analysis, and *primo* I delicately introduced a tube—"

"You would have done better," said the physician, "to introduce your fingers into her throat."

His colleague was silent, having just before privately received a severe lecture about his emetic, so that this good Canivet, so arrogant and so verbose at the time of the clubfoot, was to-day very modest. He smiled without ceasing in an approving manner.

Homais dilated in Amphytrionic pride, and the affect-

ing thought of Bovary vaguely contributed to his pleasure
by a kind of egotistic reflex upon himself. Then the presence of the doctor transported him. He displayed his eru-
dition, cited pell-mell cantharides, upas, the manchineel,
vipers.

"I have even read that various persons have found
themselves under toxicological symptoms, and, as it were,
thunderstricken by black-pudding that had been subjected
to a too vehement fumigation. At least, this was stated
in a very fine report drawn up by one of our pharmaceuti-
cal chiefs, one of our masters, the illustrious Cadet de
Gassicourt!"

Madame Homais reappeared, carrying one of those
shaky machines that are heated with spirits of wine; for
Homais liked to make his coffee at table, having, moreover, torrefied it, pulverised it, and mixed it himself.

"*Saccharum,* doctor?" said he, offering the sugar.

Then he had all his children brought down, anxious to
have the physician's opinion on their constitutions.

At last Monsieur Larivière was about to leave, when
Madame Homais asked for a consultation about her husband. He was making his blood too thick by going to
sleep every evening after dinner.

"Oh, it isn't his blood that's too thick," said the physician.

And, smiling a little at his unnoticed joke, the doctor
opened the door. But the chemist's shop was full of people; he had the greatest difficulty in getting rid of Monsieur
Tuvache, who feared his spouse would get inflammation
of the lungs, because she was in the habit of spitting on
the ashes; then of Monsieur Binet, who sometimes experienced sudden attacks of great hunger; and of Madame
Caron, who suffered from tinglings; of Lheureux, who had
vertigo; of Lestiboudois, who had rheumatism; and of
Madame Lefrançois, who had heartburn. At last the
three horses started; and it was the general opinion that
he had not shown himself at all obliging.

Public attention was distracted by the appearance of
Monsieur Bournisien, who was going across the market
with the holy oil.

Homais, as was due to his principles, compared priests
to ravens attracted by the odour of death. The sight of an
ecclesiastic was personally disagreeable to him, for the

cassock made him think of the shroud, and he detested the one from some fear of the other.

Nevertheless, not shrinking from what he called his mission, he returned to Bovary's in company with Canivet whom Monsieur Larivière, before leaving, had strongly urged to make this visit; and he would, but for his wife's objections, have taken his two sons with him, in order to accustom them to great occasions; that this might be a lesson, an example, a solemn picture, that should remain in their heads later on.

The room when they went in was full of mournful solemnity. On the work-table, covered over with a white cloth, there were five or six small balls of cotton in a silver dish, near a large crucifix between two lighted candles.

Emma, her chin sunken upon her breast, had her eyes inordinately wide open, and her poor hands wandered over the sheets with that hideous and soft movement of the dying, that seems as if they wanted already to cover themselves with the shroud. Pale as a statue and with eyes red as fire, Charles, not weeping, stood opposite her at the foot of the bed, while the priest, bending one knee, was muttering words in a low voice.

She turned her face slowly, and seemed filled with joy on seeing suddenly the violet stole, no doubt finding again, in the midst of a temporary lull in her pain, the lost voluptuousness of her first mystical transports, with the visions of eternal beatitude that were beginning.

The priest rose to take the crucifix; then she stretched forward her neck as one who is athirst, and glueing her lips to the body of the Man-God, she pressed upon it with all her expiring strength the fullest kiss of love that she had ever given. Then he recited the *Misereatur* and the *Indulgentiam*, dipped his right thumb in the oil, and began to give extreme unction. First, upon the eyes, that had so coveted all worldly pomp; then upon the nostrils, that had been greedy of the warm breeze and amorous odours; then upon the mouth, that had uttered lies, that had curled with pride and cried out in lewdness; then upon the hands that had delighted in sensual touches; and finally upon the soles of the feet, so swift of yore, when she was running to satisfy her desires, and that would now walk no more.

The curé wiped his fingers, threw the bit of cotton dipped in oil into the fire, and came and sat down by the dying woman, to tell her that she must now blend her sufferings with those of Jesus Christ and abandon herself to the divine mercy.

Finishing his exhortations, he tried to place in her hand a blessed candle, symbol of the celestial glory with which she was soon to be surrounded. Emma, too weak, could not close her fingers, and the taper, but for Monsieur Bournisien would have fallen to the ground.

However, she was not quite so pale, and her face had an expression of serenity as if the sacrament had cured her.

The priest did not fail to point this out; he even explained to Bovary that the Lord sometimes prolonged the life of persons when he thought it meet for their salvation; and Charles remembered the day when, so near death, she had received the communion. Perhaps there was no need to despair, he thought.

In fact, she looked around her slowly, as one awakening from a dream; then in a distinct voice she asked for her looking-glass, and remained some time bending over it, until the big tears fell from her eyes. Then she turned away her head with a sigh and fell back upon the pillows.

Her chest soon began panting rapidly; the whole of her tongue protruded from her mouth; her eyes, as they rolled, grew paler, like the two globes of a lamp that is going out, so that one might have thought her already dead but for the fearful labouring of her ribs, shaken by violent breathing, as if the soul were struggling to free itself. Félicité knelt down before the crucifix, and the druggist himself slightly bent his knees, while Monsieur Canivet looked out vaguely at the Place. Bournisien had again begun to pray, his face bowed against the edge of the bed, his long black cassock trailing behind him in the room. Charles was on the other side, on his knees, his arms outstretched towards Emma. He had taken her hands and pressed them, shuddering at every beat of her heart, as at the shaking of a falling ruin. As the death-rattle became stronger the priest prayed faster; his prayers mingled with the stifled sobs of Bovary, and sometimes all seemed lost in the muffled murmur of the Latin syllables that tolled like a passing bell.

Suddenly on the pavement was heard a loud noise of

clogs and the clattering of a stick; and a voice rose—a raucous voice—that sang—

"Maids in the warmth of a summer day
Dream of love and of love alway."

Emma raised herself like a galvanised corpse, her hair undone, her eyes fixed, staring.

"Where the sickle blades have been,
Nannette, gathering ears of corn,
Passes bending down, my queen,
To the earth where they were born."

"The blind man!" she cried. And Emma began to laugh, an atrocious, frantic, despairing laugh, thinking she saw the hideous face of the poor wretch that stood out against the eternal night like a menace.

"The wind is strong this summer day,
Her petticoat has flown away."

She fell back upon the mattress in a convulsion. They all drew near. She was dead.

(Translated by Eleanor Marx-Aveling)

A SUMMER TRAGEDY
ARNA BONTEMPS

The title states that this short story involves a tragedy. But is the suicide the tragedy, or does the tragedy lie in the fact that suicide is necessary for this old couple to free themselves of the loneliness, despair, and uselessness of aging? Even if we believe that suicide is never a rational solution, the harsh realities depicted in this story help us feel sympathy for Jeff and Jennie's decision. The author, Arna Bontemps, is one of the most respected of America's black writers. Born in Louisiana in 1902, he moved to Harlem and wrote in the midst of the "Harlem Renaissance"; more recently, he was librarian at Fisk University.

Old Jeff Patton, the black share farmer, fumbled with his

bow tie. His fingers trembled and the high stiff collar pinched his throat. A fellow loses his hand for such vanities after thirty or forty years of simple life. Once a year, or maybe twice if there's a wedding among his kinfolks, he may spruce up; but generally fancy clothes do nothing but adorn the wall of the big room and feed the moths. That had been Jeff Patton's experience. He had not worn his stiff-bosomed shirt more than a dozen times in all his married life. His swallow-tailed coat lay on the bed beside him, freshly brushed and pressed, but it was as full of holes as the overalls in which he worked on weekdays. The moths had used it badly. Jeff twisted his mouth into a hideous toothless grimace as he contended with the obstinate bow. He stamped his good foot and decided to give up the struggle.

"Jennie," he called.

"What's that, Jeff?" His wife's shrunken voice came out of the adjoining room like an echo. It was hardly bigger than a whisper.

"I reckon you'll have to he'p me wid this heah bow tie, baby," he said meekly. "Dog if I can hitch it up."

Her answer was not strong enough to reach him, but presently the old woman came to the door, feeling her way with a stick. She had a wasted, dead-leaf appearance. Her body, as scrawny and gnarled as a string bean, seemed less than nothing in the ocean of frayed and faded petticoats that surrounded her. These hung an inch or two above the tops of her heavy unlaced shoes and showed little grotesque piles where the stockings had fallen down from her negligible legs.

"You oughta could do a heap mo' wid a thing like that'n me—beingst as you got yo' good sight."

"Looks like I oughta could," he admitted. "But ma fingers is gone democrat on me. I get all mixed up in the looking glass an' can't tell wicha way to twist the devilish thing."

Jennie sat on the side of the bed and old Jeff Patton got down on one knee while she tied the bow knot. It was a slow and painful ordeal for each of them in this position. Jeff's bones cracked, his knee ached, and it was only after a half dozen attempts that Jennie worked a semblance of a bow into the tie.

"I got to dress maself now," the old woman whispered.

"These is ma old shoes an' stockings, and I ain't so much as unwrapped ma dress."

"Well, don't worry 'bout me no mo', baby," Jeff said. "That 'bout finishes me. All I gotta do now is slip on that old coat 'n ves' an' I'll be fixed to leave."

Jennie disappeared again through the dim passage into the shed room. Being blind was no handicap to her in that black hole. Jeff heard the cane placed against the wall beside the door and knew that his wife was on easy ground. He put on his coat, took a battered top hat from the bedpost and hobbled to the front door. He was ready to travel. As soon as Jennie could get on her Sunday shoes and her old black silk dress, they would start.

Outside the tiny log house, the day was warm and mellow with sunshine. A host of wasps were humming with busy excitement in the trunk of a dead sycamore. Gray squirrels were searching through the grass for hickory nuts and blue jays were in the trees, hopping from branch to branch. Pine woods stretched away to the left like a black sea. Among them were scattered scores of log houses like Jeff's, houses of black share farmers. Cows and pigs wandered freely among the trees. There was no danger of loss. Each farmer knew his own stock and knew his neighbor's as well as he knew his neighbor's children.

Down the slope to the right were the cultivated acres on which the colored folks worked. They extended to the river, more than two miles away, and they were today green with the unmade cotton crop. A tiny thread of a road, which passed directly in front of Jeff's place, ran through these green fields like a pencil mark.

Jeff, standing outside the door, with his absurd hat in his left hand, surveyed the wide scene tenderly. He had been forty-five years on these acres. He loved them with the unexplained affection that others have for the countries to which they belong.

The sun was hot on his head, his collar still pinched his throat, and the Sunday clothes were intolerably hot. Jeff transferred the hat to his right hand and began fanning with it. Suddenly the whisper that was Jennie's voice came out of the shed room.

"You can bring the car round front whilst you's waitin'," it said feebly. There was a tired pause; then it added, "I'll soon be fixed to go."

"A'right, baby," Jeff answered. "I'll get it in a minute."

But he didn't move. A thought struck him that made his mouth fall open. The mention of the car brought to his mind, with new intensity, the trip he and Jennie were about to take. Fear came into his eyes; excitement took his breath. Lord, Jesus!

"Jeff . . . O Jeff," the old woman's whisper called.

He awakened with a jolt. "Hunh, baby?"

"What you doin'?"

"Nuthin. Jes studyin'. I jes been turnin' things round'n round in ma mind."

"You could be gettin' the car," she said.

"Oh yes, right away, baby."

He started round to the shed, limping heavily on his bad leg. There were three frizzly chickens in the yard. All his other chickens had been killed or stolen recently. But the frizzly chickens had been saved somehow. That was fortunate indeed, for these curious creatures had a way of devouring "Poison" from the yard and in that way protecting against conjure and black luck and spells. But even the frizzly chickens seemed now to be in a stupor. Jeff thought they had some ailment; he expected all three of them to die shortly.

The shed in which the old T-model Ford stood was only a grass roof held up by four corner poles. It had been built by tremulous hands at a time when the little rattle-trap car had been regarded as a peculiar treasure. And, miraculously, despite wind and downpour it still stood.

Jeff adjusted the crank and put his weight upon it. The engine came to life with a sputter and bang that rattled the old car from radiator to taillight. Jeff hopped into the seat and put his foot on the accelerator. The sputtering and banging increased. The rattling became more violent. That was good. It was good banging, good sputtering and rattling, and it meant that the aged car was still in running condition. She could be depended on for this trip.

Again Jeff's thought halted as if paralyzed. The suggestion of the trip fell into the machinery of his mind like a wrench. He felt dazed and weak. He swung the car out into the yard, made a half turn and drove around to the front door. When he took his hands off the wheel, he noticed that he was trembling violently. He cut off the motor and climbed to the ground to wait for Jennie.

A few minutes later she was at the window, her voice rattling against the pane like a broken shutter.

"I'm ready, Jeff."

He did not answer, but limped into the house and took her by the arm. He led her slowly through the big room, down the step and across the yard.

"You reckon I'd oughta lock the do'?" he asked softly.

They stopped and Jennie weighed the question. Finally she shook her head.

"Ne' mind the do'," she said. "I don't see no cause to lock up things."

"You right," Jeff agreed. "No cause to lock up."

Jeff opened the door and helped his wife into the car. A quick shudder passed over him. Jesus! Again he trembled.

"How come you shaking so?" Jennie whispered.

"I don't know," he said.

"You mus' be scairt, Jeff."

"No, baby, I ain't scairt."

He slammed the door after her and went around to crank up again. The motor started easily. Jeff wished that it had not been so responsive. He would have liked a few more minutes in which to turn things around in his head. As it was, with Jennie chiding him about being afraid, he had to keep going. He swung the car into the little pencil-mark road and started off toward the river, driving very slowly, very cautiously.

Chugging across the green countryside, the small battered Ford seemed tiny indeed. Jeff felt a familiar excitement, a thrill, as they came down the first slope to the immense levels on which the cotton was growing. He could not help reflecting that the crops were good. He knew what that meant, too; he had made forty-five of them with his own hands. It was true that he had worn out nearly a dozen mules, but that was the fault of old man Stevenson, the owner of the land. Major Stevenson had the odd notion that one mule was all a share farmer needed to work a thirty-acre plot. It was an expensive notion, the way it killed mules from overwork, but the old man held to it. Jeff thought it killed a good many share farmers as well as mules, but he had no sympathy for them. He had always been strong, and he had been taught to have no patience with weakness in men. Women or children might be tolerated if they were puny, but a weak man was a curse. Of course, his own children—

Jeff's thought halted there. He and Jennie never men-

tioned their dead children any more. And naturally he did
not wish to dwell upon them in his mind. Before he knew
it, some remark would slip out of his mouth and that
would make Jennie feel blue. Perhaps she would cry. A
woman like Jennie could not easily throw off the grief that
comes from losing five grown children within two years.
Even Jeff was still staggered by the blow. His memory had
not been much good recently. He frequently talked to
himself. And, although he had kept it a secret, he knew
that his courage had left him. He was terrified by the least
unfamiliar sound at night. He was reluctant to venture
far from home in the daytime. And that habit of trembling when he felt fearful was now far beyond his control.
Sometimes he became afraid and trembled without knowing what had frightened him. The feeling would just come
over him like a chill.

The car rattled slowly over the dusty road. Jennie sat
erect and silent, with a little absurd hat pinned to her hair.
Her useless eyes seemed very large, very white in their
deep sockets. Suddenly Jeff heard her voice, and he inclined his head to catch the words.

"Is we passed Delia Moore's house yet?" she asked.

"Not yet," he said.

"You must be drivin' mighty slow, Jeff."

"We might just as well take our time, baby."

There was a pause. A little puff of steam was coming
out of the radiator of the car. Heat wavered above the
hood. Delia Moore's house was nearly half a mile away.
After a moment Jennie spoke again.

"You ain't really scairt, is you, Jeff?"

"Nah, baby, I ain't scairt."

"You know how we agreed—we gotta keep on goin'."

Jewels of perspiration appeared on Jeff's forehead. His
eyes rounded, blinked, became fixed on the road.

"I don't know," he said with a shiver. "I reckon it's the
only thing to do."

"Hm."

A flock of guinea fowls, pecking in the road, were
scattered by the passing car. Some of them took to their
wings; others hid under bushes. A blue jay, swaying on
a leafy twig, was annoying a roadside squirrel. Jeff held
an even speed till he came near Delia's place. Then he
slowed down noticeably.

Delia's house was really no house at all, but an aban-

doned store building converted into a dwelling. It sat near
a crossroads, beneath a single black cedar tree. There
Delia, a cattish old creature of Jennie's age, lived alone.
She had been there more years than anybody could remember, and long ago had won the disfavor of such
women as Jennie. For in her young days Delia had been
gayer, yellower and saucier than seemed proper in those
parts. Her ways with menfolks had been dark and sus-
picious. And the fact that she had had as many husbands
as children did not help her reputation.

"Yonder's old Delia," Jeff said as they passed.

"What she doin'?"

"Jes sittin' in the do'," he said.

"She see us?"

"Hm," Jeff said. "Musta did."

That relieved Jennie. It strengthened her to know that
her old enemy had seen her pass in her best clothes. That
would give the old she-devil something to chew her gums
and fret about, Jennie thought. Wouldn't she have a fit if
she didn't find out? Old evil Delia! This would be just
the thing for her. It would pay her back for being so evil.
It would also pay her, Jennie thought, for the way she
used to grin at Jeff—long ago when her teeth were good.

The road became smooth and red, and Jeff could tell by
the smell of the air that they were nearing the river. He
could see the rise where the road turned and ran along
parallel to the stream. The car chugged on monotonously.
After a long silent spell, Jennie leaned against Jeff and
spoke.

"How many bale o' cotton you think we got standin'?"
she said.

Jeff wrinkled his forehead as he calculated.

" 'Bout twenty-five, I reckon."

"How many you make las' year?"

"Twenty-eight," he said. "How come you ask that?"

"I's jes thinkin'," Jennie said quietly.

"It don't make a speck o' difference though," Jeff reflected. "If we get much or if we get little, we still gonna
be in debt to old man Stevenson when he gets through
counting up agin us. It's took us a long time to learn that."

Jennie was not listening to these words. She had fallen
into a trance-like meditation. Her lips twitched. She
chewed her gums and rubbed her gnarled hands ner-
vously. Suddenly she leaned forward, buried her face in the

nervous hands and burst into tears. She cried aloud in a
dry cracked voice that suggested the rattle of fodder on
dead stalks. She cried aloud like a child, for she had
never learned to suppress a genuine sob. Her slight old
frame shook heavily and seemed hardly able to sustain
such violent grief.

"What's the matter, baby?" Jeff asked awkwardly. "Why
you cryin' like all that?"

"I's jes thinkin'," she said.

"So you the one what's scairt now, hunh?"

"I ain't scairt, Jeff. I's jes thinkin' 'bout leavin' eve'-
thing like this—eve'thing we been used to. It's right sad-
like."

Jeff did not answer, and presently Jennie buried her
face again and cried.

The sun was almost overhead. It beat down furiously
on the dusty wagon-path road, on the parched roadside
grass and the tiny battered car. Jeff's hands, gripping the
wheel, became wet with perspiration; his forehead sparkled. Jeff's lips parted. His mouth shaped a hideous grimace. His face suggested the face of a man being burned.
But the torture passed and his expression softened again.

"You mustn't cry, baby," he said to his wife. "We gotta
be strong. We can't break down."

Jennie waited a few seconds, then said, "You reckon we
oughta do it, Jeff? You reckon we oughta go 'head an' do
it, really?"

Jeff's voice choked; his eyes blurred. He was terrified to
hear Jennie say the thing that had been in his mind all
morning. She had egged him on when he had wanted more
than anything in the world to wait, to reconsider, to
think things over a little longer. Now she was getting cold
feet. Actually there was no need of thinking the question
through again. It would only end in making the same painful decision once more. Jeff knew that. There was no
need of fooling around longer.

"We jes as well to do like we planned," he said. "They
ain't nothin' else for us now—it's the bes' thing."

Jeff thought of the handicaps, the near impossibility, of
making another crop with his leg bothering him more and
more each week. Then there was always the chance that
he would have another stroke, like the one that had
made him lame. Another one might kill him. The least it
could do would be to leave him helpless. Jeff gasped—

Lord, Jesus! He could not bear to think of being helpless, like a baby, on Jennie's hands. Frail, blind Jennie.

The little pounding motor of the car worked harder and harder. The puff of steam from the cracked radiator became larger. Jeff realized that they were climbing a little rise. A moment later the road turned abruptly and he looked down upon the face of the river.

"Jeff."

"Hunh?"

"Is that the water I hear?"

"Hm. Tha's it."

"Well, which way you goin' now?"

"Down this-a way," he said. "The road runs 'long 'side o' the water a lil piece."

She waited a while calmly. Then she said, "Drive faster."

"A'right, baby," Jeff said.

The water roared in the bed of the river. It was fifty or sixty feet below the level of the road. Between the road and the water there was a long smooth slope, sharply inclined. The slope was dry, the clay hardened by prolonged summer heat. The water below, roaring in a narrow channel, was noisy and wild.

"Jeff."

"Hunh?"

"How far you goin'?"

"Jes a lil piece down the road."

"You ain't scairt, is you, Jeff?"

"Nah, baby," he said trembling. "I ain't scairt."

"Remember how we planned it, Jeff. We gotta do it like we said. Brave-like."

"Hm."

Jeff's brain darkened. Things suddenly seemed unreal, like figures in a dream. Thoughts swam in his mind foolishly, hysterically, like little blind fish in a pool within a dense cave. They rushed, crossed one another, jostled, collided, retreated and rushed again. Jeff soon became dizzy. He shuddered violently and turned to his wife.

"Jennie, I can't do it. I can't." His voice broke pitifully.

She did not appear to be listening. All the grief had gone from her face. She sat erect, her unseeing eyes wide open, strained and frightful. Her glossy black skin had become dull. She seemed as thin, as sharp and bony, as a starved bird. Now, having suffered and endured the sadness of tearing herself away from beloved things, she showed no anguish. She was absorbed with her own thoughts, and she didn't even hear Jeff's voice shouting in her ear.

Jeff said nothing more. For an instant there was light in his cavernous brain. The great chamber was, for less than a second, peopled by characters he knew and loved. They were simple, healthy creatures, and they behaved in a manner that he could understand. They had quality. But since he had already taken leave of them long ago, the remembrance did not break his heart again. Young Jeff Patton was among them, the Jeff Patton of fifty years ago who went down to New Orleans with a crowd of country boys to the Mardi Gras doings. The gay young crowd, boys with candy-striped shirts and rouged-brown girls in noisy silks, was like a picture in his head. Yet it did not make him sad. On that very trip Slim Burns had killed Joe Beasley—the crowd had been broken up. Since then Jeff Patton's world had been the Greenbriar Plantation. If there had been other Mardi Gras carnivals, he had not heard of them. Since then there had been no time; the years had fallen on him like waves. Now he was old, worn out. Another paralytic stroke (like the one he had already suffered) would put him on his back for keeps. In that condition, with a frail blind woman to look after him, he would be worse off than if he were dead.

Suddenly Jeff's hands became steady. He actually felt brave. He slowed down the motor of the car and carefully pulled off the road. Below, the water of the stream boomed, a soft thunder in the deep channel. Jeff ran the car onto the clay slope, pointed it directly toward the stream and put his foot heavily on the accelerator. The little car leaped furiously down the steep incline toward the water. The movement was nearly as swift and direct as a fall. The two old black folks, sitting quietly side by side, showed no excitement. In another instant the car hit the water and dropped immediately out of sight.

A little later it lodged in the mud of a shallow place. One wheel of the crushed and upturned little Ford became visible above the rushing water.

from THE HEART
IS A LONELY HUNTER
Carson McCullers

Suicide, as we can see in this excerpt from one of the best-known works of twentieth-century American novelist Carson McCullers, is often a reaction to a loss of immense significance, usually the severance of a deep human relationship. Singer, the chief character in the novel, can neither hear nor speak. His closest friend is an awkward, goodhearted man named Antonapoulos, who lives in a home for the retarded a considerable distance away. They have known each other for many years. Antonapoulos offers Singer genuine companionship in a world where people's reactions to his handicap frustrate his attempts to communicate with them. When Antonapoulos dies, it is a devastating blow. Singer's only significant link with life has been severed, and there is no one with whom he can share his grief. Inability to make human contact and share feelings of despair for whatever reason is a factor in' many suicide attempts. Carson McCullers, who lived from 1917 to 1967, is also well known as the author of Member of the Wedding, Clock without Hands, *and several plays and poems for children.*

The time had come for Singer to go to Antonapoulos again. The journey was a long one. For, although the distance between them was something less than two hundred miles, the train meandered to points far out of the way and stopped for long hours at certain stations during the night. Singer would leave the town in the afternoon and travel all through the night and until the early morning of the next day. As usual, he was ready far in advance. He planned to have a full week with his friend this visit. His clothes had been sent to the cleaner's, his hat blocked, and his bags were in readiness. The gifts he would carry were wrapped in colored tissue paper—and in addition there was a deluxe basket of fruits done up in cellophane and a crate of late-shipped strawberries. On the morning before his departure Singer cleaned his room. In his ice box he found a bit of left-over goose liver and took it out to the alley for the neighborhood cat. On his door he

231

tacked the same sign he had posted there before, stating
that he would be absent for several days on business.
During all these preparations he moved about leisurely
with two vivid spots of color on his cheekbones. His face
was very solemn.

Then at last the hour for departure was at hand. He
stood on the platform, burdened with his suitcases and
gifts, and watched the train roll in on the station tracks.
He found himself a seat in the day coach and hoisted his
luggage on the rack above his head. The car was crowded,
for the most part with mothers and children. The green
plush seats had a grimy smell. The windows of the car
were dirty and rice thrown at some recent bridal pair lay
scattered on the floor. Singer smiled cordially to his
fellow-travelers and leaned back in his seat. He closed
his eyes. The lashes made a dark, curved fringe above
the hollows of his cheeks. His right hand moved ner-
vously inside his pocket.

For a while his thoughts lingered in the town he was
leaving behind him. He saw Mick and Doctor Copeland
and Jake Blount and Biff Brannon. The faces crowded in
on him out of the darkness so that he felt smothered.
He thought of the quarrel between Blount and the Negro.
The nature of this quarrel was hopelessly confused in his
mind—but each of them had on several occasions
broken out into a bitter tirade against the other, the
absent one. He had agreed with each of them in turn,
though what it was they wanted him to sanction he did
not know. And Mick—her face was urgent and she said
a good deal that he did not understand in the least. And
then Biff Brannon at the New York Café. Brannon with
his dark, iron-like jaw and his watchful eyes. And strangers who followed him about the streets and buttonholed
him for unexplainable reasons. The Turk at the linen shop
who flung his hands up in his face and babbled with his
tongue to make words the shape of which Singer had
never imagined before. A certain mill foreman and an
old black woman. A businessman on the main street and
an urchin who solicited soldiers for a whorehouse near the
river. Singer wriggled his shoulders uneasily. The train
rocked with a smooth, easy motion. His head nodded to
rest on his shoulder and for a short while he slept.

When he opened his eyes again the town was far behind
him. The town was forgotten. Outside the dirty window

there was the brilliant midsummer countryside. The sun slanted in strong, bronze-colored rays over the green fields of the new cotton. There were acres of tobacco, the plants heavy and green like some monstrous jungle weed. The orchards of peaches with the lush fruit weighting down the dwarfed trees. There were miles of pastures and tens of miles of wasted, washed-out land abandoned to the hardier weeds. The train cut through deep green pine forests where the ground was covered with the slick brown needles and the tops of the trees stretched up virgin and tall into the sky. And farther, a long way south of the town, the cypress swamps—with the gnarled roots of the trees writhing down into the brackish waters, where the gray, tattered moss trailed from the branches, where tropical water flowers blossomed in dankness and gloom. Then out again into the open beneath the sun and the indigo-blue sky.

Singer sat solemn and timid, his face turned fully toward the window. The great sweeps of space and the hard, elemental coloring almost blinded him. This kaleidoscopic variety of scene, this abundance of growth and color, seemed somehow connected with his friend. His thoughts were with Antonapoulos. The bliss of their reunion almost stifled him. His nose was pinched and he breathed with quick, short breaths through his slightly open mouth.

Antonapoulos would be glad to see him. He would enjoy the fresh fruits and the presents. By now he would be out of the sick ward and able to go on an excursion to the movies, and afterward to the hotel where they had eaten dinner on the first visit. Singer had written many letters to Antonapoulos, but he had not posted them. He surrendered himself wholly to thoughts of his friend.

The half-year since he had last been with him seemed neither a long nor a short span of time. Behind each waking moment there had always been his friend. And this submerged communion with Antonapoulos had grown and changed as though they were together in the flesh. Sometimes he thought of Antonapoulos with awe and self-abasement, sometimes with pride—always with love unchecked by criticism, freed of will. When he dreamed at night the face of his friend was always before him, massive and gentle. And in his waking thoughts they were eternally united.

The summer evening came slowly. The sun sank down behind a ragged line of trees in the distance and the sky paled. The twilight was languid and soft. There was a white full moon, and low purple clouds lay over the horizon. The earth, the trees, the unpainted rural dwellings darkened slowly. At intervals mild summer lightning quivered in the air. Singer watched all of this intently until at last the night had come, and his own face was reflected in the glass before him.

Children staggered up and down the aisle of the car with dripping paper cups of water. An old man in overalls who had the seat before Singer drank whiskey from time to time from a Coca-Cola bottle. Between swallows he plugged the bottle carefully with a wad of paper. A little girl on the right combed her hair with a sticky red lollipop. Shoeboxes were opened and trays of supper were brought in from the dining-car. Singer did not eat. He leaned back in his seat and kept desultory account of all that went on around him. At last the car settled down. Children lay on the broad plush seats and slept, while men and women doubled up with their pillows and rested as best they could.

Singer did not sleep. He pressed his face close against the glass and strained to see into the night. The darkness was heavy and velvety. Sometimes there was a patch of moonlight or the flicker of a lantern from the window of some house along the way. From the moon he saw that the train had turned from its southward course and was headed toward the east. The eagerness he felt was so keen that his nose was too pinched to breathe through and his cheeks were scarlet. He sat there, his face pressed close against the cold, sooty glass of the window, through most of the long night journey.

The train was more than an hour late, and the fresh, bright summer morning was well under way when they arrived. Singer went immediately to the hotel, a very good hotel where he had made reservations in advance. He unpacked his bags and arranged the presents he would take to Antonapoulos on the bed. From the menu the bellboy brought him he selected a luxurious breakfast—broiled bluefish, hominy, French toast, and hot black coffee. After breakfast he rested before the electric fan in his underwear. At noon he began to dress. He bathed and shaved and laid out fresh linen and his best seersucker suit. At three o'clock the hospital was open for visiting hours. It was Tuesday and the eighteenth of July.

At the asylum he sought Antonapoulos first in the sick ward where he had been confined before. But at the doorway of the room he saw immediately that his friend was not there. Next he found his way through the corridors to the office where he had been taken the time before. He had his question already written on one of the cards he carried about with him. The person behind the desk was not the same as the one who had been there before. He was a young man, almost a boy, with a half-formed, immature face and a lank mop of hair. Singer handed him the card and stood quietly, his arms heaped with packages, his weight resting on his heels.

The young man shook his head. He leaned over the desk and scribbled loosely on a pad of paper. Singer read what he had written and the spots of color drained from his cheekbones instantly. He looked at the note a long time, his eyes cut sideways and his head bowed. For it was written there that Antonapoulos was dead.

On the way back to the hotel he was careful not to crush the fruit he had brought with him. He took the packages up to his room, and then wandered down to the lobby. Behind a potted palm tree there was a slot machine. He inserted a nickel but when he tried to pull the lever he found that the machine was jammed. Over this incident he made a great to-do. He cornered the clerk and furiously demonstrated what had happened. His face was deathly pale and he was so beside himself that tears rolled down the ridges of his nose. He flailed his hands and even stamped once with his long, narrow, elegantly shoed foot on the plush carpet. Nor was he satisfied when his coin was refunded, but insisted on checking out immediately. He packed his bag and was obliged to work energetically to make it close again. For in addition to the articles he had brought with him he carried away three towels, two cakes of soap, a pen and a bottle of ink, a roll of toilet paper, and a Holy Bible. He paid his bill and walked to the railway station to put his belongings in custody. The train did not leave until nine in the evening and he had the empty afternoon before him.

This town was smaller than the one in which he lived. The business streets intersected to form the shape of a cross. The stores had a countrified look; there were har-

nesses and sacks of feed in half of the display windows.
Singer walked listlessly along the sidewalks. His throat
felt swollen and he wanted to swallow but was unable to
do so. To relieve this strangled feeling he bought a drink
in one of the drugstores. He idled in the barber shop
and purchased a few trifles at the ten-cent store. He looked
no one full in the face and his head drooped down to
one side like a sick animal's.

The afternoon was almost ended when a strange thing
happened to Singer. He had been walking slowly and ir-
regularly along the curb of the street. The sky was over-
cast and the air humid. Singer did not raise his head, but
as he passed the town pool room he caught a sidewise
glance of something that disturbed him. He passed the
pool room and then stopped in the middle of the street.
Listlessly he retraced his steps and stood before the open
door of the place. There were three mutes inside and they
were talking with their hands together. All three of them
were coatless. They wore bowler hats and bright ties. Each
of them held a glass of beer in his left hand. There was a
certain brotherly resemblance between them.

Singer went inside. For a moment he had trouble taking
his hand from his pocket. Then clumsily he formed a
word of greeting. He was clapped on the shoulder. A cold
drink was ordered. They surrounded him and the fingers
of their hands shot out like pistons as they questioned him.

He told his own name and the name of the town where
he lived. After that he could think of nothing else to tell
about himself. He asked if they knew Spiros Antonapoulos.
They did not know him. Singer stood with his hands dangling loose. His head was still inclined to one side and
his glance was oblique. He was so listless and cold that
the three mutes in the bowler hats looked at him queerly.
After a while they left him out of their conversation. And
when they had paid for the rounds of beers and were
ready to depart they did not suggest that he join them.

Although Singer had been adrift on the streets for half
a day he almost missed his train. It was not clear to him
how this happened or how he had spent the hours before.
He reached the station two minutes before the train pulled
out, and barely had time to drag his luggage aboard and
find a seat. The car he chose was almost empty. When he
was settled he opened the crate of strawberries and picked
them over with finicky care. The berries were of a giant

size, large as walnuts and in full-blown ripeness. The
green leaves at the top of the rich-colored fruit were like
tiny bouquets. Singer put a berry in his mouth and though
the juice had a lush, wild sweetness there was already a
subtle flavor of decay. He ate until his palate was dulled
by the taste and then rewrapped the crate and placed it on
the rack above him. At midnight he drew the window-
shade and lay down on the seat. He was curled in a ball,
his coat pulled over his face and head. In this position
he lay in a stupor of half-sleep for about twelve hours.
The conductor had to shake him when they arrived.

Singer left his luggage in the middle of the station floor.
Then he walked to the shop. He greeted the jeweler for
whom he worked with a listless turn of his hand. When
he went out again there was something heavy in his
pocket. For a while he rambled with bent head along the
streets. But the unrefracted brilliance of the sun, the
humid heat, oppressed him. He returned to his room with
swollen eyes and an aching head. After resting he drank
a glass of iced coffee and smoked a cigarette. Then when
he had washed the ash tray and the glass he brought out
a pistol from his pocket and put a bullet in his chest.

RÉSUMÉ
DOROTHY PARKER

*Dorothy Parker was born in 1893 and died in 1967. During
her lifetime she worked for* Vogue, Vanity Fair, *the New
Yorker, and* Esquire *and wrote plays, screenplays, poems, and
stories. She is best known for being one of the sharpest,
most biting wits in American letters. "Résumé" is a witty renun-
ciation of suicide and an ironic justification for life.*

Razors pain you;
Rivers are damp;
Acids stain you;
And drugs cause cramp.
Guns aren't lawful;
Nooses give;
Gas smells awful;
You might as well live.

from PATRIOTISM
YUKIO MISHIMA

The classical Japanese reaction to experiencing overwhelming shame or disgrace has been ceremonial suicide, or hara-kiri, a formalized, prescribed ritual. Unlike suicide, hara-kiri is considered both noble and honorable. This excerpt is from a short story by one of Japan's most popular twentieth-century writers. The story takes place in 1936, when Lieutenant Shinji Takeyama discovers that some fellow officers whom he trusted are mutineers. The thirty-one-year-old lieutenant believes he has no choice but hara-kiri. He disembowels himself in his home and his twenty-three-year-old wife stabs herself to death. The graphic description of the couple's deaths is given even more impact by the fact that Yukio Mishima himself committed hara-kiri in November, 1970.

Toward sundown on the twenty-eighth Reiko was startled by a furious pounding on the front door. She hurried downstairs. As she pulled with fumbling fingers at the bolt, the shape dimly outlined beyond the frosted-glass panel made no sound, but she knew it was her husband. Reiko had never known the bolt on the sliding door to be so stiff. Still it resisted. The door just would not open.

In a moment, almost before she knew she had succeeded, the lieutenant was standing before her on the cement floor inside the porch, muffled in a khaki greatcoat, his top boots heavy with slush from the street. Closing the door behind him, he returned the bolt once more to its socket. With what significance, Reiko did not understand.

"Welcome home."

Reiko bowed deeply, but her husband made no response. As he had already unfastened his sword and was about to remove his greatcoat, Reiko moved around behind to assist. The coat, which was cold and damp and had lost the odor of horse dung it normally exuded when exposed to the sun, weighed heavily upon her arm. Draping it across a hanger, and cradling the sword and leather belt in her sleeves, she waited while her husband removed his top boots and then followed behind him

238

into the "living room." This was the six-mat room down-stairs.

Seen in the clear light from the lamp, her husband's face, covered with a heavy growth of bristle, was almost unrecognizably wasted and thin. The cheeks were hollow, their luster and resilience gone. In his normal good spirits he would have changed into old clothes as soon as he was home and have pressed her to get supper at once, but now he sat before the table still in his uniform, his head drooping dejectedly. Reiko refrained from asking whether she should prepare the supper.

After an interval the lieutenant spoke.

"I knew nothing. They hadn't asked me to join. Perhaps out of consideration, because I was newly married. Kanō, and Homma too, and Yamaguchi."

Reiko recalled momentarily the faces of high-spirited young officers, friends of her husband, who had come to the house occasionally as guests.

"There may be an Imperial ordinance sent down to-morrow. They'll be posted as rebels, I imagine. I shall be in command of a unit with orders to attack them. . . . I can't do it. It's impossible to do a thing like that."

He spoke again.

"They've taken me off guard duty, and I have permission to return home for one night. Tomorrow morning, without question, I must leave to join the attack. I can't do it, Reiko."

Reiko sat erect with lowered eyes. She understood clearly that her husband had spoken of his death. The lieutenant was resolved. Each word, being rooted in death, emerged sharply and with powerful significance against this dark, unmovable background. Although the lieutenant was speaking of his dilemma, already there was no room in his mind for vacillation.

However, there was a clarity, like the clarity of a stream fed from melting snows, in the silence which rested between them. Sitting in his own home after the long two-day ordeal, and looking across at the face of his beautiful wife, the lieutenant was for the first time experiencing true peace of mind. For he had at once known, though she said nothing, that his wife divined the resolve which lay beneath his words.

"Well, then . . ." The lieutenant's eyes opened wide. Despite his exhaustion they were strong and clear, and now for the first time they looked straight into the eyes of his wife. "Tonight I shall cut my stomach."

Reiko did not flinch.

Her round eyes showed tension, as taut as the clang of a bell.

"I am ready," she said. "I ask permission to accompany you."

The lieutenant felt almost mesmerized by the strength in those eyes. His words flowed swiftly and easily, like the utterances of a man in delirium, and it was beyond his understanding how permission in a matter of such weight could be expressed so casually. . . .

"Well, let's make our preparations," said the lieutenant. The note of determination in the words was unmistakable, but at the same time Reiko had never heard her husband's voice so warm and tender.

After they had risen, a variety of tasks awaited them.

The lieutenant, who had never once before helped with the bedding, now cheerfully slid back the door of the closet, lifted the mattress across the room by himself, and stowed it away inside.

Reiko turned off the gas heater and put away the lamp standard. During the lieutenant's absence she had arranged this room carefully, sweeping and dusting it to a fresh cleanness, and now—if one overlooked the rosewood table drawn into one corner—the eight-mat room gave all the appearance of a reception room ready to welcome an important guest.

"We've seen some drinking here, haven't we? With Kanō and Homma and Noguchi . . ."

"Yes, they were great drinkers, all of them."

"We'll be meeting them before long, in the other world. They'll tease us, I imagine, when they find I've brought you with me."

Descending the stairs, the lieutenant turned to look back into this calm, clean room, now brightly illuminated by the ceiling lamp. There floated across his mind the faces of the young officers who had drunk there, and laughed, and innocently bragged. He had never dreamed then that he would one day cut open his stomach in this room.

In the two rooms downstairs husband and wife busied themselves smoothly and serenely with their respective preparations. The lieutenant went to the toilet, and then to the bathroom to wash. Meanwhile Reiko folded away her husband's padded robe, placed his uniform tunic, his trousers, and a newly cut bleached loincloth in the bathroom, and set out sheets of paper on the living-room table for the farewell notes. Then she removed the lid from the writing box and began rubbing ink from the ink tablet. She had already decided upon the wording of her own note.

Reiko's fingers pressed hard upon the cold gilt letters of the ink tablet, and the water in the shallow well at once darkened, as if a black cloud had spread across it. She stopped thinking that this repeated action, this pressure from her fingers, this rise and fall of faint sound, was all and solely for death. It was a routine domestic task, a simple paring away of time until death should finally stand before her. But somehow, in the increasingly smooth motion of the tablet rubbing on the stone, and in the scent from the thickening ink, there was unspeakable darkness.

Neat in his uniform, which he now wore next to his skin, the lieutenant emerged from the bathroom. Without a word he seated himself at the table, bolt upright, took a brush in his hand, and stared undecidedly at the paper before him.

Reiko took a white silk kimono with her and entered the bathroom. When she reappeared in the living room, clad in the white kimono and with her face lightly made up, the farewell note lay completed on the table beneath the lamp. The thick black brushstrokes said simply:

"Long Live the Imperial Forces—Army Lieutenant Takeyama Shinji."

While Reiko sat opposite him writing her own note, the lieutenant gazed in silence, intensely serious, at the controlled movement of his wife's pale fingers as they manipulated the brush.

With their respective notes in their hands—the lieutenant's sword strapped to his side, Reiko's small dagger thrust into the sash of her white kimono—the two of them stood before the god shelf and silently prayed. Then they put out all the downstairs lights. As he mounted the stairs the lieutenant turned his head and gazed back at the striking, white-clad figure of his wife, climbing behind him, with lowered eyes, from the darkness beneath.

The farewell notes were laid side by side in the alcove

of the upstairs room. They wondered whether they ought not to remove the hanging scroll, but since it had been written by their go-between, Lieutenant General Ozeki, and consisted, moreover, of two Chinese characters signifying "Sincerity," they left it where it was. Even if it were to become stained with splashes of blood, they felt that the lieutenant general would understand.

The lieutenant, sitting erect with his back to the alcove, laid his sword on the floor before him.

Reiko sat facing him, a mat's width away. With the rest of her so severely white the touch of rouge on her lips seemed remarkably seductive.

Across the dividing mat they gazed intently into each other's eyes. The lieutenant's sword lay before his knees. Seeing it, Reiko recalled their first night and was overwhelmed with sadness. The lieutenant spoke, in a hoarse voice:

"As I have no second to help me I shall cut deep. It may look unpleasant, but please do not panic. Death of any sort is a fearful thing to watch. You must not be discouraged by what you see. Is that all right?"

"Yes."

Reiko nodded deeply.

Looking at the slender white figure of his wife the lieutenant experienced a bizarre excitement. What he was about to perform was an act in his public capacity as a soldier, something he had never previously shown his wife. It called for a resolution equal to the courage to enter battle; it was a death of no less degree and quality than death in the front line. It was his conduct on the battlefield that he was now to display.

Momentarily the thought led the lieutenant to a strange fantasy. A lonely death on the battlefield, a death beneath the eyes of his beautiful wife . . . in the sensation that he was now to die in these two dimensions, realizing an impossible union of them both, there was sweetness beyond words. This must be the very pinnacle of good fortune, he thought. To have every moment of his death observed by those beautiful eyes—it was like being borne to death on a gentle, fragrant breeze. There was some special favor here. He did not understand precisely what it was, but it was a domain unknown to others: a dispensation granted to no one else had been permitted to himself. In the radiant, bridelike figure of his white-robed wife the lieutenant seemed to see a vision of all those things he had loved and for which he was to lay down his life—the Imperial Household, the Nation, the Army Flag. All these, no less than the wife who sat before him, were presences observing him closely with clear and never-faltering eyes.

Reiko too was gazing intently at her husband, so soon to die, and she thought that never in this world had she seen anything so beautiful. The lieutenant always looked well in uniform, but now, as he contemplated death with severe brows and firmly closed lips, he revealed what was perhaps masculine beauty at its most superb.

"It's time to go," the lieutenant said at last.

Reiko bent her body low to the mat in a deep bow. She could not raise her face. She did not wish to spoil her make-up with tears, but the tears could not be held back.

When at length she looked up she saw hazily through the tears that her husband had wound a white bandage around the blade of his now unsheathed sword, leaving five or six inches of naked steel showing at the point.

Resting the sword in its cloth wrapping on the mat before him, the lieutenant rose from his knees, resettled himself cross-legged, and unfastened the hooks of his uniform collar. His eyes no longer saw his wife. Slowly, one by one, he undid the flat brass buttons. The dusky brown chest was revealed, and then the stomach. He unclasped his belt and undid the buttons of his trousers. The pure whiteness of the thickly coiled loincloth showed itself. The lieutenant pushed the cloth down with both hands, further to ease his stomach, and then reached for the white-bandaged blade of his sword. With his left hand he massaged his abdomen, glancing downward as he did so.

To reassure himself on the sharpness of his sword's cutting edge the lieutenant folded back the left trouser flap, exposing a little of his thigh, and lightly drew the blade across the skin. Blood welled up in the wound at once, and several streaks of red trickled downward, glistening in the strong light.

It was the first Reiko had ever seen her husband's blood, and she felt a violent throbbing in her chest. She looked at her husband's face. The lieutenant was looking at the blood with calm appraisal. For a moment—

though thinking at the same time that it was hollow comfort—Reiko experienced a sense of relief.

The lieutenant's eyes fixed his wife with an intense, hawklike stare. Moving the sword around to his front, he raised himself slightly on his hips and let the upper half of his body lean over the sword point. That he was mustering his whole strength was apparent from the angry tension of the uniform at his shoulders. The lieutenant aimed to strike deep into the left of his stomach. His sharp cry pierced the silence of the room.

Despite the effort he had himself put into the blow, the lieutenant had the impression that someone else had struck the side of his stomach agonizingly with a thick rod of iron. For a second or so his head reeled and he had no idea what had happened. The five or six inches of naked point had vanished completely into his flesh, and the white bandage, gripped in his clenched fist, pressed directly against his stomach.

He returned to consciousness. The blade had certainly pierced the wall of the stomach, he thought. His breathing was difficult, his chest thumped violently, and in some far deep region, which he could hardly believe was a part of himself, a fearful and excruciating pain came welling up as if the ground had split open to disgorge a boiling stream of molten rock. The pain came suddenly nearer, with terrifying speed. The lieutenant bit his lower lip and stifled an instinctive moan.

Was this *seppuku?*—he was thinking. It was a sensation of utter chaos, as if the sky had fallen on his head and the world was reeling drunkenly. His will power and courage, which had seemed so robust before he made the incision, had now dwindled to something like a single hairlike thread of steel, and he was assailed by the uneasy feeling that he must advance along this thread, clinging to it with desperation. His clenched fist had grown moist. Looking down, he saw that both his hand and the cloth about the blade were drenched in blood. His loincloth too was dyed a deep red. It struck him as incredible that, amidst this terrible agony, things which could be seen could still be seen, and existing things existed still.

The moment the lieutenant thrust the sword into his left side and she saw the deathly pallor fall across his face, like an abruptly lowered curtain, Reiko had to struggle to prevent herself from rushing to his side. Whatever happened, she must watch. She must be a witness. That was the duty her husband had laid upon her. Opposite her, a mat's space away, she could clearly see her husband biting his lip to stifle the pain. The pain was there, with absolute certainty, before her eyes. And Reiko had no means of rescuing him from it.

The sweat glistened on her husband's forehead. The lieutenant closed his eyes, and then opened them again, as if experimenting. The eyes had lost their luster, and seemed innocent and empty like the eyes of a small animal.

The agony before Reiko's eyes burned as strong as the summer sun, utterly remote from the grief which seemed to be tearing herself apart within. The pain grew steadily in stature, stretching upward. Reiko felt that her husband had already become a man in a separate world, a man whose whole being had been resolved into pain, a prisoner in a cage of pain where no hand could reach out to him. But Reiko felt no pain at all. Her grief was not pain. As she thought about this, Reiko began to feel as if someone had raised a cruel wall of ⬤ss high between herself and her husband.

Ever since her marriage her husband's existence had been her own existence, and every breath of his had been a breath drawn by herself. But now, while her husband's existence in pain was a vivid reality, Reiko could find in this grief of hers no certain proof at all of her own existence.

With only his right hand on the sword the lieutenant began to cut sideways across his stomach. But as the blade became entangled with the entrails it was pushed constantly outward by their soft resilience; and the lieutenant realized that it would be necessary, as he cut, to use both hands to keep the point pressed deep into his stomach. He pulled the blade across. It did not cut as easily as he had expected. He directed the strength of his whole body into his right hand and pulled again. There was a cut of three or four inches.

The pain spread slowly outward from the inner depths until the whole stomach reverberated. It was like the wild clanging of a bell. Or like a thousand bells which jangled simultaneously at every breath he breathed and every throb of his pulse, rocking his whole being. The lieutenant

could no longer stop himself from moaning. But by now
the blade had cut its way through to below the navel,
and when he noticed this he felt a sense of satisfaction,
and a renewal of courage.

The volume of blood had steadily increased, and now
it spurted from the wound as if propelled by the beat of
the pulse. The mat before the lieutenant was drenched
red with splattered blood, and more blood overflowed onto
it from pools which gathered in the folds of the lieutenant's
khaki trousers. A spot, like a bird, came flying across to
Reiko and settled on the lap of her white silk kimono.

By the time the lieutenant had at last drawn the sword
across to the right side of his stomach, the blade was already cutting shallow and had revealed its naked tip,
slippery with blood and grease. But, suddenly stricken by
a fit of vomiting, the lieutenant cried out hoarsely. The
vomiting made the fierce pain fiercer still, and the stomach, which had thus far remained firm and compact,
now abruptly heaved, opening wide its wound, and the
entrails burst through, as if the wound too were vomiting.
Seemingly ignorant of their master's suffering, the entrails
gave an impression of robust health and almost disagreeable vitality as they slipped smoothly out and spilled over
into the crotch. The lieutenant's head drooped, his shoulders heaved, his eyes opened to narrow slits, and a thin
trickle of saliva dribbled from his mouth. The gold mark-
ings on his epaulettes caught the light and glinted.

Blood was scattered everywhere. The lieutenant was
soaked in it to his knees, and he sat now in a crumpled
and listless posture, one hand on the floor. A raw smell
filled the room. The lieutenant, his head drooping,
retched repeatedly, and the movement showed vividly
in his shoulders. The blade of the sword, now pushed back
by the entrails and exposed to its tip, was still in the lieutenant's right hand.

It would be difficult to imagine a more heroic sight than
that of the lieutenant at this moment, as he mustered his
strength and flung back his head. The movement was
performed with sudden violence, and the back of his head
struck with a sharp crack against the alcove pillar. Reiko
had been sitting until now with her face lowered, gazing
in fascination at the tide of blood advancing toward her
knees, but the sound took her by surprise and she looked
up.

The lieutenant's face was not the face of a living man. The eyes were hollow, the skin parched, the once so lustrous cheeks and lips the color of dried mud. The right hand alone was moving. Laboriously gripping the sword, it hovered shakily in the air like the hand of a marionette and strove to direct the point at the base of the lieutenant's throat. Reiko watched her husband make this last, most heart-rending, futile exertion. Glistening with blood and grease, the point was thrust at the throat again and again. And each time it missed its aim. The strength to guide it was no longer there. The straying point struck the collar and the collar badges. Although its hooks had been unfastened, the stiff military collar had closed together again and was protecting the throat.

Reiko could bear the sight no longer. She tried to go to her husband's help, but she could not stand. She moved through the blood on her knees, and her white skirts grew deep red. Moving to the rear of her husband, she helped no more than by loosening the collar. The quivering blade at last contacted the naked flesh of the throat. At that moment Reiko's impression was that she herself had propelled her husband forward; but that was not the case. It was a movement planned by the lieutenant himself, his last exertion of strength. Abruptly he threw his body at the blade, and the blade pierced his neck, emerging at the nape. There was a tremendous spurt of blood and the lieutenant lay still, cold blue-tinged steel protruding from his neck at the back.

Slowly, her socks slippery with blood. Reiko descended the stairway. The upstairs room was now completely still.

Switching on the ground-floor lights, she checked the gas jet and the main gas plug and poured water over the smoldering, half-buried charcoal in the brazier. She stood before the upright mirror in the four-and-a-half-mat room and held up her skirts. The bloodstains made it seem as if a bold, vivid pattern was printed across the lower half of her white kimono. When she sat down before the mirror, she was conscious of the dampness and coldness of her husband's blood in the region of her thighs, and she shivered. Then, for a long while, she lingered over her toilet preparations. She applied the rouge generously to her cheeks, and her lips too she painted heavily. This was no longer make-up to please her husband. It was make-up for the world which she would leave behind, and there was a touch of the magnificent and the spectacular in her brushwork. When she rose, the mat before the mirror was wet with blood. Reiko was not concerned about this.

Returning from the toilet, Reiko stood finally on the cement floor of the porchway. When her husband had bolted the door here last night it had been in preparation for death. For a while she stood immersed in the consideration of a simple problem. Should she now leave the bolt drawn? If she were to lock the door, it could be that the neighbors might not notice their suicide for several days. Reiko did not relish the thought of their two corpses putrefying before discovery. After all, it seemed, it would be best to leave it open. . . . She released the bolt, and also drew open the frosted-glass door a fraction. . . . At once a chill wind blew in. There was no sign of anyone in the midnight streets, and stars glittered ice-cold through the trees in the large house opposite.

Leaving the door as it was, Reiko mounted the stairs. She had walked here and there for some time and her socks were no longer slippery. About halfway up, her nostrils were already assailed by a peculiar smell.

The lieutenant was lying on his face in a sea of blood. The point protruding from his neck seemed to have grown even more prominent than before. Reiko walked heedlessly across the blood. Sitting beside the lieutenant's corpse, she stared intently at the face, which lay on one cheek on the mat. The eyes were opened wide, as if the lieutenant's attention had been attracted by something. She raised the head, folding it in her sleeve, wiped the blood from the lips, and bestowed a last kiss.

Then she rose and took from the closet a new white blanket and a waist cord. To prevent any derangement of her skirts, she wrapped the blanket about her waist and bound it there firmly with the cord.

Reiko sat herself on a spot about one foot distant from the lieutenant's body. Drawing the dagger from her sash, she examined its dully gleaming blade intently, and held it to her tongue. The taste of the polished steel was slightly sweet.

Reiko did not linger. When she thought how the pain which had previously opened such a gulf between herself and her dying husband was now to become a part of her

own experience, she saw before her only the joy of herself
entering a realm her husband had already made his own.
In her husband's agonized face there had been something
inexplicable which she was seeing for the first time. Now
she would solve that riddle. Reiko sensed that at last she
too would be able to taste the true bitterness and sweetness of that great moral principle in which her husband
believed. What had until now been tasted only faintly
through her husband's example she was about to savor
directly with her own tongue.

Reiko rested the point of the blade against the base of
her throat. She thrust hard. The wound was only shallow.
Her head blazed, and her hands shook uncontrollably.
She gave the blade a strong pull sideways. A warm sub-
stance flooded into her mouth, and everything before her
eyes reddened, in a vision of spouting blood. She gathered her strength and plunged the point of the blade deep
into her throat.

(Translated by Geoffrey W. Sargent)

ABOUT THE EDITORS

Charles S. Adler is a psychiatrist currently in private practice in Denver, Colorado. He completed his B.A. at Cornell University, his M.D. at Duke University, and psychiatric residency at the University of Colorado Medical Center. He wrote "The Meaning of Death to Children" and has delivered or published more than fifty papers and tapes in the areas of biofeedback, death, and psychosomatic disorders.

Gene Stanford is associate professor of education and Director of Teacher Education Programs at Utica College of Syracuse University. A former high school English teacher, he earned his B.A. in English at Washington University and his Ph.D in Guidance and Counseling at the University of Colorado. Dr. Stanford has published some twenty books and twenty-five articles in the field of education, including a number of paperback anthologies for young people on topics ranging from the generation gap to the nature of love to mental illness. He is coauthor of *Death Out of the Closet*, a handbook for teaching about death in the classroom.

Sheila Morrissey Adler is a psychologist in private practice in Denver, Colorado. She has studied at George Washington University, Sophia International University (Tokyo), the University of Hong Kong (Hong Kong, B.C.C.), Duke University (B.A., M.A.), and the University of Colorado (Ph.D). Her research has covered the attitudes of young people with terminal illness and their families, cross-cultural attitudes toward death, the reactions of hospital personnel toward terminally ill patients, and the early development of the concept of death. In her thirty-five lectures and publications Dr. Adler has combined her interests in these areas with her ongoing work and observations in biofeedback and stress disorders.

Questions for study and discussion over selections in this anthology are available in *Death Out of the Closet: A Curriculum Guide to Living with Dying,* a comprehensive handbook for death education, by Gene Stanford and Deborah Perry, published by Learning Ventures, a division of Bantam Books, 666 Fifth Avenue, New York, New York 10020.